ABOUT THIS BOOK

In this book, Australian economist Graham Dunkley explains and critiques the crucial concept of free trade. A policy of free trade is central to today's world-dominating globalization project. The more euphoric globalists uncritically assume that it has universal and unequivocal benefits for all people and countries. And the perpetual negotiations of the World Trade Organization are wholly based on this presumption.

Graham Dunkley shows, however, that leading economists have always been more sceptical about free trade doctrine than the dogmatic globalizers realize. There are more holes in free trade theory than its advocates grasp. And the benefits of free trade in practice are more limited and contingent than they acknowledge.

He also argues that the World Bank's long-time push for export-led development is misguided. A more democratic world trading order is necessary and possible. And more interventionist, self-reliant trade policies are feasible, especially if a more holistic view of economic development goals is adopted.

'An incisive and informative analysis of why free trade derails development…. An indispensable road map for those seeking to hack their way out of the neoliberal thicket.'

Walden Bello, Focus on the Global South; author of
Deglobalization: Ideas for a New World Economy

'This thought-provoking book is a valuable contribution to one of the greatest debates of our time, namely, trade and development.'

Ha-Joon Chang, University of Cambridge, author of *Kicking Away the Ladder: Development Strategy in Historical Perspective*

A BRAVE NEW SERIES

GLOBAL ISSUES
IN A CHANGING WORLD

This new series of short, accessible think-pieces deals with lead-ing global issues of relevance to humanity today. Intended for the enquiring reader and social activists in the North and the South, as well as students, the books explain what is at stake and ques-tion conventional ideas and policies. Drawn from many different parts of the world, the series' authors pay particular attention to the needs and interests of ordinary people, whether living in the rich industrial or the developing countries. They all share a com-mon objective – to help stimulate new thinking and social action in the opening years of the new century.

Global Issues in a Changing World is a joint initiative by Zed Books in collaboration with a number of partner publishers and non-governmental organizations around the world. By working together, we intend to maximize the relevance and availability of the books published in the series.

PARTICIPATING NGOS

Both ENDS, Amsterdam
Catholic Institute for International Relations, London
Corner House, Sturminster Newton
Council on International and Public Affairs, New York
Dag Hammarskjöld Foundation, Uppsala
Development GAP, Washington DC
Focus on the Global South, Bangkok
IBON, Manila
Inter Pares, Ottawa
Public Interest Research Centre, Delhi
Third World Network, Penang
Third World Network–Africa, Accra
World Development Movement, London

FREE TRADE

Myth, Reality and Alternatives

———————

GRAHAM DUNKLEY

UNIVERSITY PRESS LTD
Dhaka

WHITE LOTUS
Bangkok

FERNWOOD PUBLISHING LTD
Nova Scotia

BOOKS FOR CHANGE
Bangalore

SIRD
Kuala Lumpur

DAVID PHILIP
Cape Town

ZED BOOKS
London & New York

Free Trade was first published in 2004 by

In Bangladesh: The University Press Ltd,
Red Crescent Building, 114 Motijheel C/A, PO Box 2611, Dhaka 1000

In Burma, Cambodia, Laos, Thailand and Vietnam:
White Lotus Co. Ltd, GPO Box 1141, Bangkok 10501, Thailand

In Canada: Fernwood Publishing Ltd,
8422 St Margaret's Bay Road (Hwy 3) Site 2A, Box 5,
Black Point, Nova Scotia, BOJ 1BO

In India: Books for Change,
139 Richmond Road, Bangalore 560 025

In Malaysia: Strategic Information Research Development (SIRD),
No. 11/4E, Petaling Jaya, 46200 Selangor

In Southern Africa: David Philip (an imprint of New Africa Books),
99 Garfield Road, Claremont 7700, South Africa

In the rest of the world: Zed Books Ltd,
7 Cynthia Street, London N1 9JF, UK
and Room 400, 175 Fifth Avenue, New York, NY 10010, USA

Distributed in the USA exclusively by Palgrave Macmillan, a division of
St. Martin's Press, Inc., 175 Fifth Avenue, New York, NY 10010

www.zedbooks.co.uk

Cover designed by Andrew Corbett
Designed and typeset in Monotype Bembo by Illuminati, Grosmont
Printed and bound in the United Kingdom by Cox & Wyman, Reading

A catalogue record for this book is available from the British Library
US CIP data is available from the Library of Congress
Canadian CIP data is available from the National Library of Canada

ISBN 1 55266 119 9 Pb (Canada)
ISBN 81 87380 85 3 Pb (India)
ISBN 983 2535 20 4 Pb (Malaysia)
ISBN 0 86486 647 x Pb (Southern Africa)

ISBN 1 85649 862 x Hb (Zed Books)
ISBN 1 85649 863 8 Pb (Zed Books)

Contents

List of Tables, Figures and Boxes   viii

Abbreviations Used   ix

Acknowledgements and Dedication   xii

Preface   xiii

1   Introduction: Trade, Myth and Obsession   1

Trade: The Making of an Obsession   3
In-Your-Face Globalisation   4
Globalism: Three Myths   5
Free Trade: Five Myths   8
Challenging TINA – There are Alternatives!   11
Different Goals for Different Trade and Development   16

2   That's the Theory! Debating Free Trade
Doctrine Forever   18

The Smith–Ricardo Revolution   19
Free Trade Doctrine: Models, Assumptions and Question
    Marks   22
Comparative Advantage   24
Gains from Trade   26
Assumptions, Assumptions!   34
Here Come the Corollaries   41
The Rise of Not-Quite-Free Trade   43
Conclusion   46

3   A Confederacy of Heretics: Two Centuries
of Free Trade Dissent   48

Heresy before Orthodoxy   49
The Keynesian Bombshell   54
History versus Equilibrium   56
Heretics in the Temple   59
Conclusion   62

4   What about the Practice? Trading and
Free Trade in History and Reality   63

A Clash of Propensities   64
Trade and Markets Embedded   66
Trade's Loss of Innocence   70
The Necessity of Virtue: The Myth of Free Trade
    Beneficence   76
Free Trade, War and Peace   80
The Legend of the Thirties   83
Trade and Manifest Destiny   86
Conclusion   95

5   Development, Myths and Alternatives:
A Critique of Globalising Growth   97

Inventing Development   98
There Are Alternatives!   100
Trading Development   103
Of Ladders, Lock-in and Scale Economies   105
Two Steps Backwards: The Terms-of-Trade Problem   106
Two Cheers for the Poor: Globalisation, Poverty and
    Inequality   108
Belaboured Playing Fields   112
Human Development and the r-Curve   114
Greening Trade or Trading the Green?   117
Don't Forget the Ladies! Development, Globalisation
    and Women   119
A Poor Relation: The Neglect of Agriculture   121
Small Farms Are Beautiful   123
Re-greening My Valley: The Organic Agriculture
    Revolution   124

The Four Lost Causes: Culture, Community, Values and
    Tradition   125
Conclusion   134

6 THE EXPORT CULT: THE IMPORT-SUBSTITUTION
    VERSUS EXPORT-ORIENTATION DEBATE   136

An Elite Consensus   137
Models, Numbers and Export Cults   139
Welfare Methods   142
Modelling Methods   143
Case Study Methods   149
Industry Policy Does Work!   155
Conclusion   158

7 THE SELF-RELIANCE OPTION: GLOBAL MYTHS
    AND ALTERNATIVE DEVELOPMENT   161

Self-Reliance: A Respectable Lineage   162
Defining Self-Reliance   163
The Case for Self-Reliance   165
The Feasibility of Self-Reliance   167
Ten Reasons Why Self-Reliance Is More Feasible
    than Globalisers Admit   172
Alternative Development and Self-Reliance   183
Conclusion   185

8 THE FREE TRADE ADVENTURE: THE WTO,
    GLOBAL MYTHS AND ALTERNATIVES   188

Foundation Assumptions   189
The WTO in Principle   191
The WTO in Practice   194
Alternatives: Global Free Trade versus Co-operative
    World   213
A More Participatory, Cooperative World Order   215
Conclusion   219

9 CONCLUSION   221

REFERENCES   230

INDEX   247

LIST OF TABLES, FIGURES AND BOXES

Box 1.1	What is free trade?	9
Table 2.1	Ricardo's model	23
Figure 2.1	Harberger triangles	28
Box 2.1	Consumer surplus	32
Table 4.1	World merchandise and service exports	88
Table 4.2	Growth rates of world trade and world industrial/manufacturing production	91
Table 4.3	Trade ratios: merchandise exports as % of GDP	92
Figure 5.1	The r-curve	116
Box 5.1	Some costs of development	132
Box 6.1	CGE models	145
Figure 6.1	The relationship between trade and economic growth	148
Box 8.1	The WTO in brief	192
Box 8.2	GATS and the water monsters	197
Box 8.3	The Banana War	210
Box 9.1	Summary of arguments against Free Trade	225

Abbreviations Used

CGE	Computable General Equilibrium (mathematical models)
EO(I)	Export-Orientation (Oriented Industrialisation)
EU	European Union
FDI	Foreign Direct Investment
GATS	General Agreement on Trade in Services (of the WTO)
GATT	General Agreement on Tariffs and Trade
GDP	Gross Domestic Product
GNP	Gross National Product
HD	Human Development
HO	Heckscher/Ohlin (theory of international trade)
ILO	International Labour Organisation
IIT	Intra-Industry Trade
IMF	International Monetary Fund
IS(I)	Import-Substitution (Industrialisation)
IT	Information Technology
MFN	Most Favoured Nation (WTO principle)
NIET	New International Economic Theory
NGOs	Non-Governmental Organisations
OECD	Organisation for Economic Cooperation and Development
PPP GDP	GDP (above) based on Purchasing Power Parities

R&D	Research and Development
SAP	Structural Adjustment Programme (of IMF/World Bank)
S and D	Special and Differential Treatment (of Third World Countries in the WTO)
SPS	Sanitary and Phytosanitary (food and health provisions)
TNCs	Trans-National Corporations
TRIMs	Trade-Related Investment Measures
TRIPs	Trade-Related Intellectual Property Rights
UNCTAD	United Nations Conference on Trade and Development
WIDER	World Institute for Development Economics Research (UN)
WTO	World Trade Organisation

In Memory of
Jennifer Gail Crawford,
1950—2000

Swadeshi is that spirit in us which restricts us to the use and service of our immediate surroundings to the exclusion of the more remote. Thus, … I must restrict myself to my ancestral religion. If I find it defective, I should serve it by purging it of its defects. In the domain of politics I should make use of the indigenous institutions and serve them by curing them of their proved defects. In that of economics I should use only things that are produced by my immediate neighbours and serve those industries by making them efficient and complete where they might be found wanting.

MAHATMA GANDHI (1962: 54)

ACKNOWLEDGEMENTS
AND DEDICATION

The completion of this book was greatly delayed by the tragic death, on 20 July 2000, of my wife, Jenny Crawford, from breast cancer. The book is dedicated to her memory. I wish to express my profoundest gratitude to my brother, Bryce Dunkley, Professor Ken Wilson, Donald Feaver and the many other people who helped me at that time. I also thank Robert Molteno of Zed Books for his prolonged patience and my daughter, Kiran, for her acceptance of time devoted to the book.

I am also indebted to John King, P.J. Gunawardana, Alex Millmow, Donald Feaver, Jamie Doughney and Tom Weber for reading and commenting upon all or parts of the manuscript, though they are, of course, absolved from responsibility for it. Finally, I wish to thank Angela Tassone and Anthea Simpson for their indispensable and excellent typing services.

PREFACE

When I was asked to write a book on trade, I at first hesitated. Usually when I tell people that I teach and study trade (among other things), I'm given that 'Why's a nice bloke like you studying such a boring topic?' sort of look. Trade is probably meant to be boring, and arguably some things in life should be routine.

Then I recollected that this was not always so. In the days of merchant adventurers and caravan trains to exotic places, trade was the most glamorous (and dangerous) pursuit on earth. Early trade was an innocent, routine and limited process of acquiring requisite resources and a few luxuries. It was marginal to the domestic economy and 'embedded' in the social order. Society and people took precedence. In time it lost this innocence, with drugs, slaves, arms and avalanches of products, extending now to services trade, capable of destroying entire national industries. Trade gradually became 'disembedded' and threatening to whole societies and cultures, hence its controversial status today.

For this book I was asked to critically analyse Free Trade doctrine, as well as to revisit questions such as whether there are credible arguments against free trade and globalisation, whether a greater degree of self-reliance is feasible in a globalising world and whether there are more desirable alternatives to the emerging global free trade order. To all three questions I answer yes, particularly if we take a broader view of trade and globalisation, linking them more organically to technology and development, considering ethical issues and setting deeper, non-materialist goals. Indeed, the mainstream Free Trade–Protection debate has always taken maximisation of national income, or GDP, as the goal, the case for Free Trade being weaker, even irrelevant, if other goals are adopted. In other words, Free Trade and Protection are ideologies representing two differing, in many ways incompatible, world-views.

In so arguing I express many heretical views – the much-hailed benefits of free trade are contingent, not automatic; globalisation is discretionary, not inevitable; economic growth is much more desirable in the early stages of development than later, so should not now be a core human goal; Western-style development, to which globalisation is supposedly ideally suited, should not be a model for the world; the virtues of competition, technology, scale economies and national competitiveness are over-rated and should be optimised, not maximised. I even question the value of trade itself and the sheer obsession with trade which currently grips the leaders of our planet, an obsession I am sure will one day be adjudged by historians as misplaced, even bizarre.

The three main elements of my methodology are: first, a reassessment of orthodox trade theories, revealing a surprising amount of scepticism amongst classic writers; second, the use of historical and current data or studies for evidence against the claimed virtues of free trade and globalisation; third, the application of a wider range of criteria to economic questions than economics, being an extraordinarily narrow discipline, customarily does.

I identify four main (schematic) perspectives on this topic and espouse the one I call Community-Sovereignty, inspired by Gandhi (quoted above) and Schumacher. I suggest that Gandhi held a philosophy which I call 'adaptive traditionalism', as exemplified in the epigraph to this book, an approach which draws on traditional values but not unquestioningly, modifying them with newer, democratically shaped ideas where desired. I follow, in a general way, this notion rather than more fashionable doctrines such as nationalism, postmodernism, developmentalism or the like, and I will explain it in more detail.

I draw on a range of work and ideas which I label 'mainstream' (accepting of Free Market orthodoxy), 'sub-mainstream' (only partly accepting) and 'non-mainstream' (not generally accepting or totally rejecting Free Market ideology). I use some of my own jargon where desirable: Free Trade(rs) has capitals when referring to the ideological side and its ideologues, extremists being 'Free Trade Fundamentalists'; Protection(ism) has a capital when referring to ideas and is used interchangeably with 'trade intervention', which applies to a wider range of policies; 'globalists' and 'globalisers' are general advocates of globalisation; 'global fatalists' are sure it is inevitable and unstoppable; 'globo-euphorists' attribute all good things to globalisation (but seldom any bad things); 'internationalisation' (-ism) is cross-border cooperation and 'good', whereas 'globalisation' (-ism) is elite-led integration and 'bad'.

I use the old-fashioned First, Second and Third World terminology because I consider it well known, still useful and slightly poetic, whereas, being from Australia, I feel North–South to be less than accurate. For Free Market doctrine I use the Australian term Economic Rationalism (and variants) rather than Neo-Liberalism, 'liberal' traditionally connoting tolerance, democracy and other 'nice' things. This book is more about theory and philosophy than detailed policies, but I try to keep the presentation accessible. Chapter 2 is more technical in the interests of understanding orthodox theory.

This book follows on from, and draws heavily upon, my *Free Trade Adventure* (1997 and 2000b) in arguing that the benefits of free trade and globalisation are overrated and the costs thereof underestimated. Here I give more reasoning and further indications of alternatives.

CHAPTER I

INTRODUCTION:
TRADE, MYTH AND OBSESSION

The driving idea behind globalization is free-market capitalism –
the more you let market forces rule and the more you open your
economy to free trade and competition, the more efficient and
flourishing your economy will be. Globalization [is spreading] to
virtually every country in the world ... has its own set of economic rules [requiring] opening, deregulating and privatizing ...
and its own dominant culture, which [is] homogenizing [and
spreading] Americanization – from Big Macs to iMacs to Mickey
Mouse – on a global scale.

Thomas Friedman (1999: 8)

For me free trade is not a policy, free trade is just economic theory.

François Loos, French trade minister,
during trade negotiations with Australia
(*The Age*, 20 March 2003)

Today the world is in the grip of a doctrine which preaches 'Free
Market' solutions to all problems and which is espoused by an
'elite consensus' among world bodies, most governments, 'oppo-
sitions', business, and mainstream media, as well as by some
economists, but by few others. Actually, sceptics abound but they
are not in power, and, once in power, miraculously adopt orthodoxy, with the notable exception of French trade ministers (quoted
above). This doctrine has various names but I call it Free Market
Economic Rationalism, or variants thereof, and I designate its
practitioners Free Marketeers, though in Australia they are some-

times called Eco Rats! Free Marketeers advocate free trade for
international commerce, globalisation for most economic
transactions (in goods, services, capital, labour, law, accounting,
regulation or the like) and free markets for almost everything,
domestically and globally. A new world order centred on the
World Trade Organisation (WTO) is being constructed on the
basis of this doctrine and its assumptions, an endeavour which I
call the Global Free Trade Project, and I claim it is based more
on myth than reality.

I employ the metaphor of 'mythology' because in the two
centuries since Adam Smith the Free Trade debate has thrown up
many legends which are part truth, part shibboleth. One of the
great myths of the age is that free trade and related forms of
globalisation can generate a new era of prosperity, a view widely
espoused by non-economist businessmen, bureaucrats, politicians,
journalists and other public commentators. For instance Australia-
based US commentator Bruce Wolpe (*The Age*, 23 April 2003),
who opposed the war in Iraq, has said that the tragedy of the War
on Terror and the Iraq War is that they have damaged 'the secret
of the prosperity of the 1990s – free trade'. The WTO makes
similar claims for Free Trade. But this statement contains three
misconceptions: the 1990s did not see a major economic recovery, only minor trade liberalisation was achieved, and even mainstream economists doubt that this contributed much to the world
economy. Indeed, economists have always been more circumspect
in their claims for Free Trade than the more euphoric globalists,
of whom US journalist Thomas Friedman (quoted above) is an
extreme example. The core argument of this book is that Free
Trade and related globalisation cannot bring as many benefits as
claimed, and that any 'gains from trade' are contingent rather
than certain. I agree with the French trade minister (quoted above)
that the purported virtues of free trade are more theory than
reality, and even the theory has some fundamental flaws. In fact,
Free Trade is as much an ideology or a 'world-view' as a policy or
a theory.

Trade: The Making of an Obsession

In earlier English the word *trade* meant a *path* or *beaten track*, implying a routine social function, ancient trading being mainly for basics and 'embedded' in other social institutions. Some historians see trade as static and state-controlled over long periods, others seeing dynamism and embryonic entrepreneurship. Either way, many see trading as socially and culturally disruptive, thus eliciting a universal desire for 'protection' in the literal, cushioning sense. Thus, trade is a natural, ancient activity, but so is Protection, as is the widespread pre-industrial desire to embed trading in more fundamental institutions, rendering it very much subservient to society and culture (Polanyi, 1957; Clark, 1974; see also Chapter 4).

In time trading became more adventurous, luxurious and disembedded, the early trade theorists called 'Mercantilists' proclaiming it essential to development, and Adam Smith declaring it needed to be free, or unencumbered by state imposts, for maximum benefits, although he did not want trading to disrupt society and did not think capital should move across borders. By the late nineteenth century brave new trading ventures were thought essential for industrial revolution, and liberalisation became fashionable until it was realised, as economic historian Paul Bairoch (1972) later discovered, that protection was better for growth in many countries. But the myth that free trade is best for growth thrives and is the key to present-day trade obsessions.

The post-war GATT-centred trading order was based on both this myth and the 'legend of the thirties', as I call it, that inter-war protectionism nearly ruined the world. In Chapter 4 I question these and other myths. Unexpected success at the famed Uruguay Round of GATT (1986–93) entrenched these myths, created a system of permanent trade negotiations, generated images of 'trade determinism', as I call the belief that trade causes growth or other 'good' things, and gave rise to 'globo-euphoria', which attributes all good things to free trade and globalisation. In a clear statement of 'trade determinism', former WTO director general, Renato Ruggiero (in Aga Khan, 1998: 22) has stated that 'Trade liberalisation is not just a recipe for growth, but also for security and peace, as history has shown us.' The WTO has credited recent economic improvements in poor countries to their greater integration into its global order, debiting the 'ugly alternatives' of poverty and conflict to lack of such integration (quoted p. 188, below). Free Trade economists often describe the goal of globalisation as 'deep integration', or the convergence of nations' fundamental economic structures and policy systems, extending 'far beyond trade or strictly economic criteria' (Ruggiero in Aga Khan, 1998: 234).

Trade obsession reached an apogee at the 2002 Johannesburg Summit on Sustainable Development, when Australia and other trade-obsessed Western countries moved to include in key environmental and justice resolutions the clause: 'while ensuring WTO consistency', implying that we can only save the planet if the WTO approves! This clause was dropped when howled down by dissident Third World countries (TWN, September 2002, 145–6), but a strong trade determinist obsession still grips world leaders.

In-Your-Face Globalisation

Trade obsession is paralleled by an equal obsession with wider globalisation, variously defined as closer contact between societies, compression of space/time, dissolution of boundaries or integration of markets, the last of these being a definition often used by economists, who did not invent the term and are not always comfortable with it. I define globalisation as displacement of local and national factors in people's lives by transnational ones, and I describe 'cooperative internationalism', my preferred form of supranationalism, as arms' length, mutually beneficial interchange between sovereign societies.

The more iconoclastic globalists variously depict globalisation as the end of geography and the demolition of nations (Wriston);

as a borderless world and an invisible cyberspace country called 'Cyberia' (Ohmae); or as an 'electronic herd' trampling through nations at will, a 'golden straitjacket' of strict but supposedly beneficial Free Market policies and a 'brutal in-your-face, Schumpterian capitalism' which leaves laggards as 'roadkill on the global investment highway' (Friedman, 1999: 214, 333 and *passim*). Curiously, these boffins think such prognostications are *recommendations* for globalisation and wonder why there are anti-globalisation movements!

Not all mainstream writers are so globo-euphorist, however. Economists such as Bhagwati (1998) and Krugman stoutly defend free trade but query the benefits of free investment, speculative capital and extreme economic deregulation. A former top OECD official, Louis Emmerij (2000), has criticised globalisation as private-sector driven, benefiting mainly private firms and creating many new social or equity problems. And, of course, there is an array of sub- and non-mainstream critiques of globalisation, some of them conspiratorial or ill informed, but many producing well-documented critiques, which will be touched on throughout the book.

Globalism: Three Myths

The Global Free Trade Project and the general globalisation push are posited on three assumptions which I consider inaccurate, even mythological: (1) that globalisation is now well advanced; (2) that it is inevitable or unstoppable; and (3) that it is overwhelmingly good for virtually everyone.

The first myth is widely criticised on grounds such as that global integration and centralisation of power were greater in the late nineteenth century (Streeten, 1998: 14ff); that TNCs are still largely home-based; that world prices, profits and interest rates are not sufficiently uniform to indicate advanced market integration (Pryor, 2000) and that regionalism is much stronger than globalism (Rugman, 2000). I partly agree, and cite evidence that trade and FDI are less in relation to the real economy than is usually thought (Chapter 4). The idea of global takeover by Coca-Cola, McDonald's and Americanisation should not be ignored (see Chapter 5, esp. Box 5.1), even the World Bank (2002: 156) conceding this to be a concern, but it can be exaggerated. I have travelled in parts of India where little seems to have changed since the Raj, even in the cities, icons of the West and 'Cyberia' being present but largely lost in the vast squalor of Indian semi-modernity.

The second myth, that of inevitable globalism, is greatly over-drawn because, whilst there are globalising forces like improved transport and communications, the prime integrating process appears to be discretionary deregulation by governments, which today are committing what I call 'sovereignty suicide'. Even Free Traders such as Bhagwati (1998: 360) or Krugman (1995: 328) and some populist globalists like Legrain (2002) concede the vol-untary nature of deregulatory globalism, as do some more radical economists (e.g. Kitson and Michie, 2000: 13ff), while the WTO regularly warns of deregulatory backsliding and uses 'lock-in' devices to prevent this (Chapter 8), clearly implying that globalis-ation is not preordained or assured.

The third myth, that free trade and globalisation are beneficial for virtually all people in all countries at all times, is based on oversimplified research methods and questionable results, a former OECD official Emmerij (2000) hinting that the World Bank is over-optimistic to an extent which borders on dishonesty in its globo-euphorist claims (e.g. in 2002). Globalism is complex, with crosscutting impacts. There can be beneficial mechanisms, such as what I call 'referential effects' ('modelling' of good laws from other countries) and 'regulatory effects' (international pressure for improved standards – see Held, 1999; Braithwaite and Drahos, 2000) alongside mixed or adverse impacts ranging from 'integra-tive effects' (homogenisation of legal or administrative practices) and 'displacement effects' (destruction of one culture by another) to 'disruption effects' (social or other dislocation). Such costs of globalism are inadequately considered by globo-euphorists, although the World Bank (2002: 128–30) now obliquely acknowledges them; some of these will be touched on throughout this book.

In particular, I argue that the worst impacts are from the latter two effects – displacement and disruption. The much quoted British globo-euphorist, Philippe Legrain (2002), who claims to have discovered the 'truth' about globalisation, glibly decrees that it brings overwhelmingly beneficial cultural change and that 'most people in the Third World quite like our Western "trash"' (2002: 31ff). But it is nonsense to claim to know what several billion people want or how they are affected by major changes. My reading, from travel and some work with NGO grassroots projects in India (Dunkley, 1993), is that people's views are mixed, with some burgeoning consumerism but with many people resistant to undue Westernisation. Most want modest improvements in areas such as income, health and education, but many also wish to preserve their own traditions, adapted where necessary. One Middle Eastern economist and advocate of greater self-reliance, Yusif A. Sayigh (1991: 206), suggests that external economic, technological, consumption, educational and cultural dependence in the Arab World is a major factor in the rise of Islamic fundamentalism.

As the well-known development economist Paul Streeten has assessed it, globalisation is good for the richer countries, asset-holders, the educated, risk-takers, profits, large firms, the private sector in general, men, purveyors of global culture and so forth, but adversely effects, for instance, poorer countries, workers, the unskilled, the public sector, small firms, women, children and local communities or cultures (Streeten, 2001). Where benefits such as increased growth or reduced poverty *do* appear to be associated with freer trade or globalisation, often the real causes of these are factors such as domestically generated development, macroeconomic stabilisation or recent improvements in social stability. Increased trade or globalisation is often an effect rather than a cause of these factors (see Chapter 6). In any case, economic growth appears to provide its greatest benefits at low income levels, beyond which these benefits may level off and the costs may rise (see Chapter 5).

There are many facets of globalisation, but this book focuses primarily on the role of trade, debates about Free Trade and the crucial links between trade, technology and development.

Free Trade: Five Myths

Free trade is usually defined as the absence of government restrictions upon the cross-border flows of goods or services, with minor regulation allowed, although as a result of the growing trade obsession discussed above, an increasing number of policies are now being deemed trade-restrictive and slated for liberalisation or abolition (see Box 1.1 and Chapter 8).

Some mild global critics, such as trade unions and certain NGOs (e.g. Oxfam, 2002), argue that free trade is all right so long as the benefits are distributed equitably or provided exchange is 'fair' (non-exploitative – see Chapter 8). Others say free trade is good, but more so in theory than practice, or that it could be good but does not exist in reality because countries 'cheat' too much (by using a variety of hidden protection devices). I disagree with such views, arguing instead that the Free Trade doctrine is fundamentally flawed, and that Protectionism is often justified, both in theory and in practice.

I argue that, related to the three myths of globalisation, there are five myths of Free Trade: (1) trading is anciently integral to human nature; (2) free trade, free markets and private initiative are best for most exchange; (3) 'comparative advantage' is the best basis for all exchange of goods and services; (4) trading and free trade have, on balance, overwhelmingly net positive benefits for all concerned; (5) the amount of trading has gradually increased over time, indicating inevitable globalism. Myths by their nature

Box 1.1 What is free trade?

Free trade is the absence of artificial barriers to the free flow of goods and services between countries. There are five types of barrier to trade in goods and services:

1. Natural barriers: transport and communications costs, physical distance, geographical impediments (mountainous terrain, etc.).
2. Cultural barriers: language, traditions, negative attitudes to trading or foreign contacts and divergent commercial practices.
3. Market barriers: imperfect competition, market-sharing tactics, monopolistic or oligopolistic strategic trading (Chapter 3), and TNC profit maximising devices such as transfer pricing or differential 'pricing to market' (considerably differing prices in different countries – see Pryor, 2000: 201).
4. Policy barriers: tariffs (customs duties); quotas or import licensing; subsidies to local production; import bans; export promotion schemes; and a wide range of 'non-tariff' barriers such as administrative technicalities and 'voluntary export restraints'. Free Traders even tend to argue that tax, quarantine, environmental or other such policies which discriminate against imports, even if inadvertently, are trade barriers.
5. Service regulations: trade in services is said to be constrained by national regulations such as bans or limits on entry of foreign providers (banks, insurance companies etc), restrictions on the operations of foreign providers or limits on the movement of foreign service personnel.

Protection is the deliberate use of policy barriers or regulations to assist local industries or to promote exports.

Free Traders claim that protection, by increasing inefficiency and inflating import prices, raises costs for local firms. Protectionists reply that such costs can be outweighed by its social benefits.

Free Traders want as many of these barriers removed as possible, by elimination of protection, deregulation, global regulatory harmonisation and even reduction of cultural barriers through pro-global attitudes. The aim of this is to create a 'level playing field' – equal access for all companies to the markets of all countries.

contain grains of truth and I do not completely reject these five assertions – trade *is* ancient and *has* risen over time, for instance – but I argue throughout the book, especially in Chapter 4, that they are generally overstated, partly misconceived, often over-simplified and not always consistent with the evidence.

In particular, much mythology derives from Adam Smith's surmise that trade and economic improvement in general are natural human instincts (quoted p. 63, below), others inferring that free trade and general development are therefore 'just human nature'. I will call this the 'Smithian Propensity', of which there are several versions, and suggest that it *is* natural but partly counterbalanced by an equally natural 'Gandhian Propensity' to seek preservation of worthwhile traditions, social institutions and natural environments (see Chapter 4).

Overall, I base my case against Free Trade doctrine on four general grounds: (1) that it is over-simplified, based unduly on questionable myths and assumptions; (2) that it is excessively narrow, omitting a range of non-economic considerations; (3) that it presents only a means, failing to adequately consider ends or goals; (4) that it entails changes which, along with many technological and developmental pressures, are undemocratic or non-consensual. Trade textbooks and monographs today look so-phisticated, often brandishing a bevy of statistics, diagrams and 'econometrics' (mathematical applications to economics), but on closer inspection they are often based on remarkably narrow, sim-plistic assumptions.

The famed US economist Milton Friedman once decreed that it does not matter if assumptions are unrealistic so long as theories are adequately tested. But the problem lies in defining 'realism' and 'adequacy', for assumptions can shape results and certainly the inclusion of non-economic criteria can completely change the way trade policies are assessed. I provide examples of such problems throughout the book, concluding that a broader view than most economists take brings Free Trade and globalisation much more into question.

Free Marketeers argue that free trade is the 'optimum' trading policy compared with protection because, in theory, it supposedly leaves everyone better off (economically) without making anyone worse off, and, in practice, because it allegedly produces higher income and faster economic growth than protection. The Free Trader's unwritten rule is that the relative virtue of the two policies, free trade or protection, depends upon which can produce the higher income, and they claim free trade almost always does. Some critics accept this rule and counterclaim that protection can often produce higher income, especially where free trade 'locks' countries onto lower rungs of the development ladder (see Chapter 5 below), and many question the underlying concept of comparative advantage. By contrast, I argue that a wider range of criteria than just income or growth should be used, and that the doctrine of 'gains from trade' is more problematic than that of 'comparative advantage' (see Chapter 2). With wider criteria than just economic ones, the case for free trade is greatly weakened.

Challenging TINA – There are Alternatives!

Those who claim that there is no alternative (TINA) to free market economics, free trade and globalisation lack both imagination and knowledge, for alternative perspectives and proposals abound, particularly among sub- and non-mainstream writers or activists, but even to some extent within the mainstream.

There are many alternative schools of thought in economics alone, but for convenience I identify four groups of approaches regarding three sets of issues covered in this book: attitudes to the key themes of trade, development and technology; attitudes to both methods and goals in policymaking; and attitudes to a wider range of criteria, including political, social, cultural, ethical, ecological and spiritual (broadly defined) considerations. The titles of the groupings are mine, the boundaries are not rigid and the cameo theorists mentioned typify rather than exclusively exemplify the approaches.

1. *Free Market Economic Rationalist (Smith/Ricardo) approach*

Smith (1776), Ricardo (1817), Mill (1848) and other 'Classical' economists pioneered the claim that free markets and free trade are beneficial, but were not dogmatic about it; 'Neo-classical' economists from the mid-nineteenth century until today greatly rigidifying the doctrine. Neo-classical theorists tend to depict people as rational, individualistic, utility-maximising consumers whose goals are materialist, whose values are largely utilitarian and who make economic decisions in isolation from wider aspects of life. Such theorists thence see the overall economy as a mere aggregation of such individuals, who are deemed 'representative' agents (see Keen, 2001). Most economists do not see people this way in real life, but accept the depiction for simplicity or even modelling convenience. Where variations are allowed, alternative results often follow, cases of which will be noted in later chapters. Most Free Market international economists focus very narrowly on trade, assume materialistic goals and neglect non-economic issues, the almost exclusive target of mainstream trade theory being maximisation of GDP and growth thereof.

Perhaps the greatest difference between Neo-classical economists or other Free Marketeers and the following three groupings is that the former believe in largely automatic self-balancing market equilibrium, with the equilibria usually 'working out for the best' via Adam Smith's 'invisible hand', routinely clearing markets, producing what people really want, ensuring full employment and balancing trade. Most other economists see equilibria as less assuredly benign, or even question the equilibrium concept itself, instead seeing a need for government and community intervention in economic processes, including trade or other international ones. Free Marketeers see the economy as a yacht adjusting itself to market breezes, while Keynesians or other 'heretics' see it as a motor boat powered by investment and requiring firm controls. This philosophical difference is a crucial distinguishing factor between Free Traders and Protectionists, who essentially reflect differing world-views.

2. Market Interventionist (Keynes/Kaldor) Approach

Those influenced by the great British economist J.M. Keynes see demand leading the economy, acknowledge far more 'market failures' than Free Marketeers do and advocate much more policy intervention, especially for macroeconomic purposes, but also for Managed Trade (Chapter 8). Keynes himself sympathised with free trade policies, though he believed that trade intervention could promote employment; he accepted some permanent protection for a balance between various industries, including for the support of traditional agriculture, and thought high levels of self-reliance quite feasible (Dunkley, 1995, 2000b: *passim*; Chapter 7).

Keynes's Hungarian–British colleague, Nicholas Kaldor (1978; 1989), placed more emphasis on microeconomic issues, investment processes, economies of scale and the multiplier benefits of manufacturing, firmly opposing free trade. Kaldor pioneered many of the current critiques of Neo-classical economics which centre on recognition of imperfect competition (monopoly and oligopoly), 'increasing returns' or 'economies of scale' (rather than the orthodox 'law of diminishing returns'), 'learning effects' (efficiency improvements due to learning processes amongst workers and managers over time) and market mechanisms alternative to the 'equilibrium' concept, particularly the notion of 'cumulative causation' (see Chapter 3).

US Kaldorians like Lester Thurow (1992) and Laura D'Andrea Tyson go even further, urging industry policy-type protection to promote competitive high-tech industries. Most Keynesians share the same pro-growth, pro-technology goals as Economic Rationalists, placing minimal emphasis on values or socio-cultural factors, although they are usually concerned about equity issues, while Keynes himself (1930) forecast a post-avarice return to religion and tradition.

3. Human Development (Marx/Sen) Approach

A more diverse grouping than the previous two, Human Development theorists more fundamentally question Free Market theory, capitalist economies and orthodox development processes, stressing social or welfare goals and 'human capacity development', a concept made famous by Indian–British economist/philosopher, Amartya Sen (1983; 2001), but which he derived extensively from Marx (see Cowen and Shenton, 1996: 449 and *passim*). Marxists are usually considered, not necessarily accurately, to be materialists with little interest in cultural or spiritual traditions and bent on radical social change, although they do seek a more creative, equitable, cooperative utopia in the long term. Marx himself advocated free trade to hasten social development and revolution (see Chapter 3), but 'dependency' Marxists (e.g. Amin, 1990) are famous for advocating self-reliance as a development tool to overcome 'imperialist' blockages.

By contrast, Sen, a fairly mainstream Nobel laureate, accepts general market principles, current forms of globalisation, reasonably free trade and longer-term growth-oriented goals. His most radical contributions are, first, his 'capacity expansion' concept, which implies the provision of collective benefits such as infrastructure, health, education, literacy, training, female employment or general social development, and, second, his notion of 'entitlement' which suggests that people's sustenance stems from collective security as well as from market-derived income. Indeed, Sen argues that free markets often exacerbate famines, that public redistribution has been integral to social justice since ancient times, a view popularised earlier by Polanyi (1977; 1957), and that democracy, as in India, is far more effective for this than Chinese-style dictatorial governance (Drèze and Sen, 1989; 1995). This 'human' view of development policy has been highly influential in international bodies, especially the UN, and tends to be more interventionist than the milder Keynesian approach. Although the trade views of this grouping are mixed, many advocate intervention for Managed and Fair Trade purposes (see Chapter 8).

4. Community-Sovereignty (Gandhi/Schumacher) Approach

More diverse and non-mainstream than the previous three, this grouping seeks both alternative economic methods or policies, and alternative goals such as social equity, ecological sustainability, maintenance or restoration of communities and cultures, protection of national sovereignty (along with greater international cooperation), less materialistic values and, for some, a more holistic, spiritual framework for living. Virtually everyone in this grouping opposes Free Trade and integrative globalisation, mostly advocating intervention for what I call Fair and Self-Reliant Trade reasons (see Chapter 8). Community-Sovereignty theorists and activists draw on many sources, but for many a profound underlying inspiration has been the great Indian independence leader Mahatma Gandhi, who has variously influenced peace movements, 'deep' ecologists, non-violent action groups, alternative economic doctrines, self-reliance theories and alternative technology groups, much of this through the German-born British heterodox economist E.F. Schumacher (Schumacher, 1973; King, 1988: ch. 10).[1]

Gandhi's ideas are wholly steeped in a spiritual view of life and the world, with individuals ideally seeking self-realisation through a search for spiritual truth. This leads to traditional Hindu precepts such as peace, love, right action, and *Ahimsa* (Non-violence), applied to all walks of life, and thence entails political actions such as *Satyagraha* (non-violent rectification of wrongs), *Sarvodaya* (respect and justice for all) and *Swadeshi* (sovereignty and self-reliance for communities and nations).

Gandhi opposed rampant economic growth as morally corrupting, free trade as socially destructive and copying of the West as degrading. He variously advocated self-reliant villages (1962), national self-reliance (quoted p. xi, above), priority for locals over more distant peoples, simple technologies and lifestyles, self-restraint in consumption, or what the Indian guru Satya Sai Baba has called 'a ceiling on desires', and 'adaptive traditionalism' or the preservation of traditions shorn of those which are destructive.

Such ideas are potentially revolutionary alternatives to globalising materialism (see Chapter 5).

Schumacher (1973) was heavily influenced by Gandhi, although he called his political economy framework 'Buddhist economics', Buddhism having long anticipated some of these ideas. He placed particular emphasis on the Buddhist precept of 'right livelihood', implying that in all things, including work and consumption, individuals should do what is morally right and environmentally requisite. Schumacher is best known for his beliefs that economic policies should be set in ethical, ecological, people-centred and spiritual frameworks, that development goals should entail small-scale, decentralised communities and that technologies should be 'intermediate' (see Chapter 5) or 'appropriate' to human scale, to community needs, to local and national sovereignty and to environmental maintenance. On this basis he founded the remarkable London-based Intermediate Technology Group, which now promotes this sort of technology and development worldwide. Schumacher (1973: 56–7) opposed free trade and globalisation on the grounds that unnecessary mobility created structural vulnerability, community decay and general 'footlooseness'. Both he and Gandhi clearly saw links between trade, technology, development and wider social issues.

Of these four groupings I identify most closely with the fourth, but I draw on the others where appropriate, including some near-Interventionist Free Traders like Krugman and Rodrik, whose informative work reveals many cracks in Free Trade doctrine, even though they do not embrace extensive Protectionism.

Different Goals for Different Trade and Development

In sum, this book is a general, critical survey of the Free Trade question, covering both theory and practice, in which I conclude that the proclaimed benefits of free trade and globalisation are contingent and part mythical rather than automatically assured, and that there are credible alternatives. I do not tackle all issues equally: the labour and environmental issues, for instance, already have plenty of coverage, although I do touch on them and have examined these two topics in separate papers (Dunkley, 1996 and 1999).

In Chapter 2 I critically analyse orthodox Free Trade theory, and I outline alternative 'heretical' perspectives in Chapter 3. In Chapter 4 I recount some historical and statistical evidence against Free Trade mythologies, while in Chapter 5 I list equity, environmental, cultural and other grounds for an alternative approach to development and trade. The next two chapters provide unusual case studies, one criticising the famed World Bank/WTO case for free-market, 'export-oriented' development; the other arguing for the feasibility of what I call Self-Reliant Trade. In Chapter 8 I critically examine the WTO's new world trading order, alternative forms of trade, Managed, Fair and Self-Reliant, suggesting some new architecture for a fairer, more cooperative world.

Overall, I argue against Free Trade on the grounds that its benefits are overrated and its costs underestimated, its main effects being undemocratic, 'non-consensual' social change. More than Free Traders seem to realise, the virtue of their doctrine depends on the goals sought. If we want an entrepreneurial, business-led, high-tech, free-flowing globally engaged Cyberia, then we probably need techno-globalism, although theorists like Thurow (1992) say that completely free trade is not the way to do even this. If, however, our goals are for a more just, equitable, ecological, holistic society, then full-blast Free Trade or techno-globalisation are not required, and there is a case for allowing nations to find their own more self-reliant trading and development models. Throughout the book I suggest some alternative goals which could be sought, particularly three which I describe as social justice, environmental sustainability and cultural integrity.

Note

1. On Gandhian ideas and influences, see Weber, 1999; Murphy, 1990.

CHAPTER 2

THAT'S THE THEORY!
DEBATING FREE TRADE
DOCTRINE FOREVER

> If a foreign country can supply us with a commodity cheaper than
> we ourselves can make it, better buy it of them with some part of
> the produce of our own industry, employed in a way in which we
> have some advantage.
>
> Adam Smith (1776, 1: 478–9)

The theory of comparative advantage has a lot to live up to. US Nobel laureate Paul Samuelson has pronounced it the only proposition in the social sciences which can be displayed to mathematicians as both true and non-trivial (Maneschi, 1998: 1); trade theorist Ronald Findlay paints it the 'deepest and most beautiful result in all economics'; Södersten's leading international economics textbook dubs it 'one of the oldest, still unchallenged theories of economics'. Today there is a widespread view amongst the more ideological globalists (Chapter 1), a view not shared by all economists, that the case is now closed – free trade is generally best for all people in all countries at all times and that it brings assured gains, leading to long-term economic growth and development. The WTO and World Bank posit their new world order on such assertions, but this chapter will question the underlying logic, assumptions and corollaries of Free Trade theory. I argue that the implications of free trade are more complex, the theory less watertight and its benefits less assured than globalisers claim.

The Smith–Ricardo Revolution

Actually, trade theory is two theorems in one, the first holding that each country has a 'comparative advantage' in certain exports and the second avowing that specialisation in those export lines will bring 'gains from trade'. The idea that trade stimulates the economy has been around for a long time, the earlier trade interventionists known as 'Mercantilists' arguing it strongly, their version aiming at the accumulation of bullion and national power, although some anticipated the concept of industry policy (Hudson, 1992; Maneschi, 1998).

But the real revolution began with Smith (1776), who pioneered much of modern economics, including: the trade notions of 'absolute advantage' (below) and 'gains from trade' (above quotation); the development concepts of 'division of labour' (1776, 1: 8ff), economic growth, productivity expansion (1776, 1: 9), economies of scale, surplus generation, capital accumulation and technical change; and even the consumerist philosophy, hinted at by earlier Enlightenment writers, that luxury was the right of all, not just a social elite.

Smith also had a touch of the Community-Sovereignty theorist, his softer side having emerged in an earlier more philosophical book, *The Theory of Moral Sentiments*. He variously condemned the merchant's 'contrivance to raise prices' (1776, 1: 44), hoped that investment and employment would remain local rather than shift overseas (1776, 1: 476–7), warned that machines could make workers 'stupid and ignorant' (1776, 2: 303), suggested that people had a predilection for traditional agriculture (1776, 1: 403) and implied eventual limits to growth once a country had that 'full complement of riches which the nature of its soil and climate, and its situation with respect to other countries, allowed it to acquire' (1776, 1: 106).

Although Smith advocated 'self-love', profit-seeking and the 'invisible hand' of the market, which, he supposed, led merchants to incidentally benefit society (1776, 1: 477–8), he also urged 'civil society' institutions which could subvert the profit-oriented 'passions' of rapacious merchants and manufacturers (1776, 1: 519) to the broader 'interests' of all. For such subversion he recommended up to several dozen forms of market intervention, including various taxes, restraints on monopolies, price controls, state provision of schools and public works, export bans on scarce food items and even regulation of ale houses. He also accepted protection for defence, revenue and adjustment purposes.

Less scholastic but more technical than Smith, David Ricardo, a wealthy London stockbroker, one-time MP and amateur economist, systematised the earlier labour theory of value (later influencing Marx) and developed a pioneering production theory in which the 'law of diminishing returns' caused rents (income to land) to rise, manufacturing profits to fall and the economy to eventually reach a 'stationary state' (zero growth). Free trade could alleviate this state by reducing food and wage costs, but not prevent it.

However, Ricardo has been immortalised primarily for his seminal theory, which others partly anticipated, that trade is driven by 'comparative advantage' based on what today is called 'relative opportunity costs', not by Smith's 'absolute advantage' based on total costs (Table 2.1). This clearly implied the still fashionable idea that every country has a comparative advantage in something and can gain from trading in that specialty, although Ricardo did not favour complete free trade or the export of private capital (1817: 55) and he acknowledged that trade could be disruptive for more developed, trade-dependent countries (1817: ch. 19).

Thus, the Smith–Ricardo revolution involved recognising the role of market mechanisms, gains from trade and general links between economic factors, including between trade, technology and development, but neither theorist was dogmatic about the implications of his doctrines or thought that trade should dominate society.

After Mill (1848) the perceived importance of trade rose as the Industrial Revolution expanded trade volumes and GNP shares, most theorists assuming the veracity of 'gains from trade' doctrine and confining debate to the sources of comparative advantage or the mechanics of trade policy – if protection *had* to be used subsidies were better than tariffs, which were better than quotas, and so on. The most famous theory of comparative advantage arose in the 1930s with a hypothesis by Swedish economists, Heckscher and Ohlin (HO), that it is based on resource abundance – for example, labour-abundant countries would have comparative advantage in, and would export, labour-intensive goods.

From this now widely accepted theorem there emerged three important corollaries. The first was that as a country shifts from protection to free trade, prices of factors (land, labour and capital) adjust without the factors having to migrate to other countries, so that trade is a *substitute* for migration, and movements of labour or capital (the latter dominating the global economy today) are not really necessary for the world to benefit from exchange. The second corollary was that trading will move factor prices towards international convergence, or equalisation, which tallied with the 'law of one price', formulated earlier by Jevons and other Neoclassical theorists, that all prices will gradually equalise via 'arbitrage' (i.e. people buying in lower-price markets and selling in higher-price ones). The key implication of this was that trade can affect the distribution of income and thus have political repercussions.

The third, and most famous, corollary of HO theory, formulated by Stolper and Samuelson in 1941 (reprinted in Bhagwati, 1969), was that, following from the first two corollaries, free trade will increase the relative price (and income) of a country's abundant factor, which is capital in rich countries and labour in the poor. This occurs because the increased trade normally raises product and factor prices in industries which enjoy comparative advantage and which are intensive in that abundant factor. Protection does the reverse – that is, raises the price (income) of the scarce factor, which is labour in rich countries, and hence workers in those countries tend to favour Protectionism.

HO theory is now regarded as useful for explaining some trade, especially of Third World countries, but not all aspects, so that other theories of comparative advantage and trading have emerged (see below). But the corollaries are particularly interesting. The first corollary, that trade can be a substitute for factor flows, means that TNCs *need not* exist (see Krugman and Obstfeld, 1994: 161) and it is only since the 1970s that new theories of location, imperfect competition and various semi-political issues have emerged to explain their existence in reality (see Chapter 3). Regarding the second corollary, the 'law of one price' has not eventuated, large world-wide price differences still being common (Pryor, 2000: 20–21). This partly reflects trade barriers, but also suggests that the world is more complex than HO theory assumed (see below), that markets are imperfect and that globalisation is neither as advanced nor inevitable as global fatalists claim. The third corollary, the Stolper–Samuelson theorem, is still used to explain some distributional issues, suggesting that trade can affect equity, does have political impacts, is not socially neutral and, as Samuelson (1996) himself has said, creates many losers, even if in theory these can be compensated by the 'winners' (see below).

Free Trade Doctrine:
Models, Assumptions and Question Marks

Since Ricardo, trade has been said to be based on 'comparative advantage' or 'comparative costs', this referring to how much of one product each country has to forgo to produce one unit of another. The country which has to forgo least has a comparative advantage. What counts is how good a country is at producing one thing compared with another. A man who is better at both football and management than his mate can still earn more by employing his inferior friend to run his business while he specialises in football. Ricardo's model (Table 2.1) shows Portugal with lower absolute costs than England in both cloth and wine, but

Table 2.1 Ricardo's model

	Labour cost (worker-hours)		Opportunity cost (wine compared with cloth)	
	Cloth (1 unit)	Wine (1 unit)	1 cloth unit (/wine units)	1 wine unit (/cloth units)
England	100	120	$\frac{100}{120} = \frac{0.83}{\text{wine}}$	$\frac{120}{100} = \frac{1.2}{\text{cloth}}$
Portugal	90	80	$\frac{90}{80} = \frac{1.12}{\text{wine}}$	$\frac{80}{90} = \frac{0.89}{\text{cloth}}$

Notes

1. Labour costs are based on Ricardo's (1817: 153–4) example, except that he calls these numbers 'men required' to produce a set amount of output per year. Opportunity cost column provided by myself.
2. Model shows Portugal to have an *absolute advantage* in both products – i.e. lower labour costs (Labour cost column); Portugal is one-tenth better at cloth production but one-third better at wine, suggesting a *comparative advantage* in the latter.
3. 'Opportunity cost' is the opportunity forgone in doing one thing rather than another; the column shows the cost of one product in terms of the amount of the other forgone (based on the labour cost ratios).
4. Despite an absolute disadvantage in both products, England has a *comparative advantage* in cloth because she has to forgo less wine (0.83) than Portugal (1.12), and so is less inferior at cloth than wine. For the converse reason Portugal has a comparative advantage in wine. Thus, if money units reflect wine units, cloth will be cheaper in England than wine and the obverse in Portugal.
5. Trade is always likely to occur when there are different opportunity cost ratios between countries. Exchange will occur somewhere between the two countries' ratios, i.e. between 0.83 and 1.12 for cloth and between 0.89 and 1.2 for wine, the exact rate being indeterminate in economic theory, so is likely to be determined by bargaining or power relations. Mill later recognised that if a weaker country were forced to trade at or above the top exchange ratio (e.g. Portugal at 1.12 wine for 1 cloth), then that partner would not gain from trade.

enjoying a *comparative advantage* in wine because Portugal has to forgo less cloth than England to produce the wine – her superiority is greater in wine. Trade only occurs if there are differences in cost ratios between countries (as in Table 2.1), though the causes of such differences are still in some dispute (see below).

The bare logic of Ricardo's model and the basic validity of comparative advantage doctrine seem unassailable, although many theorists, too numerous to mention here, still have quibbles. Some still jumble the concepts of *absolute*, *comparative* and *competitive* advantage, such as in a recent pronouncement by Australian political economist Hugh Stretton that 'most trade arises from *competitive* rather than comparative advantage' (Stretton, 1999: 666–7). This sort of statement drives mainstream economists mad, especially as *competitive advantage* is not an orthodox concept but an umbrella term which includes comparative advantage as well as exchange rates and firm-specific factors. However, Stretton's description of this term sounds like *absolute* advantage and some still claim this is a valid concept, others questioning whether *comparative* advantage still drives trade (see below).

In short, I argue that the concept of comparative advantage is valid, but complex, variable and multi-facetted in ways explained below. However, I also argue that Free Trade theory in general is more contentious, contingent and assumption-dependent than Free Traders admit.

Comparative Advantage

If the concept of comparative advantage can be accepted as reality, then three other elements are more questionable – its basis, stability and assumptions. Traditionally the basis of national advantage, whether absolute or comparative, was seen as a combination of nature, tastes and factor productivities, particularly related to production techniques. Smith (1776, 1: 10) described its basis as 'soil, climate and situation', and Ricardo (1817: 151) as a country's 'situation, its climate, and its other natural or artificial advantages'.

Thus comparative advantage was often taken as natural or God-given and static, although Smith and Ricardo also related it to technology, HO theory (above) later added 'factor abundance' and, more recently, 'increasing returns' or 'economies of scale' have been invoked as a possible basis of trade (see below). For modelling convenience the two most likely bases of comparative advantage are often stated as 'technology' (Ricardo) versus 'factor abundance' (HO), but this oversimplifies its causes (see Maneschi, 1998).

Regarding the question of whether comparative advantage is constant or changing, Smith and Ricardo were vague, but referred sufficiently often to machinery, structural shifts towards industry and skill improvements to imply changeability. Smith (1776, 1: 19–20) depicted skills as deriving 'not so much from nature, as from habit, custom and education' – that is, from traditions, policies and changes therein. Over time, however, the convenient assumption of constancy was used for theoretical and modelling purposes and is still used today, even though nobody takes it literally. As will be further discussed below, it is now generally held that, in practice, comparative advantage is natural and fairly static for resources and agriculture but induced and dynamic for most industrial, technological and service sectors, this malleability potentially having far-reaching trade policy implications.

As regards the underlying assumptions of comparative advantage theory, Smith and Ricardo presumed little beyond competitive conditions, internal factor mobility and external immobility. But for quantification Neo-classical economists wanted tighter limits, so the HO model assumed two countries, two goods and two factors (2 × 2 × 2), which is often chided as unrealistic, arguably unfairly as multi-country/multi-good models of comparative advantage have been devised, though at the cost of greater complexity.

Less realistic or justifiable is the HO model's presumption of perfect competition, constant returns to scale, uniform technologies, fixed factor endowments and homogeneous tastes, which effectively assumes away most other possible causes of comparative advantage. One critic surmises that such a narrowing of assumptions is designed to obtain pro-market, pro-Free Trade results (Hudson, 1992: ch. 8), but I consider the excessively 'scientific', apolitical analysis which typifies Neo-classical theory a more likely cause of the narrowing.

Many trade economists now concede that analytical results can vary with the way assumptions are applied and that the questions of the causes and variability of comparative advantage are still open. Further assumptions, particularly relating to 'gains from trade', are examined below.

Gains from Trade

In most mainstream literature the focus of trade theory has long been on comparative advantage versus other explanations of trade, with the 'gains from trade' side of the coin taken as proven. Most critics of Free Trade doctrine have done likewise, although they are more likely to question the validity of comparative advantage as a concept, whereas I argue that it is a valid concept, with 'gains from trade' being the more questionable of the two sides. This is a crucial issue because the entire Global Free Trade Project is posited on the 'gains from trade' doctrine that nations will normally obtain higher consumption and income from trading freely than from autarky or extensive trade restrictions. I wish to question this belief.

Textbooks illustrate the 'gains from trade' in a number of complex ways, of which I will outline two as simply as possible. The first, known as the 'consumption possibility frontier', purports to show how a country can, by trading, consume more than it produces. It does this by specialising in products for which it has a comparative advantage, rather than trying to produce everything; then it exports the surpluses of its specialties in exchange for imports, this supposedly providing greater efficiency of resource-use.

There are two key elements to this story, both of which need questioning. The first is that the 'gains from trade' take the form of increased import consumption and only *indirectly* the form of income (see below). This assumes that higher import consumption is truly an increase in 'welfare', as economists like to put it, and that people always prefer more to less, so they will jump at the chance of more goodies even if these are imported. Certainly importing is likely to increase the quantity and variety of products available, but some critics believe it is not possible to show theoretically, as Neo-classical doctrine tries to, that people always prefer 'more to less' (see Keen, 2001: ch. 2), while the well-known British economic theorist Frank Hahn says that it is possible to have *too much* variety (see below).

The second key element is that when a country specialises, in order to seek 'gains from trade', it must restructure its economy, but this can entail the decline of some industries, the rise of others and even the complete elimination of certain sectors. This process can have many costs, which are acknowledged but underestimated by Free Traders, including relocation of employment, long-term unemployment, family disruption, devastation of certain towns or regions, loss of some industry-specific skills and changes in the nature of society – in other words a range of personal and social costs which need to be in some way subtracted from the gains from trade (see Prasch, 1996). People are seldom consulted about these changes, which are almost entirely 'non-consensual'.

A second method of illustrating the 'gains from trade' I wish to outline could be called the 'Harberger Triangles' technique, and is common in international economics textbooks. It is complex but I outline it in Figure 2.1 because it is a key to crucial trade issues. Readers who find Figure 2.1 unduly difficult may omit it, as the text explains the essentials. Free Traders say that protection is effectively a tax (on imports) which raises local prices (P_T) above world prices (P_W). This has several benefits: it encourages new local firms, which receive a so-called 'producer surplus' (area *a*) and government gets some customs revenue (rectangle *c*), as well as rectangle *e* as a bonus if the country's 'terms of trade' improve. This last concept is a complex but crucial

Figure 2.1 Harberger triangles

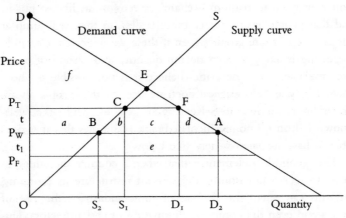

Notes

1. D is the domestic demand curve for a product and S is the domestic supply curve (without imports). Here the world price (P_W) is below the domestic equilibrium (E), thus tariffs are tempting so as to protect the local industry.

2. A Protectionist country can maintain a price P_T above the world price P_W by a tariff t. If that country is large with world market power, its lower post-tariff demand may force other countries to reduce the product's price to, say, P_F, encouraging imports and raising government revenue (rectangle e) from the additional tariff t_1.

3. A shift to free trade by removing $t + t_1$ will move the price to P_W. The various gains and losses of this are indicated by triangles and rectangles as marked. Area a, known as 'producer surplus', is bonus income to firms which arises when tariffs provide a price which is higher than previously prevailed. Triangle b is a production inefficiency due to higher production costs under tariffs. Rectangle c is the additional tariff revenue ($t \times S_1 D_1$) under a protectionist policy. Triangle d is a consumption inefficiency due to lower consumption ($D_2 - D_1$) and higher prices ($P_T - P_W$) under tariffs. Triangles b and d are called 'deadweight losses' because they are created by the tariff but allegedly have no counter-benefits for anyone, though it could be argued that they are not a complete loss (see text). These triangles are named after Arnold Harberger, a US economist who first used them to illustrate efficiency losses from monopoly and other market 'distortions'. The triangle f (P_TDF) is known as 'consumer surplus' (see below and Box 2.1), which represents consumption benefits. This concept is not direct income as non-economist globalists think, but an indirect 'psychic income' for consumers, as Ricardo (1817: 147) realised when he wrote that 'No extension of foreign trade will immediately increase the amount of value [production] in a country' although it will powerfully contribute to increase the mass of commodities, and therefore the sum of enjoyments [consumption].'

4. Under free trade, domestic producers lose area a due to new imports $S_1 - S_2$; government loses rectangle c due to elimination of tariff t as well as forgoing e if it is a large country and loses the terms of trade benefit, while triangles b and d go to consumers. In other words, areas $a + b + c + d$ all go to the consumers as an addition to 'consumer surplus', whose new total is the augmented triangle f (P_WDA). Triangles b and d are the net gains from trade, the entire Global Free Trade Project being based primarily on the presumption that these are real inefficiencies which can be eliminated by trade liberalisation.

one. The 'terms of trade' (the ratio of a country's export prices to import prices) will improve if the country is large enough to influence world prices, so that its lower import demand under protection will pull world prices down (to say P_F). At the lower price there will be a few extra imports, and the revenue goes to the government.

The problem, according to Free Traders, is that firms in the protected industries will be selling less but at higher prices (P_T), and this is said to be inefficient, the two (Harberger) triangles b and d being socalled 'deadweight losses' to the economy, which represent the alleged costs of protection.

With free trade all this is reversed. Prices in the protected industries fall to the world-parity level (from P_T to P_W), local firms lose area a, the government loses rectangle c (due to less customs revenue) and perhaps rectangle e if the terms of trade deteriorate. In fact, such deterioration is likely for a large country, and this 'terms of trade' case is the only one which most Free Traders accept as an instance of protection unambiguously making a country better off in terms of income than with free trade. However, under free trade the Harberger triangles of inefficiency disappear, and this represents the 'gains from trade'. Areas a, c and e, along with triangles b and d (the 'lost' inefficiency, so to speak) all go to consumers (triangle f, whose bottom drops from P_T to P_W).

So free trade has winners and losers – local firms (along with their workers) and governments lose while consumers win, but the wins supposedly outweigh the losses by the size of the eliminated 'triangles of inefficiency', which are said to be 'net gains from trade'. The Global Free Trade Project is basically about eliminating these quaint little triangles as completely as possible.

This is a persuasive and, at present, world-conquering doctrine, but it has several problems. First, the inefficiency supposedly represented by the Harberger triangles may be at least partly countered over time if the new enterprises or industries encouraged by protection improve their efficiency through 'learning effects' –

that is, the gradual accumulation of knowledge and experience. Free Traders tend to discount such effects and claim that protection fosters various inefficiencies, but there is evidence that it can also foster viable new activities (see Chapter 6).

Second, the 'gains from trade' do not provide direct cash income to consumers, but involve an indirect, swings-and-roundabouts redistribution which people receive as 'consumer surplus', or a 'psychic' bonus as a result of prices being lower than they expect. In Box 2.1 I outline some ways in which this 'consumer surplus' may be less beneficial than Free Traders claim. In fact, many economists admit that this concept is theoretically questionable. Third, the 'gains from trade' doctrine is based on a number of simplifying, not always realistic, assumptions and leads to various (questionable) corollaries, which I critically examine below.

Paul Krugman once said that economics has a 'dirty little secret' – Free Trade theory is true but the 'gains from trade' are very small (quoted in Dunkley, 2000b: 14). I agree, except that I see *three* dirty little secrets. Secret No. 1 is that there is an unwritten golden rule of Free Trade: 'thou shalt accept structural change for it will be good for you in the long run'. Secret No. 2 is that this structural change is 'non-consensual', with few people having a say in it, and the social or other 'non-economic' adjustment costs can be high. Secret No. 3 is that the benefits of free trade, or the 'gains from trade', arise not as direct cash-in-hand but in the form of an indirect, theoretical, concept called 'consumer surplus' whose real value can be questioned (Box 2.1), and so these gains, as Krugman has admitted, are probably small, unless the even more uncertain 'dynamic gains' (below) are invoked. Below and in later chapters I will argue that 'gains from trade' are contingent on many factors and could be negative more often than Free Traders admit.

In sum, even in mainstream trade theory the 'gains from trade' is not a clear-cut unambiguous concept, but an indirect outcome of inefficiency reduction and transfers of 'consumer surplus', a concept which is less meaningful in practice than in theory and is of uncertain value. Mainstream economists accept that some individuals can lose, but claim that because there are overall net gains, the 'winners' can compensate the losers and still be better off, the compensation preferably being via low-cost lump-sum transfers, though the actual implementation of compensation is seldom monitored. If compensation is by a method other than lump-sum transfers, there will be administrative costs, which further eat into the gains from trade. But I also argue that factors such as the uncertain meaning of 'consumer surplus' (Box 2.1), possible unequal trade impacts and forgone terms of trade benefits for some countries, can, to a greater extent than globalisers admit, minimise any gains from trade or even ensure overall nett losses. These, probably overstated, gains are the main reason why I claim that Free Trade doctrine is partly mythological.

The type of trade gains outlined above are called 'static gains' and were the only type discussed until fairly recently, most economists accepting that, because triangles b and d are small, trade gains would be relatively minor in practice, usually less than 1 per cent of GDP (Chapters 4 and 6). But many economists claim there are further 'dynamic gains' from trade due to capital accumulation stimulated by the 'static gains', to import competition and to resultant new technological development. Dynamic gains are usually divided into two categories: 'capital accumulation gains' and 'productivity gains', with one Australian modelling group, Stoeckel et al., adding 'risk premium gains'. The latter consist of the lower interest rates which countries can supposedly obtain when they liberalise, either unilaterally or under IMF/ World Bank SAPs, credit-rating agencies such as Standard & Poor's apparently being impressed by such obedient behaviour. Some estimate that 'dynamic gains' are half the static gains, the latter remaining as the main trade gain (e.g. Dowrick, 1994), but others now say they are double the static gains, and Stoeckel et al. claim they are several times as large (Stoeckel et al., 2000; Dunkley, 2000b: 138–9).

Box 2.1 Consumer surplus

Neo-classical economists use the term 'surplus' in a different way
to Marxists, deeming it a sort of bonus. 'Producer surplus' arises
when price is above marginal cost, as shown by the supply curve.
In Figure 2.1, the triangle OCP_T shows producer surplus under
tariffs while the smaller triangle OBP_W is the surplus under free
trade, which thus reduces the surplus of local producers. 'Consumer surplus' was defined by Alfred Marshall (1920: 103–10), who
invented the concept, as the difference between what a person is
willing to pay for a product, rather than go without it, and the
market price which has to be paid, the two usually being different.
Consumer surplus is the triangle P_TDF under tariffs and P_WDA
under free trade, the latter thus delivering an extra bonus of areas
$a + b + c + d$ (in Fig. 2.1). This concept is used to measure benefits
of various policies, including trade. The 'producer surplus', as a
direct income, seems real enough, but how real is consumer surplus?

Economists regard consumer surplus as bonus 'utility' (satisfaction) which people subjectively feel when prices are less than they
are willing to pay. In Figure 2.1 some people, possibly the wealthier,
are willing to pay up to D, but only have to pay P_T under tariffs,
or P_W under free trade. Is this an equivalent of direct money income which they rush out and spend? Probably not! Marshall said
it was measurable in money terms, but economists now tend to
call it 'psychic income' because it makes people feel richer without
putting money directly into their pockets. Trade economists simply
assume that there is a one-for-one income equivalent of consumer
surplus, seemingly unaware that this has been extensively debated
by their 'welfare' economics colleagues for decades. As far back as
the 1930s, most welfare economists agreed that 'aggregate consumer surplus' (triangle f in Fig. 2.1) was not very meaningful
because the respective 'utilities' (satisfaction) of individuals could
not be adequately compared or aggregated. But the trade economists have never caught up, still thinking that gains from trade in
the form of 'consumer surplus' is a solid, measurable concept, which
it is not!

Marshall (1920: 110) believed consumer surplus was more significant for necessities than luxuries and was 'highly conjectural' for larger-than-customary price changes. Silberberg (1972: 942ff) argued that valuing 'utility' was arbitrary, and that a one-for-one income equivalent of the consumer surplus bonus was unlikely, especially where the bonus was abrupt or discontinuous. Currie et al. (1971: 741ff) argued that 'consumer surplus' was a meaningful income equivalent via the 'income effect' – i.e. lower prices raise disposable income – but was still a limited notion due to conceptual uncertainties, measurement difficulties, the impossibility of knowing or meaningfully aggregating individual consumer preferences, the possibility of heterogeneous preferences and the likelihood that people's desire for income will differ considerably and unpredictably. Samuelson (1974: 197ff) had earlier played down the concept for similar reasons, being one of the few trade theorists to do so. Blaug (1985: 400–401) questions the measurability of consumer surplus for large price changes and major budget items, as well as because of the aggregation problem (above). Joan Robinson (1962: 123) declared the whole concept 'bogus' because it involved a 'pseudo-quantitative treatment of something which by its nature cannot be measured'.

Thus 'consumer surplus' probably denotes some real income effect, but cannot be accurately measured in practice, despite attempts by trade and other modellers to do so (see Doughney, 2002). The concept of 'gains from trade' is, therefore, probably real but of a much more contingent and uncertain value than Free Traders make out.

However, there are problems with the 'dynamic gains' concept. First, it assumes that all the 'static gains' will flow through to 'dynamic gains', whereas the above critique of 'consumer surplus' (Box 2.1) gives reason to doubt this. Second, it is difficult to separate trade from other causal factors in 'dynamic gains' whose two main components, investment and productivity improvements, can have many inter-related causes besides any impetus which may come from trade. Third, it is implicitly assumed that all capital accumulation and productivity growth from technological innovation are equally beneficial, whereas some social costs are likely. Fourth, the 'risk premium gain' (above) is arguably a subjective, political concept generated by global credit-ratings agencies, and it is questionable whether governments should tailor their policies to please such bodies. Fifth, dynamic gains are longer-term and many economists admit they are rather speculative (Krugman, 1999: 178–9; and see Dunkley, 2000b: 138–9). The mainstream US economist Rachel McCulloch (1999) quips that the theory of static gains is 'leaky and incomplete' while dynamic gains are 'notoriously hard to formalise and measure', so the latter requires an even greater leap of faith than the former. Thus, it could be said that 'dynamic gains' from trade tend to add something to 'static gains' (Figure 2.1) but by an uncertain amount.

Assumptions, Assumptions!

The above theoretical framework depends heavily on assumptions which vary in their degree of realism and are easily caricatured, sometimes unfairly, by critics. We need to distinguish between convenience assumptions such as, 'two countries – two goods – two factors', 'no transport costs', or 'no government', the failure of which will not seriously undermine trade theory, and the more substantive assumptions, discussed below, whose failure could partly invalidate the doctrine. Certain simplifying assumptions are necessary to make reality manageable, but the compatibility of these with reality has to be scrutinised. Some criticisms are, I think, invalid. A few critics assert, for instance, that orthodox trade theory does not work in the presence of floating exchange rates or trade imbalances, but mainstream theorists deny that such macro-factors affect comparative advantage, which is primarily a micro-level concept. I partly concur with the latter view, although external forces can affect prices and some resource allocation to an extent (Chapter 3).

The following is a list of explicit or implicit assumptions apparently underlying Free Trade theory, and I comment on the ways in which these can fail.

1. *'Perfect' competition* The basic requirements for competitive markets, domestically and internationally, are: many buyers and sellers; each unit small in relation to the market; homogeneous products; rational maximising behaviour by 'agents' (firms and consumers); no entry or exit barriers, and so forth. Failure of too many of these criteria will mean inefficient markets and the possibility of profits being drained away from countries without monopolies or oligopolies, along with other problems now being identified even by mainstream economists (Chapter 3). The present-day rage for deregulation and competition policies is aimed at 'perfecting' markets, as well as being an acknowledgement of assumption failures.

2. *Constant returns* 'Returns' in this context means the rate of output growth relative to factor inputs (land, labour and capital) and, conversely, the rate of change of costs relative to scale of production. Economists have always been ambivalent as to whether diminishing, constant or increasing returns were the relevant production pattern, so constant returns were often assumed for simplicity, even though increasing returns or 'economies of scale' were noted as early as Adam Smith. In earlier times diminishing or constant returns seemed the relevant pattern in crafts and agriculture, possibly still being so, but many, even among mainstream commentators, now think that increasing returns are the norm in modern industry, especially with mass production and higher technologies, though this may be overstated (Chapter 7). The implications for production and trade are immense, including the possibility that free trade is not universally beneficial (Chapter 3 and Keen, 2001: ch. 3).

3. *No learning effects* As mentioned above, the 'deadweight loss' (Harberger) triangles (*b* and *d* in Figure 2.1), which

supposedly prove the inefficiency of protection and the virtues of free trade, implicitly assume protected industries will
not improve their efficiency through 'learning-by-doing' (i.e.
on-the-job learning by workers), skill improvements or the
like. But many economists have shown these beneficial
mechanisms do exist and *may* justify some protection (see
Chapter 3).

4. *External immobility of factors*   Ricardo and others once assumed
   that factors of production (labour and capital) did not generally
   move internationally, and HO theory (above) suggests factor
   movements are unnecessary when trading is adequate, but
   clearly this is not true in practice. The implications of this
   assumption failure are not clear; many Post-Keynesian and
   other theorists arguing that mobile factors cause trade to
   switch to an *absolute* rather than *comparative* advantage basis
   because TNC capital can shape production costs in host
   countries. Mainstream economists insist that factors may move
   in accordance with *absolute* advantage but trade is still based
   mainly on comparative advantage, although other possible
   bases for trade have been identified (below), so the question is
   arguably still open. If trade was based on *absolute* advantage
   under factor mobility conditions, then exploitation-based trade
   would be more likely, intervention would be more justifiable
   and less trading may be conducted (e.g. in Table 2.1 Portugal,
   with an absolute advantage in both products, would not bother
   to trade).

5. *Internal mobility of factors*   A classic assumption since Smith
   has been that factors can move to new employment sufficiently smoothly that the costs of free trade will not outweigh the benefits. Recently the WTO (2001: 8) has glibly
   claimed that firms 'adapt gradually and in a relatively painless
   way' better under free trade than protection. Real world
   experience shows that this is simply not so, even Adam Smith
   (1776, 1: 491) having advocated protection for short-term
   adjustment if necessary. Capital can have 'sunk' (irrecover-

able) costs and workers can find it hard to get new jobs at equivalent pay (Prasch, 1996).

6. *Full employment* Deriving from the previous assumption, permanent full employment would ensure no-cost redeployment of workers displaced by imports, but this seldom occurs in reality. Mainstream economists often admit this but claim that it reduces rather than eliminates gains from trade. However, even a few mainstream modellers concede that lost profits, reduced wages and long-term unemployment are social costs which can outweigh gains from trade, and which the famous Post-Keynesian economist Joan Robinson has said would reduce Free Trade doctrine to 'wreckage' (see Dunkley, 2000: 116, 152, 289).

7. *Small-country terms of trade* Early theorists assumed that all countries were small traders who could not influence world prices, but, as discussed above, in practice many can, thus potentially obtaining gains from protection or losses from free trade via the 'terms of trade effect' (Figure 2.1).

8. *Lump-sum compensation* As already touched on, trade theory clearly acknowledges that there are both winners and losers from free trade (Figure 2.1) and that the former must compensate the latter, both domestically and worldwide, by costlessly raised lump-sum payment, for the full gains from trade to be reaped. Failure on any of these points, by way of uncompensated losers or high cost compensation transfers, will reduce the gains, and although structural adjustment assistance is common now, few if any countries monitor its adequacy. Many Fundamentalist Free Traders still oppose such compensation on the grounds that net gains exist even if not redistributed, an argument I regard as invalid (see No. 12 below).

9. *No externalities* The economist's euphemism for side-benefits or side-costs of a transaction, 'externalities' will arise if trade prices deriving from comparative costs (Table 2.1) do not reflect all costs, such as social and environmental problems or

labour exploitation (see later chapters). Any such externalities will offset gains from trade, a point readily acknowledged but often underplayed by mainstream economists.

10. *Voluntary, arm's-length trade* An implicit assumption in trade theory is that trading transactions are voluntary and 'arm's length' between independent firms from each country. In practice, involuntary trade can occur due to slavery, 'gunboat diplomacy', debt-induced exchange or IMF–World Bank pressure, and non-arm's-length trade is rising, with much world trade now being intra-firm (between subsidiaries of a TNC). Commercially, exchange will not be conducted outside the two trading countries' opportunity cost ratios (Table 2.1), but politically it is quite possible for one country's exchange to be pushed up to or outside this ratio (e.g. Portugal to more than 1.12 wine for one cloth) by these involuntary and non-arm's length mechanisms, which would eliminate gains from trade for that country. Non-arm's-length transactions now include frequent use of transfer pricing by a TNC to induce paper losses, for tax purposes, by its subsidiaries in higher tax countries.

11. *The good consumer* Mainstream Free Market Economic Rationalist theory assumes, contrary to Gandhi, that consumption is the chief goal of economic activity, and perhaps of life itself, so that higher consumption and consumer surplus via trade constitute true welfare gains. However, if, for the reasons suggested above, people do not always seek to maximise consumption and the consumer surplus concept is fuzzy, then free trade might not be as optimal, nor trade *per se* as desirable, as globalisers claim.

12. *Uniform preferences* Because the gains from trade are a 'swings and roundabouts' affair and partly subjective, with gains or losses shared around unevenly, gains from free trade are only positive if the gainers appreciate them. For convenience economists and modellers assume that everyone equally appreciates higher consumption, but in the quite feasible event

of this not being so, perhaps due to high income groups getting most of the gains, some groups being less consumerist or certain people resisting imported consumer goods, then the theoretical benefits of free trade are at least partly negated, a fact which trade texts seldom mention (though see Krugman and Obsfeld, 1994: 204). This also makes compensation, which supposedly rectifies uneven trade gains, more difficult to implement precisely or fairly.

13. *Gains to locals* 'Gains from trade' theory is posited on the assumption that the 'static gains' mostly remain in the country. But in an age of globalisation and 'demonstration effects' (i.e. copycatting of other country's consumption habits) people may increase their 'marginal propensity to import' (i.e. spend more of their 'consumer surplus' on imports than they traditionally did) or send more of their savings overseas rather than reinvest it locally as required for 'dynamic gains'. In such cases the gains from trade may be less than implied by the theory. Further, free trade tends to redistribute benefits from government and local firms (Figure 2.1), many of which may be small, cooperative or public enterprises, to private individuals and exporters, so that free trade is inherently a privatising process and this may not equate to the public good.

14. *Let them eat structural change!* As noted above, a key unwritten rule of Free Trade is that 'thou shalt accept structural change', Free Traders assuming that such change brings efficiency, development and acceptance by people because of those benefits. But the reality is more complex because 'efficiency' and 'development' are often a matter of judgement, alternatives do exist (see Chapters 5–7 below) and most trade- or technology-induced structural change is undebated, undemocratic and non-consensual, thus always tending to elicit some resistance (Polanyi, 1957; Dunkley, 2000b). Bill Gates (1996: 11) has decreed that because we cannot vote on technological change we have to accept it, the same un-

democratic fatalism being frequent in relation to trade-induced structural change.

15. *Material goals* A final assumption of Free Trade doctrine is that the key goals of economic policy are income maximisation in the short term and rapid economic growth and development in the longer term, this being more critical than is generally realised. Free Traders claim that free trading is almost always best for such purposes; although I question this in Chapter 6, the more important point is whether or not income and growth *should* be a central goal – if they should not, many other more self-reliant trade and development policies are justifiable even if they sacrifice some income or growth.

This list of assumptions is not exhaustive, others occurring in specific contexts such as the WTO's crucial assumption, in pushing service trade liberalisation, that goods and services are equivalent for this purpose (Chapter 8). But the list does indicate the remarkable number of hidden assumptions underlying Free Trade theory and the possible effects where these prove unrealistic.

More broadly, I suggest two major implications of this assumption-dependent nature of Free Trade theory. First, assumption failures mean that trade may be less beneficial or free trade less justified than claimed, to an extent which depends on the number and degree of the failures. Second, countries may differ in their degrees of assumption failure, and thus in their 'capacity to gain' from trade. For instance, a large country with 'terms of trade' benefits, many oligopolistic firms, major 'increasing returns' sectors and high unemployment might lose badly from free trade, whereas a smaller country with small-scale competitive industries and internally mobile factors may readily gain from free trade, a situation which seems to have prevailed in late-nineteenth-century Europe (see Chapter 4). I do not suggest that such assumption failures leave trade doctrine 'in tatters' as some critics proclaim, but I do suggest that they render free trade and globalisation more ambiguous, more contingent and subject to a wider range of qualifications than Free Traders admit.

Here Come the Corollaries

Corollaries are implications which flow from rather than underlie trade theory and which are usually alluded to in mainstream literature, though the following listing and critiques are my own.

1. *Universal benefits* The greatest single myth of Free Trade is the standard claim by globo-euphorists that all people in all countries virtually always gain from free trade, the entire GATT/WTO system being largely built on this corollary. Yet, curiously, mainstream economists have never really claimed this, admitting to various costs of free trade (see below). A country with a negative terms-of-trade effect, chronic unemployment, adverse externalities, inequalities, wide preference diversities and high structural adjustment costs may not benefit from free trade at all, while non-economic costs such as environmental effects or compromised sovereignty may mean overall losses from trade. Thus, gains from trade are contingent rather than guaranteed.

2. *Everybody's good at something* The related mythology and corollary that every country will have comparative advantage in something is partly true by definition (Table 2.1) but this misses the key point that a country must *benefit* from trading for this to be so. But, as already discussed, gains are not guaranteed, for the costs of free trade may outweigh the benefits, or a country's comparative advantage may be in a weak-price sector (see Chapter 5 below).

3. *Unilateral benefit* This is my term for the Free Traders' claim that because gains from trade derive from specialisation-induced efficiency, any country can benefit from reducing its own protection unilaterally. However, I dispute this claim on the grounds, first, that gains are not automatic, and, second,

that failure of assumptions 1, 2 and 7 above may enable one country to gain at the expense of another (see Chapter 3).

4. *Redistribution*   Between the times of Ricardo and Hecksher–Ohlin (HO) Neo-classical economists largely ignored the distributive effects of trade, and present-day globo-euphorists claim that free trade helps the poor, but Ricardo hypothesised that trade would favour profits (see above) and the Stolper–Samulson extension of HO (see above) says that trade liberalisation will disadvantage the scarce factor, which for rich countries is unskilled labour in the labour-intensive industries most commonly protected. Thus, the globalisers' claim that free trade helps the poor is by no means fully supported even by mainstream economics, let alone by the range of more complex issues to be discussed in Chapter 5.

5. *Vested interests*   Free Market Economic Rationalists, especially the so-called 'Public Choice' school, claim that free trade is so good it could only be opposed by a (supposedly small) number of noisy self-interested losers. But this rather cynical hypothesis ignores, first, the wide range of possible losers due to the assumption failures discussed earlier, second, the fact that for non-economic reasons many oppose free trade on principle and, third, that there can be vested interests in free trade as well (see Chapter 4 and Dunkley, 2000b: 413).

6. *Engine for growth*   One of the most acclaimed corollaries and mythologies of trade theory is that free trade, via 'dynamic gains' (see above, and later), can spark continuing economic growth, but the various assumption failures discussed, as well as issues examined in the following chapters, seriously undermine this famed assertion (see Chapter 6).

7. *Cosmopolitanism*   Finally, the broad-brush claim that free trade leads to wide-ranging, beneficial cosmopolitanism (as early economists called globalisation), and perhaps to world peace, is belied by the adverse effects of globalisation outlined in Chapter 1, by the assumption failures discussed above and by the many costs potentially entailed (see Chapters 4 and 5).

In this section I have sought to examine Free Trade doctrine critically by stressing uncertainties, assumption failures and questionable corollaries of trade theory, as well as some logical vagaries in two core concepts of Free Trade doctrine – the Harberger triangles and 'consumer surplus'. In my view, many critics focus unduly on the meaningfulness or otherwise of comparative advantage, a notion which I regard as valid, albeit subject to arbitrary definition and change. I distinguish between this concept and the 'gains from trade' side of the coin, which is the more critical to arguments for the globalisation project. I have pointed out that in conventional trade theory the 'gains from trade' is not an automatic single-number concept but a tortuous 'swings and roundabouts' process whose outcome, given uncertainties, assumption failures and the like, can often be less favourable than Free Traders imply. In claiming vast benefits for globalisation, globo-euphorists rely heavily on a faith that economists have got the numbers right, but I argue that this is somewhat misplaced, one mainstream economist (McCulloch, 1999) quipping that, because of this faith, Free Trade theory is more like religion than science. Certainly the Free Trade debate has not been resolved, with many question marks remaining.

The Rise of Not-Quite-Free Trade

Few mainstream economists have given free trade a completely blank cheque, and in this section I briefly examine the reasons for their hesitation, with more far-reaching challenges outlined in the next chapter.

Despite his zeal for free trade, Adam Smith accepted protection for revenue, retaliation, defence and social adjustment purposes. Malthus accepted food security grounds for protection (Gomes, 1987: 175ff) and by the time of J.S. Mill (1848) the 'infant industry' and 'terms of trade' (Box 2.1) cases were also being widely acknowledged, though the latter was not formally proven until the work of Charles Bickerdike in 1906 (Irwin, 1996:

113ff). By the late nineteenth century leading Neo-classical economists such as Edgeworth and Marshall were describing free trade
as uncertain in theory but the best policy in practice because
governments could get their protection policies wrong (now called
'government failure') or resources could be wasted in lobbying
efforts (now called 'rent seeking' – see Chapter 6). However,
Marshall (1923: 760ff) conceded that the case for Free Trade was
often overstated in relation to developing countries seeking industry and scale economies.

During the 1920s there emerged major new challenges to free
trade doctrine by Frank Graham (USA), Allyn Young (UK and
USA) and James Brigden (Australia) on the basis of increasing
returns and learning effects – that is, failure of assumptions 2 and
3 above – while John Williams (USA) queried the factual basis of
the internal mobility and external immobility assumptions (Nos 4
and 5 above), avowing that society was too 'organic' for such
rigid presumptions (Young, 1928; Gomes, 1990; Irwin, 1996).
During the 1930s Keynes and his colleagues questioned Free Trade
on macroeconomic grounds, paramountly the need to restore full
employment (see Chapter 3). In the 1940s Samuelson (in
Bhagwati, 1969) showed that free trade need not benefit all
individuals, that some countries (but not all together) could benefit
from an 'optimum tariff' and that net gains from trade may often
rely heavily on efficient lump-sum compensation of losers
(assumption No. 8 above), which, of course, involved political
decisions.

During the 1950s many economists proposed various Protectionist arguments for development reasons (Chapters 3 and 4),
while Lipsey and Lancaster formulated their landmark 'second
best' theorem. This theorem holds that if full market efficiency is
to be achieved, all 'distortions', including government interventions, must be removed together, and if this is not administratively or politically possible then continuing protection may be
better than free trade. This is one reason why Free Market Economic Rationalists now demand the deregulation of all markets

in close sequence. Bhagwati and others pointed out that protection may be better than free trade in the presence of 'distortions' – government intervention, imperfect competition, externalities and so forth – of which a remarkable number were identified, although the 'first best' solution is elimination of distortions if possible. Mainstream economists, of course, used this as an argument for all-round liberalisation and competition policy rather than protection and general interventionism, thus demonstrating that Free Trade is not an ideology-free concept – it needs free competitive markets to work.

Thus, the early post-war period saw a marked transition from confidence in, to ambivalence about, the veracity of Free Trade theory, the reliability of doctrinal assumptions and the universality of benefits from trade. Many mainstream economists asserted no more than that 'some trade is better than no trade for the world as a whole', with possible losses to certain people and countries conceded. Certainly it was widely acknowledged that free trade is not always the best policy (Kitson and Solomou, 1990).

Leading British economic theorist Frank Hahn once remarked that extreme Free Marketeers 'say much more than even pure theory allows them to say, and infinitely more than the applicability of that theory permits'. Regarding free trade, he has said that, whilst often beneficial, it can bring *too much* variety and *excessive* 'new knowledge', along with 'psychic and other costs', so that not all countries or people may benefit (Hahn, 1982, 1998). French Nobel laureate Maurice Allais, whose main work is in arcane general equilibrium theory, has criticised Free Trade and advocated mild protection both within the EU and globally, because he believes comparative advantage to be so dynamic and volatile now that countries may be 'left behind', at very high social costs (Chandra, 1997: 188; Dunkley, 2000: 120).

Conventional trade theory has proved unable to explain trends such as trade imbalances, the rise of TNCs, Third World underdevelopment or, in particular, the phenomenon of 'intra-industry trade' (IIT – see Chapter 3). In response, new theories of the causes of trade have emerged, including the 'availability' thesis (available supply of suitable resources and products); Samuelson's 'specific factors' model (multiple factors with mobile labour); Linder's theorem based on demand and tastes; the 'product cycle model' (phases of innovation, production and export); several technology-based theories and an 'economies of scale' model (Chapter 3). Abstruse mathematical testing has shown the Ricardian and HO models to be useful but vulnerable to assumption failures, while the 'technology gap', Linder and 'economies of scale' theories have often proved better at explaining technology-intensive trade and IIT than did comparative advantage theory, although none is regarded as a complete explanation (see Krugman and Obstfeld, 1994; Irwin, 1996; Maneschi, 1998).

Conclusion

Since Smith and Ricardo it has been generally taken for granted that free trade is economically better than protection, globo-euphorists claiming that it is best for all people and all countries at all times and the WTO's Global Free Trade Project being largely based on this presumption. However, many mainstream economists have been more cautious than this, admitting to cases where free trade is not unambiguously best and accepting a few arguments for protection such as 'terms of trade', infant industry, externalities, 'second best' and adjustment costs (see Box 9.1 for a fuller list).

In this chapter I have argued that of the two linked trade theorems, 'comparative advantage' is valid but more complex than traditionally painted, while the 'gains from trade' element involves 'swings and roundabouts' rather than direct monetary benefits, so is contingent rather than automatic. Countries may therefore differ in their capacities to gain from trade. Trade theory is too dependent upon questionable assumptions and corollaries to guarantee benefits for all countries and people. Losses are possible, especially when account is taken of the costs of (non-consensual) structural change or other social impacts.

For these and other reasons examined in the next chapter, the critical thinking US Free Trader, Paul Krugman (1987), has said that Free Trade theory is now in more doubt than at any time since Ricardo and that the case for Free Trade is not overwhelming, but is 'a more subtle [and] … political case than we are used to making' (1999: 362). I suggest that Free Trade doctrine is like modern drug therapy: miracles are theoretically possible, but the costs can be high, there can be adverse side effects, resistance increases over time and effectiveness depends upon the patient's own response mechanisms.

CHAPTER 3

A CONFEDERACY OF HERETICS:
TWO CENTURIES OF FREE
TRADE DISSENT

[T]he cheapness of the articles produced by machinery, and the improved means of transport and communication furnish the weapons for conquering foreign markets. By ruining handicraft production in other countries, machinery forcibly converts them into fields for the supply of raw material.... A new and international division of labour, a division suited to the requirements of the chief centres of modern industry springs up.

Karl Marx (1967: 451)

It is the policy of an autonomous rate of interest, unimpeded by international preoccupations, and of a national investment programme directed to an optimum level of domestic employment which is twice blessed in the sense that it helps ourselves and our neighbours at the same time.

J.M. Keynes (1936: 349)

[F]ree trade is not passé, but is an idea that has irretrievably lost its innocence. Its status has shifted from optimum to reasonable rule of thumb ... [and] can never again be asserted as the policy that economic theory tells us is always right.

Paul Krugman (1987: 132)

Depending on where the boundaries are drawn in defining an economic theorist, there have probably been many more 'heretics' than followers of orthodoxy in the Free Trade debate. Unlike early theological heretics, economic dissenters have never been burnt at the stake, although ostracism in university departments or other orthodox circles has not been unknown. As sub-mainstream or non-mainstream economists, trade heretics variously question the logic, assumptions, corollaries, values or goals of mainstream trade theory, abandon or modify the concept of equilibrium (Chapter 1), usually eschew simplistic, linear mathematical models, often employ more complex notions of causality and mostly reject trade-deterministic versions of trade–development links. In some areas of economics, goals do not matter much as certain universals apply – for example, whatever its goals, a society must balance its external payments; or if it wishes to invest more it must save more; or to avoid inflation it must avoid excess demand. But in trade, goals can matter – the goal of self-reliance precludes trade-dependence; interest rate autonomy as advocated by Keynes (above) precludes extreme financial deregulation; domestically oriented 'import substitution' development precludes the 'export-oriented' models favoured by the IMF/World Bank and the WTO (Chapter 6). This chapter briefly examines a few of the remarkable variety of alternative perspectives in the trade field.

Heresy before Orthodoxy

Although the idea of 'freedom to trade' has existed beside trade interventionism for a long time, historically by far the greater number of economic thinkers and policymakers favoured Protection in some form or another, most ancient Greek philosophers, including Aristotle, opposing trade altogether. Many pre-Smithian economists, loosely known as 'Mercantilists', were scorned by Smith and others for allegedly holding quaint (or dangerous) notions such as export promotion, inducement of trade surpluses, accumulation of bullion (precious metals) or enhancement of national mercantile power. Later research suggested, however, that many Mercantilists were actually astute forerunners of modern Market Interventionism (Hudson, 1992), Keynes (1936: ch. 23) explaining that bullion accumulation was at that time the only way of forcing down interest rates to expand investment (his own famous policy preference). The Nobel laureate Sir John Hicks has said that the Mercantilists' early trade and policy Interventionism would have worked better if contemporary administrative capacity had been more developed.

Adam Smith sought to debunk the Mercantilists in favour of what today we would call deregulation and trade liberalisation, without being a dogmatic Free Trader, but the famed population theorist Thomas Malthus (1766–1834) wanted population control, opposed industrial development in favour of agrarianism and queried free trade on food security and social stability grounds. Ricardo's contemporary, Robert Torrens, identified the role of demand, not just Ricardian cost, in trade, also anticipating comparative advantage, the terms of trade issue (Chapter 2), the 'Australian' case for protection (below) and the trade policy of reciprocal concessions. Thereafter he was ostracised by mainstream Free Traders and condemned as a Mercantilist (Irwin, 1996: ch. 7).

Mercantilist influence continues to the present day, even Keynes (1936: ch. 23) hailing them as forebears of his investment 'motor-boat' view of the economy (my metaphor – Chapter 1). Perhaps the first great Mercantilist political figure was US leader Alexander Hamilton (1755–1804) who advocated early versions of 'infant industry' protection, tariff-led industrial development and national self-reliance, all of which were adopted to some degree during the nineteenth century and were more common than Free Traders acknowledge (Gomes, 258ff; Irwin, 1996: 121ff; Maneschi, 1998: ch. 5; Chang, 2002).

Two key figures in nineteenth-century economic and trade heresy were the German scholar-rebel Friedrich List (1789–1846) and the Swiss economist–philosopher J.C.L. Simonde de Sismondi (1773–1842). List saw manufacturing as the heart of development and living standards, criticising the anti-industrialism of Malthus and Sismondi (List, 1841: 127–8), proclaiming industry to be the path from barbarism to civilisation (1841: 183) and documenting the fact that protection-led development had been very common throughout Europe in the past. List argued against Smithian free trade on the grounds that it only worked for countries of relatively equal development, that private business interests did not equate to those of society and that political intervention was required to promote development. For List the core development process lay not in markets, but in dynamic 'productive power' which inheres in a 'national system', not in a 'cosmopolitan system of universal trade' (1841: 120ff). However, List's Protectionism was a limited one, as he recommended trade intervention only for the catch-up phase of industrialisation in order to prevent the lagging country being locked into inferior sectors. List's 'national system' theory strongly influenced German, US, Japanese and Australian ideas about protection-led development, but has always been rejected by mainstream economists as fuzzy and Mercantilist (see Chang, 2002: 3ff and *passim*).

Sismondi insightfully anticipated Marx's class struggle doctrine, the welfare state and Gandhian alternative development, opposing Smithian laissez-faire doctrine, Free Trade and industrial develop-ment in favour of a harmonious balance between capital, labour and small farmers. Sismondi's US contemporary, Henry Carey (1793–1879), similarly advocated Gandhi/Schumacher-style small rural enterprises to 'bring the loom to the field or the anvil to the mine' and urged Protection for self-reliant development, which he thought would improve local employment, community maintenance, the status of women, intellectual life and even morals (by keeping men in jobs near home). Carey also perceptively opposed large-scale rural exports to prevent overcultivation and soil degradation, probably the world's first environmental argument against free trade. Despite Mill's rejection of the latter argument (1848: 285ff), Carey helped shape later US isolationist and self-reliance sentiment.[1]

Marxists are usually supposed to be the archetypal political-economic heretics, but Marx himself was ambivalent about trade-development doctrine, querying aspects of Ricardian logic but generally accepting comparative advantage. He thought capitalist trade exploitative and destructive (above quotation), but believed that in the long term it would enhance accumulation and 'constant capital' (i.e. encourage machines to displace labour), thus reducing domestic profits, destabilising the system and hastening the collapse of capitalism, thus paving the way for socialism. Like Carey, Marx (1967: 505–6) forecast soil depletion, but via competitive capitalist exploitation rather than trade, and he thought capitalist destruction of rural society would eventually result in more progressive social formations. In fact, contra List, Marx supported free trade in agrarian countries for the backhanded reason that, whilst protection was pro-business, free trade would hasten colonial catch-up and eventual revolution – 'The protectionist system conserves, while the free trade system destroys' (quoted in Hudson, 1992: 256). However, many later Marxists favoured protection for Listian social development and productivity-enhancing reasons.[2]

The late nineteenth century saw an upsurge of Protectionist sentiment, academically and politically, the former thrust led by a scholarly, though now forgotten, school known as 'historical economists'. Some of this group, as devoted Nonconformists or Anglican clerics, anticipated Gandhi in attacking Free Trade for inducing excessive individualism and materialism. The best-known member of this school, Archdeacon William Cunningham, was for his 'sins' squeezed out of his Cambridge lectureship by economic doyen of the era, Alfred Marshall (Cunningham, 1914; Koot, 1987). However, Marshall himself (1920: 112–13), following Mill and partly anticipating Schumacher, urged a mid-course between material incentives and the Buddhist principle of 'paucity of wants' so as to 'increase the beauty of things' rather than consume excessively, and he thought the case for free trade overstated (see Chapter 2).

Politically, campaigns for Protection, led in Britain by Joseph Chamberlain (1836–1914), were unsuccessful there but very influential in many European countries which were feeling the structural impacts of contemporary trade liberalisation (Chapter 4). Common grounds for opposing Free Trade included: declining terms of trade (mainly argued among scholars), adverse effects on income distribution, loss of revenue, reduced effectiveness of domestic taxes, the decline of agriculture and severe adjustment costs. Grounds for Protection included: infant industry assistance, revenue raising, anti-dumping, employment, economic growth, a more desirable industry mix, defence and food security (Koot, 1987).

This period also saw popularisation of the 'pauper labour' argument against Free Trade (see Chapter 5) and establishment (from 1890) of the first international organisations for labour protection, these being forerunners of today's ILO (formed in 1919). As early as Ricardo's time Robert Owen and others observed that his model (Table 2.1) assumed workers were paid in proportion to their efforts ('marginal product'), failing which countries could obtain an unfair competitive trading advantage, an issue hotly debated ever since (Dunkley, 1996; Chapter 5).

In the 1920s there emerged a so-called 'Australian case for Protection', earlier versions dating back to Torrens (above), which argued that countries dependent upon exporting agriculture, which is a diminishing returns industry, could raise wages, accelerate development and avoid labour emigration by protecting increasing returns sectors in manufacturing. Free Traders insisted this was only a distributional issue, the country being better off overall from trade liberalisation, but the Australian economist James Brigden showed that as a major primary exporter Australia also faced a terms-of-trade loss (Chapter 2) if agriculture expanded too much, a problem which manufacturing protection could rectify. Leading US economist Paul Samuelson and his wife Marion later confirmed Brigden's view (Irwin, 1996: ch. 11). During the following decades several variants of the 'Australian case' were used to advocate Protection for Third World development purposes, particularly the idea that tariffs could raise manufacturing wages and attract resources into higher returns industries. Free Traders have always opposed such arguments, and the evidence is mixed (see Chapter 6). Many pre-war Third World leaders began a thrust for more self-reliant development, and Gandhi led a campaign to symbolically destroy imported textile products for that purpose (see later chapters).

The Keynesian Bombshell

Unquestionably one of the greatest and most influential economists of all time, John Maynard Keynes (1883–1946) grew up in a Cambridge academic family, studied under and revered Alfred Marshall, began as a dutiful Free Trader, then shook the economics world with a bombshell conversion to Protectionism in the early 1930s as he composed his revolutionary *magnum opus* (Keynes, 1936). Standing orthodoxy on its head, Keynes said that demand, not supply, drove the economy; that government spending should expand, not contract, in a slump; and that protection could generate employment. In my metaphor (Chapter 1) he saw the economy as a self-powered motorboat rather than as a yacht awaiting the right world market winds.

Free Traders have always flatly denied that protection could raise employment, free trade being deemed a microeconomic policy capable of improving efficiency and generating employment, so long as the 'market breezes' were right. Keynes, however, said that trade was a macroeconomic issue, that the trade balance could affect aggregate demand, and that the market interest rate was 'not self-adjusting at a level best suited to the social advantage' (1936: 351). State control over interest and investment was the best way of powering employment growth, which would also boost import demand via what was later called the 'trade multiplier', thus helping other countries as well – see quotation p. 48 (also Keynes, 1930). Some modelling research work suggests that this mechanism can work – that is, protection can generate employment – especially if the targets for assistance are well chosen and bilateral trade agreements are used to prevent retaliation by other countries (cited in Dunkley, 2000b: 117). Some argue that protection has worked this way historically (see Chapter 4).

Keynes thought that the requisite trade intervention could be implemented via tariffs, quotas and other such border measures or through exchange rate adjustment, preferably only temporarily while demand stimulus was needed, although he accepted some permanent protection to maintain a desired industry balance – that is, to retain sectors crucial to self-reliance such as agriculture or steel (Dunkley, 1995). Later Keynesians, led by Kaldor (1978, 1989), advocated more radical policies such as industry policy and national planning for generating economies of scale, research capacity and national competitiveness. Kaldor's approach was based on a fundamental challenge to orthodox theories of equilibrium and diminishing or constant returns (esp. see Kaldor, 1989: ch. 15).

The influential sub-mainstream Post-Keynesian school, following Keynes, Marx and Joan Robinson, among other influences, fundamentally challenges Free Market Economic Rationalist theory in seeing prices as set by corporate power; private, globalised speculative finance as destabilising; and government intervention as necessary for macro-stability and full employment. As regards trade, many Post-Keynesians see trading as determined by absolute rather than comparative advantage (see p. 36 above), and trade balance rather than deficits as important for full employment, both of which suggest much more macro- and micro-trade intervention. Joan Robinson followed Keynes (1936: 338ff) in arguing that export-led growth can be 'beggar-thy-neighbour' or 'neo-Mercantilist' when it forces other countries into a trade deficit, implying a case for managed trade intervention for balanced trade rather than export-oriented Free Trade (Chapter 6). Robinson also argued that Free Trade doctrine is invalid when there is chronic unemployment.[3]

A related 'Neo-Ricardian' school makes similar criticisms, producing theoretical modelling to show that the 'gains from trade' may be indeterminate rather than mostly positive, and suggesting that protection can often make a country better off economically.[4] These theories have not as yet developed full alternative policy systems but strongly suggest extensive intervention, although both of these schools tend to favour rapid economic growth and materialist goals much more than Community-Sovereignty thinkers.

History versus Equilibrium

These latter two schools, following path-breaking leads by Kaldor, challenge more fundamentally than do moderate Keynesians the underlying nature of markets, development and equilibrium. US Interventionists like Thurow and Tyson advocate trade intervention via industry policy for the creation of high technology, high value-added, increasing returns sectors. Such sectors are thought capable of generating high-skill workforces, new learning economies, enhanced national competitiveness and generally faster, higher 'quality' growth. Thurow advocates such an approach particularly for 'brainpower' industries like telecommunications, computers, aircraft, robotics, new materials, microelectronics and biotechnology, which are said to be highly globalised, mobile sectors crucial to national 'strategic advantage' (Thurow, 1992; and in Whalen, 1996).

This Thurowian view implies three 'heretical' arguments, some pioneered by Kaldor and Robinson, against Free Trade or for new types of protection: (1) 'increasing returns' sectors are now common and can make a country better off, but need fostering by the state; (2) many such sectors are characterised by 'imperfect competition' which generates monopoly profits, hence supporting a country's own firms in such sectors can ensure a share of these profits, Free Traders christening this 'rent snatching'; (3) the existence of 'increasing returns' and 'imperfectly competitive' sectors makes the global economy 'dynamic' and renders comparative advantage volatile or evolutionary, so 'dynamic comparative advantage' can be shaped by calculated government policies such as industry assistance or research promotion; (4) the concept of market equilibrium, which is central to Free Market Economic

Rationalist theory, may be too abstract and inaccurate to be historically meaningful or analytically useful.

Such theorising has brought out some striking 'heretical' ideas or facilitated the further development of older ones, including: 'cumulative causation', first extensively developed by Kaldor and Myrdal, which is the idea that economies develop by evolutionary build-up rather than market equilibria and need nudging in the right direction by state planning (Toner, 1999); 'path dependence', or the idea that development processes can shape their own directionality and may need guidance from governments (Arthur, 1994; later chapters below); 'first mover advantage', or the notion that the first firm into a new market gets an advanced foothold, with advantages for both the company and home country; 'phases of comparative advantage', or the hypothesis that trade patterns involve an inverse relationship between a country's market share and global demand, so that free trade may not be mutually beneficial for all countries nor the optimal policy in all development phases (Gomory and Baumol, 2000).

These ideas have several heretical implications. First, history, or the way economies develop, may be more relevant than the Neo-classical concept of 'equilibrium' for trade and general economic policymaking (Krugman, 1991). Second, trade might not be mutually beneficial for each country if there are political 'influence effects' of trading (Hirschman, 1945), strategic rivalries for 'good' industries (Thurow, 1992), or phases of comparative advantage development (Gomory and Baumol, 2000). Third, the above suggests close links between trade, technology and development patterns, so that appropriate trade policy may depend on development goals (Chapter 5). Fourth, trade and development policies are so complex and interrelated that government intervention and planning are needed to sort them out.

However, not all the implications of these new Market Interventionist theories are desirable, particularly implications such as extreme global competition, promotion-intensive marketing of new products, glorification of TNCs which champion such products, reliance on high technology, acceptance of questionable technologies like biotechnology or robotics and even the strategic clash of nations (see esp. Thurow, 1992, who preaches most of these).

Arguably more challenging to orthodoxy are those Human Development and Community-Sovereignty heresies which closely link trade to development and consider longer-term goals. One major Human Development writer, the respected British development economist Paul Streeten (1990, 1996, 1998, 2001), argues that comparative advantage is valid but is created, arbitrary and temporary (1996), so 'cannot provide the basis for either predicting the flow of trade, or recommending free trade' (1990: 51). He suggests that assumption failures such as unemployment and imperfect competition via intra-firm trade by TNCs undermines the validity of trade theory; that the explosion of speculative capital has destabilised trade; that global liberalisation and deregulation have not appreciably increased world investment or growth; that globalisation, on balance, exacerbates inequity and damages cultures; that some reduction in trading for non-economic goals and the 'quiet life' is legitimate; and that greater national self-reliance is feasible.

The more radical Community-Sovereignty approach is well exemplified by US ecological economist Herman Daly, who, whilst accepting the validity of comparative advantage, argues that Free Trade, along with domestic market mechanisms, produces social-ecological inefficiency due to environmental externalities, which he claims are far more extensive than mainstream economists concede. He also sees Free Trade-induced externalities arising from the 'cheap labour threat' (which I consider a dubious concept – see Chapter 5), from an excessive scale of development and from a general undermining of community. Daly advocates a range of protection systems to rectify these problems, to control TNCs, to ensure that comparative advantage reflects all social costs and to foster greater national and community self-reliance (Daly and Cobb, 1994; Daly, 1996: ch. 10).

These and other heretical views suggest that development rather than trade should be at the centre of policymaking, that development proceeds via complex historical and political processes rather than simplistic, self-balancing equilibria, and that communities have a right to control such processes, preferably through a democratic state.

Heretics in the Temple

Though a lesser blast than Keynes's, Free Traders were struck by further bombshells during the 1980s when highly 'respectable' mainstream international economists began to publish articles questioning trade orthodoxy and thence formed a loose new school embracing what became known as 'new international economic theory' (NIET). Notably articulated by Paul Krugman (1987), NIET realistically acknowledges various assumption failures (Chapter 2), employing complex mathematical models with parameters such as imperfect competition – that is, oligopolistic markets (few sellers) or 'monopolistic competition' (many sellers but differentiated products), increasing returns, barriers to entry/exit and 'learning effects'. Such models are able to explain many recently observed global corporate practices such as excess profit-making, dumping, predation or global advertising and TNC strategies such as 'first mover' advantage (above), pre-emptive R&D or market-targeted innovation. The general implication of all this is that, whilst market imperfections such as oligopoly or increasing returns may encourage more trade, they also raise the number of possible exceptions to the rule that free trade is best.[5]

There are various moderately dramatic consequences of NIET. First, the inefficiencies of imperfect competition, which economists have always acknowledged, may offset gains from trade, especially if trading encourages the expansion of oligopoly-dominated industries. Second, NIET concedes that much oligopolistic behaviour is indeterminate, giving rise to possible 'strategic', manipulative and politically motivated corporate conduct. Third,

NIET suggests it may be efficient, in 'gains from trade' terms, for governments to intervene 'strategically' via human resource development policies, industry policy, policies to promote 'dynamic comparative advantage', strategies for 'rent-snatching' (i.e. the taxing of excess oligopolistic profits) and schemes for assisting local firms to recoup R&D costs, preserve local intellectual property or establish new enterprises in monopolised or foreign-dominated domestic markets.

A fourth consequence of NIET is the inference that much trade generated by the above factors, especially by increasing returns, takes the form of 'intra-industry trade' (IIT) – that is, trade within an industry group, cars for cars, and so on – which is arguably often wasteful when ships pass each other carrying products with only minor, advertising-induced differences to satisfy finicky rich-world consumerism. Some IIT arises simply to cover R&D costs, to stave off rival TNCs, to snatch high-profit markets or to thwart potentially competitive local firms in another country, so that much First World trading today is 'distinctly expendable' (Rosecrance, 1986: 144), or is readily replaceable with domestic production (Streeten, 1998: 17). Mainstream economists like Krugman (1994: 244ff) acknowledge wasteful trade but claim it may enhance efficiency-inducing competition.

A final consequence of NIET issues is that increasing returns and learning effects, or 'learning-by-doing', make it possible for comparative advantage to be shaped and re-created over time, which some call 'cumulative advantage' (see Dunkley, 2000b: 121–2), which Krugman (1994: 112) has poetically described as 'a river that digs its own bed deeper' and which he has also conceded to be the legitimate basis for state-led industry policy. In fact some NIET writers now say that it is increasing returns, rather than comparative advantage, which drives technology-based trade.

With leading international economists such as Krugman, Dixit, Helpman and Grossman, as well as the world's top microeconomist, William Baumol (Gomory and Baumol, 2000), contributing to this literature, NIET might seem like heretics inside the sacred temple of Free Trade, but the results are not as millenarian as might be expected. Although NIET ideas generally suggest limits to free trade, a case for some 'strategic trade' intervention and politicisation of policymaking (Krugman, 1999), most NIET theorists remain largely Free Traders on grounds that NIET assigns only a marginal role to government, that the right policy balance is hard to achieve, that policymaking can be corrupted and that the 'first best' responses are competition measures or other domestic policies, points with which defenders of orthodox of course concur (Bhagwati, 1994; Irwin, 1996: 217ff). As Krugman (1999: 176) puts it: 'Free Trade is not the optimal policy ... but clever interventionist policies will do only a little better'; he estimates that a strategic trade policy to capture high returns industries would increase US GNP by only 1 per cent, although Free Marketeers bend over backwards to claim that benefits of this size from free trade are highly significant. Much of NIET was anticipated by Kaldor, Robinson, Streeten and others, who have drawn from it conclusions which are much more critical of Free Trade doctrine.

The above analysis suggests many possible criticisms of the way TNCs operate, 'oligopolistic strategies' being central to NIET, but mainstream exponents of NIET seldom venture that far. One of the virtues of NIET which even non-mainstream observers concede is that it adds a dynamic, long-term dimension to orthodox, static Neo-classical theory, but even here NIET theorists are unadventurous, blandly prescribing more trade and higher growth. One related school, New Growth Theory, sees technology as 'endogenous' (internal rather than external and random), so that government-backed research and education can combine with trade to generate 'dynamic comparative advantage' and accelerate growth, the clearly implied goal being a high-tech, high-growth materialistic society, which many others now question.

Overall, NIET tends to follow Marshall (Chapter 2) in declaring that Free Trade has theoretical weaknesses but in practice is the better and politically safer option. As McCulloch (1999: 203) notes, this is the opposite of many non-economists, who tend to say that Free Trade is alright in theory but problematic in practice. In the next chapter I will question its veracity in both respects.

Conclusion

Among Free Trade ideologues and general globalists there is a widely peddled myth that the virtues of Free Trade have been conclusively proved since Smith and that all authoritative economists concur. But this and the previous chapter have shown that such is far from the case; many, if not most, top-line mainstream economists conceding some faults in Free Trade doctrine and some grounds for Protection, even if they finally make a personal choice for Free Trade (see McCulloch, 1999). There have been at least three periods of major challenge to Free Trade doctrine from mainstream or sub-mainstream sources: in the 1890s from the 'historical economists' or others, in the 1930s from the Keynesians, and in the 1980s from NIET, though in each case the main result was to broaden the doctrine rather than bring it to its knees. All along, however, there have been 'heretics' who more fundamentally challenged orthodoxy with much deeper considerations, some of which will be touched on in later chapters.

Notes

1. For Sismondi, see Gomes, 1987: 176; Lutz, 1999. Carey's key works are *The Harmony of Interests* (1967 [1851]), and *Principles of Social Sciences* (1963 [1858]). Also see Hudson, 1992. I am indebted to John Seale of the David Syme College, Melbourne, for valuable information and discussion on Carey.

2. Marx's trade views are scattered, but see *Capital*, Volume 1 (1967): esp. Parts 1 and 4; Volume 3 (1967: 237ff). On Marx and later Marxists, see Gomes, 1987: 154ff; Hudson, 1992: 248ff.

3. King, 2002 and 2003, esp. R. Blecker 'International Economics', and sources cited therein.

4. See Steedman, 1979; Evans, 1989; Nell, 1998: esp. 694ff. On Sraffa, see Keen 2001.

5. See Dixit and Norman, 1980; Grossman, 1992; Krugman, 1994, 1999; Irwin 1996: ch. 14; Gomory and Baumol, 2000.

CHAPTER 4

WHAT ABOUT THE PRACTICE?
TRADING AND FREE TRADE
IN HISTORY AND REALITY

This division of labour ... [is a] consequence of a certain propensity in human nature ... the propensity to truck, barter, and exchange one thing for another.... But man has almost constant occasion for the help of his brethren, and it is in vain for him to expect it from their benevolence only. He will be more likely to prevail if he can interest their self-love in his favour.

Adam Smith (1776, 1: 17–18)

[In earlier times] the production and circulation of commodities is secondary to the proper functioning of a culture and operating only to satisfy its essential needs. In the modern economic model, society is deliberately reorganised in an attempt to optimise its economic sector – a reorganisation frequently to the detriment of large sections of the society's population but to the marked benefit of other sections.

David Clark (1987: 6)

[H]ee that commaunds the sea, commaunds the trade, and hee that is Lord of the Trade of the worlde is lord of the wealth of the worlde.

Sir Walter Ralegh (quoted in Andrews, 1984: 9)

The greatest enduring myth in the whole of economics, as well as in Free Trade doctrine, rests on the above quotation from Adam Smith. This multiple mythology holds that humans are naturally and unavoidably a self-loving, self-improving, privatised, market-using, trading 'animal', and that history has been a largely linear process of gradual enlightened realisation that economic rationalism, free markets, free trade and global 'deep' integration are the optimal instruments for achieving 'natural' human aspirations in practice, whatever the ambivalence in theory of the sort outlined in previous chapters. The WTO's new techno-global order is being constructed on this Smithian world-view and on five great associated myths. The present chapter questions this world-view and its myths, suggesting instead that in reality history is a complex, non-deterministic, non-linear process involving much political discretion and partly driven by interests, including vested interests in free trade and globalisation.

A Clash of Propensities

There are many grand depictions of what drives history. Early Christian writers saw it driven by battles between Good and Evil. Marx saw a dialectical class struggle and Weber an inexorable process of rationalisation, while currently Gates (1996: ch. 1) sees it driven by linear technological progress, Huntington sees a 'clash of civilisations', especially between the West and Islam at present, and Fukuyama a drive for individual recognition and liberal values, with history about to 'end' as everyone adopts 'liberal democracy'. Today most globalisers are Fukuyamaists with a strong dash of Gatesianism, Marx being out of fashion and Huntington now trendy, but I suggest that a more likely driving force is continuing tension between two human propensities which I call the Smithian and the Gandhian.

A propensity is looser, more ambivalent and less deterministic than a drive, the two not being mutually exclusive, but the predominance of one over the other can strongly shape a society's destiny. Economists frequently refer to Smith's above-quoted hint – it was no more than that – regarding a supposed natural human propensity for trade and development. Many versions of the 'Smithian Propensity' have been devised, an extreme image being that human nature is self-centred and greedy. I pose a more acceptable version that sees people desiring to exchange some surplus production for purposes of certain improvements in product quality or variety, general living standards and life prospects.

Against the 'Smithian Propensity', I argue that there is an equally natural 'Gandhian Propensity' for people to seek reasonable social justice, protection of cultural–spiritual traditions, or at least the integrity rather than exact continuity of these, and maintenance of the community's natural environment, all being pursued partially at the expense of production and income maximisation if necessary. The two propensities vie with each other to some extent and although all societies will have both, one may predominate – the Smithian Propensity in the USA, for instance, and the Gandhian in India. Historical evidence of the 'Gandhian Propensity' can be seen in earlier practices of 'embedding' economies, markets and trade within social–ethical–spiritual norms or traditions (see below), as nicely described by the late Cambridge historian David Clark (quoted above), as well as in the traditional accumulation of ecological knowledge (see Chapter 5).

In this chapter I critically examine five myths of Free Trade which globalisers regard as the practical side of Free Trade doctrine and which I suggest arise from overemphasis on the Smithian Propensity. According to Myth No. 1, trade is an ancient, natural, universal activity which has steadily increased because of its virtues. Myth No. 2 holds that free markets and private initiative have always been the best basis for almost all trade and economic activity, so that free trade and globalisation inevitably evolve eventually. Myth No. 3 is that comparative advantage-based trading has always been intuitively known as the best trade policy, hindered only by unenlightened political intervention and protectionist vested interests. Myth No. 4 claims that trading in general, and free trade in particular, has overwhelmingly positive net benefits in practice, despite any theoretical uncertainties (see previous chapter). Myth No. 5 is that the volume and ratios of trade have been increasing, especially due to technological 'miracles', thus indicating inevitable globalisation.

The standard inference from these myths is that a new global order based on Free Trade and 'deep integration' is the best policy for development and prosperity, but if the mythologies are partly or wholly untrue, as I argue is the case, then the Global Free Trade Project is seriously flawed.

Trade and Markets Embedded

Myth No. 1, that trade is an ancient, natural and universal activity, is true in a general sense, all archeological and historical evidence broadly confirming this, and formal long-distance exchange, often pushed by rulers for revenue purposes, possibly predates local markets in an age when communal barter predominated (Polanyi, 1977: ch. 13). However, this does not mean, as Myth No. 2 holds, that free markets, private enterprise or free trade are natural and universal, or that economic evolution is linear and preordained. Indeed, the well-known economic historian Karl Polanyi (1957: 139–40) has said that free markets and free trade are not natural, but require enforcing through 'continuous, centrally organised and controlled interventionism', even some mainstream economists conceding that free trade has to be encouraged, or even forced, by government (cited in Dunkley, 2000b: 20).

A long-standing debate in economic history pits the 'primitivist' view, that custom and tradition prevailed over economic rationality until relatively recently, against a 'modernist' claim that proto-modern trading, markets and capitalist practices have been latent or even apparent from the earliest times. US anthropologist Melville Herskovits (1952) is believed, inaccurately in my view (see below), to have clinched the latter view with ethnographic evidence of early profit-taking, market entrepreneurship, rational calculation and private property (Polanyi et al., 1957: esp. chs 1 and 7). Most globalisers now take such linear, rational evolution, along with the 'Smithian Propensity', for granted, there even being Marxist-inspired, class-struggle-based versions variously tracing the emergence of rational global markets to the sixteenth century

(Wallerstein), the Middle Ages (Braudel, 1982) and even 3000 BC in Asia (Frank, 1998).

However, many scholars such as Max Weber argued that human development patterns varied, with non-economic factors important. The early anthropologists Malinowski and Thurnwald observed that traditional societies often had viable non-market, non-capitalist, non-profit motivated, holistic systems in which trade or other economic processes were 'embedded' in the social, political, cultural and religious institutions of society for the various purposes of justice, social control and cultural maintenance.[1] Polanyi (1957; 1977; Polanyi et al. 1957) made famous the view that there were other exchange systems besides markets, such as redistribution, reciprocity and variants thereof, the self-regulating market only fully displacing the others in the nineteenth century when business classes sought to 'disembed' the economy from tradition and place profit-making at the centre of society. Contrary to Myths Nos. 1 and 2 (above), Polanyi and others (e.g. Clark, 1987, quoted above) suggest that the economy was traditionally a subdivision of society until this ordering was reversed in the 'great transformation' of the Industrial Revolution period.

Some critics question the accuracy and relevance of Polanyi's thesis (e.g. Braudel, 1982: 226–7; Frank, 1998: 18), although Frank badly misinterprets Polanyi as claiming that markets were non-existent until the Industrial Revolution. But Polanyi (1957; 1977) primarily argues that various exchange systems have coexisted and that the economy, markets and trading were 'embedded' in social norms or traditions until disembedded by commercial interests. In my terminology, he appears to imply that the Gandhian Propensity *should* prevail over the Smithian Propensity for purposes of 'social protection aiming at the conservation of man and nature' (1957: 132).

There is plenty of evidence for Polanyi's thesis, Clark (1987), for instance, documenting the prevalence of culture over trade and economic forces from early times until the formation of commercially based states. The South African anthropologist

Stephan Viljoen (1936: 223–4) has argued, against Smith, that there is 'no natural propensity to barter', that some societies (e.g. the Incas) had no competitive trade, that trade has major cultural impacts and that many societies have, thus, sought to control trade. Indeed, Smith himself (1776, 1: 519) referred to the 'mean rapacity, the monopolising spirit of merchants and manufacturers, who neither are, nor ought to be, the rulers of mankind'. Economic historians, including Polanyi's famed student Moses Finley, variously point out, consistently with Polanyi, that early markets were rudimentary and industries simple, craft-based activities until well after Roman times; early trade was largely confined to key materials and special needs, representing less than 2 per cent of societies' GDP until the industrial age; that traders were usually foreigners or from minority groups and of low status; that Aristotle, Hesiod and other Classical writers argued against trade and market dominance, or for 'embedding'; and that external trade was regularly supervised, taxed and generally controlled more than domestic exchange, often in the interests of cultural separation from other states.[2]

Likewise in Asia, whilst research confirms Frank's (1998) claim regarding the extensiveness of early trading networks, there is evidence that trade was usually politically controlled in order to maximise the benefits of exchange without undue disruption to traditional ways of life. Both China and Japan had periods of consciously adopted commercial isolation, or at least reduced trading contacts, for purposes of selective trade optimisation, control of foreign penetration and maintenance of cultural integrity. Braudel (1982: 117–18) suggests that in China, as late as 1949, local and town economies remained embedded in peasant society and culture.[3] Ayittey (1991: ch. 8) notes that, although in traditional African society trade and markets were extensive and relatively free, some states controlled these and they were strongly embedded in the social order, marketplaces being centres for religious, social, political, judicial and other crucial cultural functions.

Even in Europe where autonomous markets and long-distance trade rose rapidly after the Middle Ages, fairs remained under the control of local authorities and sovereigns sought intervention where necessary, while many localities remained self-reliant and relatively non-marketised for centuries (Braudel, 1982: 228). Indeed, where national commercial markets were uncontrolled they often displaced local, more embedded, exchange networks so that 'traditional habits and customs were lost or smashed' (Braudel, 1982: 42). Although the Church gradually modified its opposition to usury and mercantile values, especially for long-distance trade, hostility to excessive commercialism remained among many Christians; Luther once proclaiming, in anticipation of Gandhi, that God gave countries enough resources for self-sufficiency and he could 'not see that many good customs have ever come to a land through commerce' (Irwin, 1996: 21).

The seventeenth-century Italian scholar Alberico Gentili proposed that one country could declare war on another for withholding trade but had no right to 'alter the customs and institutions of foreign peoples' (Irwin, 1996: 22). Although arguing for the early universality of 'rational economic man', Herskovits (see above) also observed that societies sought to balance individualist, materialist, economic motives against collective, sociocultural values (Smith versus Gandhi?). He criticised crude economic determinism, characterising Western machine technology and values as an 'invasion of the evaluative processes by pecuniary considerations' (1952: 487, 490ff), noting that acquisitive market-based commerce is much less important in self-sufficient, non-literate communities than in the 'pecuniary societies of Europe and America' (205).

In sum, Myths No. 1 and 2 regarding the antiquity and naturalness of trade and private, market-led commerce are greatly overstated. A degree of trade and commerce (the Smithian Propensity) is ancient and natural, but so is the desire to control and socially 'embed' these in the sociocultural interest (the Gandhian Propensity). Polanyi was broadly correct, while Frank's (1998) claim of an ancient lineage and inevitable trajectory for market-based perpetual globalisation is narrow and probably mistaken.

Trade's Loss of Innocence

In this and following sections I will question Myth No. 3, that comparative advantage-based trade is natural and arises automatically if free, voluntary exchange is permitted and if 'good' trading interests can overcome 'bad' Protectionist interests. I will also seek to rebut Myth No. 4, that trading, especially free trade, is universally beneficial as gauged by economic growth and certain non-economic criteria, including world peace. As noted above, trade was originally simple, controlled and limited to a few basic needs, but I will argue below that this innocence was lost as in practice it became disembedded, politicised, sometimes forced and often exploitative.

Regarding comparative advantage, the renowned French historian Ferdinand Braudel (esp. 1984: ch. 1) has said that it is 'not the result of 'natural' and spontaneous tendencies, but rather an inheritance' (p. 48), and this may date back centuries as it can be 'hard to live down a dependent past' (pp. 49–50). Comparative advantage may thus reflect technology or geography, but also sociocultural factors, politics (as in access to credit or markets), dependency, unequal trade mechanisms and exploitation. Braudel (1984: ch. 4) also observes that national markets were not natural, spontaneously forming processes but political constructs imposed from above, traditional localities often resisting mergers and seeking to retain their identities. He notes that in France it was the general tide of industrial revolution rather than integrationist policies such as the abolition of internal tariffs and tolls which led to development (1984: 289ff). All this indicates that the orthodox concepts of free trade and comparative advantage may be unduly rigid, that advantage-formation is a substantially sociopolitical process and that the development of national and international markets is discretionary and political rather than natural or inevitable.

An extreme illustration of these issues, and of trade losing its innocence, is the slave trade, which is today variously blamed on monarchs, states, Mercantilism and pre-Enlightenment values, but which arguably was the epitome of comparative advantage-based free trade and free-market commerce. The Atlantic slave trade was free or minimally regulated for most of its history. Africa had a seeming comparative advantage in slavery due to factors such as a long history of slave 'exports' to the Arab world; many rulers who were experienced in slaving; a war-captives system able to supply innumerable slaves; the *allegedly* greater stamina of Africans compared with native Americans; and Africans' *supposed* general suitability to plantation labour (Thomas, 1997: 463 and *passim*). The slave trade also saw the emergence of systematic, rational commerce, possibly to a greater extent than ever before, with detailed cost–benefit calculation for everything from capture and transportation to 'acceptable' numbers of deaths and the life expectancy of slaves. Historians now think that the contribution of slavery to Old World development has been overstated, total European trade with the New World providing just 4 per cent of GNP and profit rates of about 10 per cent over time being comparable to other sectors, although many personal fortunes were made and some say slavery contributed, perversely perhaps, to the rise of modernity.[4]

In Africa slavery-based comparative advantage was by no means inevitable. Africa was not 'primitive' but a complex traditional society (Thomas, 1997: 352, 362) with advanced production and some exports of horticulture, palm oil, gold, ivory, arts, crafts and a range of raw materials. The advent of slave trading often induced or forced African leaders and societies into abandoning customary pursuits, but those which avoided slavery usually succeeded in subsistence or found alternative exports (Thomas, 1997: 562ff, 691ff, 797).

A number of striking lessons arise from all this. First, particular comparative advantages are not rigidly fixed or inevitable but are historically, socially and politically shaped. Second, exploitative, self-damaging comparative advantage can emerge 'naturally' through market processes, and thus should be sociopolitically controlled. Third, particular patterns of development shape, and are shaped by, the trading process, so that alternative development models (see later chapters) can produce different trade requirements or outcomes. Fourth, whilst slavery was primarily caused by a now unacceptable, exploitative, inhumane moral code, obsession with trade itself and with import-dependent forms of development also played a key role. Alternative consumption in Europe and more appropriate forms of development in Africa would surely have reduced the Atlantic slave trade, which saw a staggering 10–15 million souls transported and 4–6 million deaths in transit (Thomas, 1997: 805–6). Finally, patterns of development and globalisation are not inevitable but, like comparative advantage, are socially and geopolitically constructed, as indicated by Sir Walter Ralegh (quoted above) and revealed in a statement by the French general Meynier, who in 1911 said of Europeans: 'to open markets for their trade in Africa they have stamped out the last vestiges of African civilisation' (quoted in Dumont, 1962).

Similar lessons can be learnt from the equally repugnant opium trade and related aspects of imperial expansion. It is well documented, even by mainstream historians, that whilst Europeans did not initiate opium addiction or trading in Asia, they massively stimulated both for purposes of balancing their hitherto large spice trade deficit with the East. This was done by promoting opium in China, forcing that country into free trade through 'gunboat diplomacy' and two Opium Wars (1839–42 and 1856–60), as well as by forcing India to shift her trading focus from well-established traditional crafts and agriculture into large-scale opium production and processing, with peasants often forced into opium, tea or other export crops (Trocki, 1999: 73ff and *passim*). The result was a political/military forcing of palpably inappropriate consumption and development throughout Asia, with old crops sometimes physically uprooted (Trocki, 1999: 65), and extensive social disruption.

There was a close link between trade, development and imperial expansion, with trade often the initiating factor rather than the innocent bystander, and the flag followed trade rather than the reverse, as is often said (Trocki, 1999: 60). According to one historian (Andrews, 1984: ch. 16), trade, plunder and settlement were the same process, Britain stressing the first two, with promotion and balancing of oriental trade the chief goal. William Pitt once said that British policy was British trade, with trade promotion, trading rivalry and the acquisition of trading bases being the main motives for the colonisation of many areas, including Australia. From the time of Ralegh (1554–1618), who militantly favoured 'forcible trade' (Andrews, 1984: 9), the notion grew that no country had the right to withhold trade, so in time a policy of 'free trade imperialism' was implemented via 'prestige, cajolery, threat, the dangled loan reinforced occasionally with blockade, bombardment or expedition' (Robinson and Gallagher, 1967: 5; Stevens, 1983). In short, trade was, and arguably still is, a form of power as well as a goal, both power and goal being usable to create strategic comparative advantage either at home or in other states as required, extensively shaping societies via what the well-known economist Albert Hirschman (1945: 14ff) called an 'influence effect' – that is, societies influence each other in a range of ways by virtue of the very existence of trading relations.

The slave and drug trades are extreme cases, but similar issues can be seen in the more routine trading relations between Britain and Portugal, which were more complex than Ricardo's famed numbers (Box 2.1). Most historians now say Portugal spent too long trading and mining in the Americas, consumed too many luxuries at home and placed too little emphasis on agricultural or industrial development, all of which led to extreme import dependence on Britain, paid for with New World metals. Portugal did export wine, à la Ricardo, but English capital came to control the vineyards, and attempts by Portugal to promote cloth or other new industries were stymied by English influence. The 1703 Anglo-Portugese Methuen Agreements cemented a political alliance in exchange for a trade liberalisation agreement which effectively 'totally discontinued' Portugese textiles and other manufactures, as the British ambassador, Sir John Methuen, himself put it, locking Portugal into wine or other rural specialisations until the 1930s or beyond.[5] A later historian, G. Young, said that Portugese textiles were 'killed by the showier, shoddier British' products and 'Portugese native industry was smothered in its infancy' (Sediri, 1970: 56).

The lessons of this story are several. First, a country can overtrade, becoming excessively dependent on imports. Second, comparative advantage can be historically and politically shaped, including by an external power, to a nation's disadvantage − in this case by England through the 'granting of judicious credit' (Braudel, 1984: 38), 'strategic' foreign investment (see Chapter 3 above) and an unequal trade treaty (Sediri, 1970) to enforce 'market access'. Third, free trade can ensure that such disadvantageous comparative advantage is locked in for long periods, even centuries, by domestic factors − in Portugal's case by weak government and a strong landlordism reinforced by *excessive* specialisation in wine, Ricardo notwithstanding (Sediri, 1970: 6).

Overall, it is clear that Myth No. 3 regarding the supposed 'naturalness' of free trade and comparative advantage has been grossly oversimplified ever since Ricardo. Comparative advantage can be shaped by many forces, particularly relative national power, manipulated by external interests, combined unfavourably with internal mechanisms, developed in a direction which is neither desired by, nor beneficial to, local people and the resultant trade may be a *consequence* rather than the *cause* of development (Sediri, 1970: 70ff; Hirschman, 1945).

Also oversimplified is that part of Myth No. 3 which holds that there are selfish and illegitimate Protectionist interests, as opposed to benevolent, legitimate pro-Free Trade ones which governments should encourage. This is often argued in relation to the abolition of the British Corn Laws, the first great trade debate in history. Britain was not a purist Free Trader until almost the middle of the nineteenth century, maintaining, prior to that, selective tariffs, restrictions on the emigration of skilled artisans, bans on the export of machinery, and a series of Navigation Laws which favoured British shipping. The latter even had the imprimateur of Adam Smith (1776,1: 487) and the backing of many business leaders, who regularly lobbied to retain their world trade monopolies (Hirst, 1993; Chang, 2002). The Anti-Corn Law League, formed in 1839, represented a range of commercial, Free Trade interests, one historian observing that 'Free Traders were as thoroughly self-interested as their protectionist opponents' (Musson, 1992; Fielden, 1992; Bairoch, 1993: ch. 2).

It is a similar picture in relation to the spread of trade liberalisation agreements after 1860, which Free Traders often depict as a wave of enlightenment. In fact, the landmark 1860 Anglo-French trade liberalisation agreement involved both economic and geopolitical motives, the French seeking British neutrality over Italy, for instance, later bilateral agreements having similar political backdrops (Kindleberger, 1992: 459ff). In France free trade was so unpopular that the 1860 treaty was negotiated in secret and imposed by Napoleon III, who had only recently converted to Free Trade doctrine. Some say Europe only shifted to free trade (temporarily) under pressure from Britain and from emergent export interests (Bairoch, 1993: 22), while Britain herself adopted free trade mainly to reduce the power of the landed classes, to ally more closely with the USA and to prevent other countries from using protection for development by 'kicking away the ladder' as List colourfully put it.[6]

Overall, both principles and growing corporate export interests probably played a role in early trade liberalisation (Kindleberger, 1992; Fielden, 1992), but clearly Free Trade is an ideology as much as a policy. Ultimately the relative virtues of Free Trade and Protection must be decided on the basis of their real effects, and these are not as clear-cut as Free Trade ideologues claim.

The Necessity of Virtue:
The Myth of Free Trade Beneficence

Myth No. 4 – that trading in general, and free trade in particular, bring guaranteed universal benefits – is the most crucial of all Free Trade mythologies because the entire Global Free Trade Project depends upon it. Yet, just as many mainstream and other economists concede that Free Trade doctrine is flawed in theory (see Chapter 2), a surprising number also find it flawed in practice as well, as I outline in this section. The 'benefits in practice' claims began after the abolition of the Corn Laws, when Free Traders such as 'hero' of the abolition Richard Cobden (e.g. 1995: 436) attributed much of Britain's subsequent prosperity thereto, just as today's globo-euphorists attribute most economic virtues to globalisation.

The key problem in measuring gains from trade in practice is that income increments do not wear origin labels, so that the sources of gains have to be inferred, modelled, surmised or guesstimated. Also, the requisite data are often limited, some have only come to light recently, sometimes historical data are revised much later and estimates of protection levels vary. There are two main approaches to measurement, one seeking correlations of exports and/or relatively open trade with growth, the other making 'welfare' estimates of trade impacts via the 'Harberger triangles' (see Figure 2.1), though more complex modelling is used today (see Chapter 6). The long-standing claim that freer trade *did* correlate with growth in the nineteenth century, so that trade is an 'engine of growth', has mainly been based on broad correlations. Two major problems with such studies, however, are the variations used for value of protection and the estimation methods employed, there being no consensus on the 'best' approach in either case.

A major revision began around 1970 when Irving Kravis argued, from extensive cross-national studies, that trade–growth correlations are poor, trade being minor in some high-growth countries and vice versa, so that trade has only been a 'handmaiden' of growth, not an engine. Others confirmed this, one study noting that British exports only led growth in a few periods and sectors (e.g. textiles and steel).[7] In the first attempt to estimate nineteenth-century Britain's welfare-based gains from trade, the US economist Donald McCloskey startlingly concluded that free trade had reduced Britain's terms of trade (see Chapter 2 above) sufficiently to *cut* GNP by about 4 per cent (i.e. loss of area *e* in Figure 2.1). McCloskey dubbed this effect 'Magnanimous Albion' because Britain had *lost* from free trade, thereby *donating* to her trading partners. This phenomenon of trade leading to lower terms of trade and so to *negative* growth, which Bhagwati has called 'immiserising growth', depends heavily upon elasticity estimates, and some critics say McCloskey's guesses were too pessimistic, but Britain's declining terms of trade have been confirmed by others.[8]

However, the greatest embarrassment for globalisers comes from the neglected work of the Swiss-based Belgian statistician Paul Bairoch (1972; 1993), whose early research found growth spurts following trade liberalisation only in Britain, with *declines* in growth for France, Germany and Italy. He also found (1972) that free trade brought a divergence of growth rates between Britain and France rather than the equalising convergence forecast by Free Traders, as well as a *lower* rate of industrial innovation in France. Other writers have similarly found that free trade led to industrial stagnation in the Netherlands and major government revenue losses in many European countries, especially Italy (Kindleberger, 1992).

Bairoch attributed these trends mainly to imports of cheap grain from Poland and the New World, which implied only a short-term structural adjustment problem, but his later work (1993: esp. ch. 4) drew more far-reaching conclusions, including that Britain's apparent benefits from free trade were probably due to her technological lead established under protection (also see Chang, 2002); that many other European countries had marked *declines* in growth following trade liberalisation, but then experienced recoveries after renewing protection; that the Europe-wide late-nineteenth-century depression began at the peak of free trade and ended with the general mid-1890s return to protection; that in the early twentieth century growth was stronger in the more protectionist countries, especially relative to a stagnating Free Trade Britain; that the strongest US growth occurred under protection; and that the period of rising protection, after the late 1880s, actually saw an *expansion* of exports, with the fastest trade growth in the more Protectionist countries.

Bairoch's embarrassing conclusions are almost entirely contrary to the claims of both contemporary Free Traders (e.g. Cobden, 1995: ch. 25) and present-day globalisers, causing some (e.g. Senghaas, 1985: 43ff) to hypothesise that growth leads to trade, not the reverse, as is conventionally assumed. Moreover, Bairoch's results have recently been strikingly confirmed by a leading main-stream economic historian, Kevin O'Rourke (2000), who, using recently released historical data, revised national accounts, modern mathematical modelling and a sample of ten Old and New World countries from 1875 to 1914, found a clear positive correlation between protection and growth. O'Rourke (2000) suggests that the benefits of protection may have derived from factors such as learning effects, dynamic scale economies, increased productivity as rural labour shifted to protected larger-scale industry and a lower price of capital goods relative to newly protected consumer goods. Such factors vary between countries, thus making the benefits of trade or protection uncertain and contingent, as I argued in Chapter 2.

In addition to the apparently widespread negative effects of free trade, many adverse social impacts, especially the destruction of rural communities, have been widely commented upon, both at the time and since (e.g. Polanyi, 1957: esp 133). By the 1870s, grain imports from the New World and industrial recession to-gether induced a massive grain price collapse, which brought what Mancur Olson, the famed US economist who once claimed that interest groups are impediments to free trade and progress, called the 'downfall' of British farming and caused large-scale emigration from Britain to the USA. These now-forgotten emigrations began soon after the abolition of the Corn Laws, especially among small farmers from areas most affected by both abolition-induced imports and technological change. As Olson noted, 'Britain's persistence in laissez-faire policies at the price of a devastated agriculture is unique in the history of nations' (Olson and Harris, 1959; Vugt, 1988).

This episode illustrates the complex relationships between trade, technology and development. Abolition-induced farm imports appear to have elicited new farming methods, which accelerated growth but with social and environmental costs. Cobden himself (1995: 435ff) inadvertently illustrated this by revealing that on his own estate, which his friends rescued from bankruptcy, he had rationalised management, consolidated tenant holdings, removed all hedgerow trees and exterminated wildlife. Cobden (1995: 443) also admitted that his own rents had declined since abolition of the Corn Laws, and by 1890, whilst British post-abolition wages had risen by 20 per cent, rural rents, the main income for a third of the population and two-thirds in Ireland, had plummeted by 50 per cent, Irish tillage rates falling by 25 per cent and rural employment by 20 per cent. US historians O'Rourke and Williamson (1999: 91, 285) have attributed the above results to the abolition of the Corn Laws and to agricultural free trade. Such economic and social costs led to Polanyi's (1957) 'double movement' or social backlash, and thence to new Protectionism, including strong self-reliance policies in countries such as Ireland, Italy and Spain. A further tragic side effect of abolition was to boost imports from Cuba and Brazil, increase the price of slaves and thus aid continuation of the (by then partly illegal) slave trade. In parliament Free Traders like Cobden blocked the re-imposition of duties designed to stem this effect (Thomas, 1997: 733ff).

In conclusion, the benefits of nineteenth-century free trade proclaimed by Myth No. 4 were in fact contingent, country-specific and largely mythological. Trade was at best a 'handmaiden' for growth, trade liberalisation was frequently a hindrance and protection seems to have helped development ever since the Napoleonic Continental Blockade of British exports, which gave many European industries a chance to take off (Crouzet, 1964; Hudson, 1992). Thus, in the 1890s, as Marshall was declaring free trade flawed in theory but best in practice, it was also proving flawed in practice, at least in terms of economic growth, a criterion which is arguably dubious (see next chapter) but which is the one preferred by economists themselves.

Free Trade, War and Peace

Of course Free Traders claim more for their doctrine than just growth, other alleged virtues including variety, competition, 'opportunity', less parochial views and peace. Trade arguably does increase product variety, although as Hahn says (see Chapter 2), perhaps too much so, early European imports like tobacco, sugar, opium or tea having many social costs. Thus, the advantage of variety depends on the virtues of consumerism.

Competition can in principle be enhanced through imports and FDI, but displacement of local firms or industries could counter the effect. As noted in Chapter 3, monopolistic or oligopolistic trade is common today and began long ago, early Anglo-Dutch rivalry having been imperfectly competitive and boosted Dutch profits more than would have prevailed under competitive free trade (Irwin, 1991a). Also certain critics (e.g. Group of Lisbon, 1995: 103 and *passim*) point to various social, environmental, attitudinal and cultural costs of competition as a system of economic governance. So competition can be questioned both as a virtue and as an assured outcome of free trade.

Increased trade is supposed to bring 'opportunities' for innovation, skill enhancement and new markets, but Self-Reliant Trade may bring just as many such opportunities at home, especially as import surges can kill off some enterprises, industries or skills.

Trade can bring more outward-looking attitudes to a society, but it is questionable whether trading, let alone free trade, is a necessary condition for such attitudes, and it is surely not a sufficient one! Wider and deeper education, travel and cultural exchange are necessary, and probably sufficient, conditions for fostering broader, more tolerant, more understanding world outlooks, or what I call cooperative internationalism (Chapter 1).

Perhaps the most noble claim made by Free Traders is that the profits of commerce are more valuable than the spoils of war, so that trade can bring world peace, an idea first espoused by Smith, Ricardo and Mill. The great champion of this vision, Richard Cobden (1995: 394), once proclaimed Free Trade as the 'spirit of truth and justice ... [and] good-will among men', 'thrusting aside the antagonism of race and creed and language and uniting us in bonds of eternal peace' (Hirst, 1903: 229). The utopian ideal that trade can lead to peace motivated some founders of GATT, notably the US statesman Cordell Hull, and the WTO still occasionally makes such a claim (e.g. Annual Report, 1998: 37–8). A more sophisticated version, by the US scholar Richard Rosecrance (1986), holds that post-war Western governments have created 'trading states', finding that resources can be acquired more cheaply through trade than conquest. However, this idyllic notion assumes economic causes of war, particularly quests for resources and territory, whereas most scholars also identify diplomatic, ideological, revolutionary or other non-economic causes as well. Even the highly commercial post-1945 era has seen some 80 wars take 20–30 million lives throughout the world (Brogan, 1998).

The converse thesis, that trade *leads to* war, has mainly been a non-mainstream view, espoused by many radicals and some Marxists who read Marx as saying that rich countries used trade and colonial exploitation to rescue falling profits, thus conflicting with other imperial powers in the process (Grampp, 1987). Gandhi (*CW*, 47: 90) also implied this thesis, hinting that self-reliance could both limit India's vulnerability to foreign encroachment and prevent her from herself becoming exploitatively expansionist.

Keynes (1936: 381–2) did claim 'struggle for markets' as a cause of war, but this was not widely endorsed by his more orthodox colleagues.

Historical evidence does not clearly support either view. Anthropological studies variously suggest that trading can foster peaceful 'diplomatic practices' (Herskovits, 1952: 197) or can lead to 'trading blows' (Sahlins, 1974: 303) to 'plunder rather than peace' (Viljoen, 1936: 216) or to 'looting, warfare and murder in pursuit of valuable staples' (Clark, 1987: 33), and rivalry in slave trading led directly to some wars (Thomas, 1997: ch. 19). Militant statesmen like Ralegh (quoted p. 63 above) and Colbert thought trade an extension of war, while some enlightenment thinkers linked trade with peace (Gomes, 1987: 17, 121ff). Smith (1776, 1: 490) thought *tariffs* had caused the 1672 Franco-Dutch war, though later scholars say it was commercial rivalry, and historical references to trade wars are common (e.g. Clark, 1987: 64). Certainly the great trading companies were armed both with weapons and with briefs to make war in the name of trade promotion (Gomes, 1987: 15, 90). Hirschman (1945: 78ff) perceptively suggests that international conflict can arise from both *too little* trade, through resource deprivation, and *too much* trade, through countries resisting penetration by others. In general, as noted above, trade and power are more closely linked than Free Traders realise, so that trade will always be a potential cause of conflict (see Hirschman, 1945; Sediri, 1970).

Political scientists are equally undecided, some confirming a positive link between trade and peace, some saying it depends on the state of power balances, some surmising that trade may spark conflict by threatening national security, or help fund rearmament by inducing prosperity. One survey found war more associated with periods of hegemony, openness and prosperity than with eras of non-hegemony, protectionism and recession (Mansfield, 1997: 235). Some iconoclasts and a few economists attribute the Second World War partly to the inter-war trade collapse, though many economists are sceptical; while, conversely, some pre-First

World War observers like Norman Angell declared the world so integrated that war had become impossible! (Angell, 1911: esp. 266ff). Neither view is very credible today. Keynes (1933: 237) assessed that greater isolation would have been better for peace before 1914, and that macroeconomic expansion to eliminate unemployment, as he advocated, would be more conducive to peace than a policy of increasing trade (1936: 381ff).

The ideal of peace through trade cannot have been helped by the Western doctrine, dating back to Gentili (see above), that one nation could wage war on another for withholding trade, could open markets like oysters, as Lord Randolph Churchill decreed in the 1890s, or could prise other countries open with a crowbar as US trade representative Carla Hills announced a century later (O'Rourke and Williamson, 1999: 108). I suggest that education, public attitudes, elite ambitions, degrees of democracy and philosophies of tolerance are more important inducements for peace than trade, though none is infallible.

The Legend of the Thirties

One of the greatest Free Trade mythologies, and part of Myth No. 4, holds that inter-war protection at least partly caused the Great Depression, the chronic recession of the 1930s and possibly the Second World War! This legend motivated the formation of GATT and is still quoted *ad nauseum* by Free Traders as proving the need for global integration. Yet legend it largely is! Renewed protection had generally begun around 1880 (see above) with Britain and the USA being the main converts in the early 1930s, but a few countries had *reduced* tariffs after a 1927 League of Nations trade liberalisation resolution (Bairoch, 1993: 4), and in the main new tariffs *followed* rather than preceded depressed conditions. Many mainstream economists, Arndt (1967: 271), Kindleberger and Krugman (see Dunkley, 2000b: 117) for instance, have always been sceptical of the legend.

Some economists, notably Kaldor (1978, 1989), have found that the 1930s protectionism, via tariff increases, exchange rate depreciation or both, actually bolstered income and employment in many countries, thus *alleviating* the Depression. Kaldor (1989: 335–6) documented a remarkable 8 per cent per annum growth rate for British industrial output from 1932 to 1937, apparently following renewed tariffs and a halving of imports, a trend which continued until the 1950s.[9] Recent modelling evidence shows the infamous US Smoot–Hawley tariffs of June 1930 to have had a minimal adverse impact on efficiency, income or employment, most import reduction being due to the slump itself, and one study suggests that tariffs actually *raised* US GNP by 2 per cent via Keynesian-type demand stimuli.[10] Similarly, a study of the British car industry has shown that, due to scale economy effects, the 1930s tariffs in that sector *increased* efficiency, welfare and income, and so probably these would have arrested Britain's industrial decline if applied earlier (Foreman-Peck, 1979).

Free Traders always argue that protection is at the expense of other countries, a so-called 'beggar-thy-neighbour' effect, and that it risks retaliation. But some of the above evidence supports Keynes's contention at the time that all countries can benefit from protection if it boosts confidence, and thence raises income, employment and imports, an effect which seems to have occurred from the 1890s onwards (see above). Protection could be particularly beneficial where industrial development was low initially and unemployment very high, as appears to have been the case in Eastern Europe during the 1930s (Kofman, 1997). Moreover, the danger of retaliation proved less than claimed because Britain and the USA largely precluded it through bilateral agreements, while many countries did not bother to retaliate because their protection levels were already high (Kofman, 1997; Dunkley, 2000b: 117).

So the startling conclusion is that the Legend of the Thirties is probably untrue, as is the general notion of 'trade determinism'. Protection was continuously and almost universally used between the Napoleonic and Second World Wars, an era which saw utterly unprecedented industrial growth (Bairoch, 1993; Senghaas, 1985: 22ff). Recent work suggests that nineteenth-century tariffs helped growth (see above; O'Rourke, 2000), while globalisation via migration and trade brought social disruption and *more* inter-country inequality, not less as Free Traders anticipate (O'Rourke and Williamson, 1999; and see Chapter 5). On the other hand, both Bairoch (1993) and O'Rourke (2000) warn that the positive growth impact of protection might not always apply, possibly being less in the post-1945 era due to a waning of protection-amenable factors such as labour shifts from agriculture and infant industry advantages.

As regards the overall benefits of freer trade, economists were until recently surprisingly modest in their estimates of likely gains from liberalisation, conceding that these would be very small unless supplemented by 'dynamic gains', which were seen as more uncertain and harder to measure (Chapter 2). Since the 1980s trade modellers have devised more complex 'computable general equilibrium' (CGE) models, which are supposedly better able to track linkages and dynamic gains. These tend to show higher benefits from trade liberalisation than earlier 'welfare' methods (Harberger triangles, Figure 2.1), but there are various problems with these models (see Box 6.1).

However, one of the most ambitious CGE exercises to date, a joint OECD–World Bank study (Goldin Report) of likely Uruguay Round benefits, estimated these as about 1 per cent of world GDP and less for most countries, whereas more bullish projections by GATT and other groups had suggested up to several per cent (Dunkley, 2000b: ch. 7). Free Traders claim that such projections underestimate trade benefits because the models do not cover services or capture all benefits, but service benefits are hard to measure and services liberalisation has major social costs (Chapter 8). Free Traders claim that even small benefits accumulate into major gains over time, but so would gains from protection, as might the social costs of freer trade. Many, though not all, mainstream economists insist that these sorts of gains are 'non-trivial', or positively beneficial, but their criteria are elusive. Krugman (1999: 176) once estimated US gains from a 'strategic trade' protection policy as about 1 per cent of GDP, which he dismissed as trivial, yet this was the *same figure* that the Goldin Report declared to be non-trivial. Clearly 'triviality' is in the eye of the beholder, and a good deal of legend surrounds Myth No. 4 that there are wondrous gains to be had from free trade.

Trade and Manifest Destiny

Free Trade Myth No. 5 holds that, due to technological miracles, sensible policies and the 'naturalness' of trading, trade volumes and ratios have greatly increased over time, clearly manifesting a destiny of inevitable globalism. In this section I suggest that this picture is at least part mythology, as the story is more complex.

Curiously, for a long time trade economists believed that trading would eventually decline because of the maturation of industries, the satiation of trade-linked needs, the non-tradability of services and the reduction of comparative costs margins between countries due to transfer of technologies (i.e. the lessening of comparative advantage differences), among other factors (e.g. Keynes, 1933; Arndt, 1963: 272). In fact, world trade appears to have continued growing in various respects: in absolute terms from $5 billion in 1870 to over $5 trillion in 2000; as a ratio of exports to GDP (see Tables 4.1 and 4.2); in terms of 'connectivity' (most countries now conduct at least some trade with most others); and in terms of rising import content of production (Held et al., 1999: 167, 174; Pryor, 2000).

However, patterns of trading are intricate and alternative interpretations are possible, my view being that both the importance of world trade and the inevitability of globalisation are overstated. This can be seen in relation to a number of the following standard features of trading.

Products These vary in their tradability, manufacturing and high technology being fast-growing and 'over-represented' in trade compared with their shares of GDP, which is widely thought to mean that trade will inevitably grow as the world becomes more 'sophisticated'. This is only partly true. In recent years the manu-facturing share of world trade was 61 per cent, about three times its share of world output, the share of 'machinery and transport equipment' alone being 33 per cent, with 'office and telecommu-nications equipment' accounting for 10 per cent. This clearly appears to indicate the industrial specialisation which Free Traders urge, though such a disparity suggests that it may in fact represent more specialisation than necessary.

By contrast, the world trade share of agriculture is about 8 per cent, only slightly more than its 6 per cent share of world output, and the trade share of services is 20 per cent compared with a world output share of 60 per cent, exactly the reverse of the manufacturing pattern. This may suggest that such items are inherently non-tradable, or that nations wish to remain largely self-reliant in food and many services. Although trade in some commercial services is growing rapidly, that in sectors such as community services, health, education and entertainment is not increasing, which suggests that these activities are not readily tradable (see Krugman, 1995: 342–3), and that attempts by the WTO to force the growth of trade in all services (see Chapter 8) may be unwarranted.[11]

Countries and blocs Country trade shares change only gradually over time, Britain's share of world exports falling from 33 per cent in 1800 to 5 per cent in the 1980s, Spain's doing likewise (Holtfrerich, 1989: Table 1.2). Post-war patterns include rising shares for Europe, parts of Asia and the Middle East (Table 4.1). Some claim that declining shares for Africa and other poor regions are a disastrous indicator of these regions being 'marginalised' or left out of globalisation and its 'goodies'. But this is an over-simplified view because many structural and developmental factors

Table 4.1 World merchandise and service exports (% shares)

	MERCHANDISE							SERVICES
	1948	1953	1963	1973	1983	1993	1998	1998
North America	27.5	24.6	19.4	17.2	15.4	16.8	17.0	20.5
Latin America	12.3	10.5	7.0	4.7	5.8	4.4	5.2	4.0
Western Europe	31.0	34.9	41.0	44.8	39.0	43.8	44.5	48.3
Central/Eastern Europe/Baltic states/CIS	6.0	8.2	11.0	8.9	9.5	2.9	4.1	
Africa	7.4	6.5	5.7	4.8	4.4	2.5	2.0	2.4
Middle East	2.1	2.1	3.3	4.5	6.8	3.4	2.6	
Asia	13.8	13.2	12.6	15.0	19.1	26.3	24.5	19.4
Japan	0.4	1.5	3.5	6.4	8.0	10.0	7.4	4.7
China	0.9	1.4	1.3	1.0	1.2	2.5	3.5	2.6
Australia and New Zealand	3.7	3.2	2.4	2.1	1.4	1.5	1.3	
Six East Asian traders	3.0	2.6	2.4	3.4	5.8	9.7	9.6	
Other Asia	5.8	4.5	3.1	2.1	2.7	2.6	2.8	
GATT/WTO members	60.4	68.7	72.8	81.8	76.0	87.0	89.9	

Source: WTO, Statistics, 1999: p.12, Table II.2; services extracted from p. 22, Table III.4.

are involved, some more developed regions like North America and Australasia also incurring declining shares. As can be seen from Table 4.1, much of the world's trade is regional rather than global. Trade within the three largest blocs, Western Europe, East Asia and North America, represents around 50–60 per cent of world trade for many sectors – e.g. 48 per cent for agriculture, 49 per cent for all manufacturing, 55 per cent for cars and 56 per cent for textiles.[12] This suggests that, despite the widely claimed 'death of distance' or 'end of geography', inter-country space remains important and desired (see Krugman, 1995: 342).

Changing nature of trade The post-war era has seen a massive acceleration in three complex new features of trade, all of which indicate ongoing globalisation, but not necessarily its inevitability or guaranteed benefits. The first is 'intra-firm trade' (IFT), or exchange between subsidiaries of TNCs, whose value is uncertain but often estimated at around 40 per cent of world trade. When added to trade between TNCs and non-TNCs, which some put at 30 per cent of world trade or more, TNCs are involved in at least 70 per cent of all trading, some observers putting this as high as a staggering 90 per cent. The causes of this trend are complex, but include rising general trade (above), rising FDI, increasing TNC control of both trade and investment, domestic consolidation of large companies and government deregulation of all these, thus entailing corporate and national politics as much as, or more than, inevitable globalism. As TNCs are known to use oligopolistic strategies, surplus profit extraction and transfer pricing (Chapter 3), the benefits from IFT are dubious.

A second new feature of global trade is 'intra-industry trade' (IIT), or exchange within product groups – cars for cars, and so on (see Chapter 2, above). First World IIT has doubled since 1960 to some 60–80 per cent of all trade, a notable exception being the still fairly self-reliant Japan at 30 per cent (Held et al., 1999: Table 3.8). A standard textbook explanation for the rise of IIT is that 'increasing returns' or 'economies of scale' enable more countries to put more products onto world markets at competitive prices, which implies economic benefits. On the other hand, factors such as product differentiation, 'reciprocal dumping' (TNCs sneaking into each other's countries using price discrimination), brand promotion, advertising-driven consumerism and other oligopolistic controls also play a role (Chapter 3). These can have costs and constitute 'wasteful trade', arguably being due more to corporate deregulation than to inevitable globalism.

The third new feature of global trade is what I call 'supply-chain trade' (SCT), these units also being known as commodity- and value-chains. Supply-chains involve a complex of links between the 'value-added' sections of an industry from the producer through designers, processors and wholesalers to retailers, particularly using a variety of outsourcing and subcontracting systems. Where once such chains involved arm's-length independent firms, they now frequently encompass arrangements ranging from full foreign ownership to licensing and a variety of loose-knit partnerships. 'Producer-driven chains' tend to involve FDI and TNC control of key producing firms, while 'buyer-driven chains' more often involve many small producers in sectors such as food, clothing, footwear furniture or toys, supplying large retail groups. Both types, but particularly the latter, may facilitate a squeezing of small suppliers' incomes and onerous control by the end users, possibly explaining some of the unequalising effects of globalisation (see Gerefi and Korzeniewicz, 1994; Kaplinsky, 2001). As with IFT and IIT, SCT is at least partly due to deregulation of economic processes.

Trade beats output One of the most frequently cited pieces of evidence for inevitable globalisation is that rates of growth of trade have been markedly higher than those for output, supposedly indicating that the global economy is expanding faster than national economies. But the trends are not as clear-cut as claimed, one data compilation (see Table 4.2) showing that world industrial output outgrew trade until about the mid-nineteenth century, which at least suggests that correlations are uncertain, or even that growth led to trade rather than the reverse. Thereafter the trends varied, trade only outstripping output from 1840 to 1870 and since 1948. In any case, the causes and meanings of both trends are complex, as the next point will outline.

Trade ratios The statistic most commonly cited in support of Free Trade and supposedly inevitable globalisation is the trade

Table 4.2 Growth rates of world trade and world industrial/manufacturing production (annual average, %)

	World trade	World industry
1705–85	—	1.50
1720–80	1.10	—
1780–1830	1.37	2.60
1820–40	2.81	2.90
1840–60	4.84	3.50
1860–70	5.53	2.90
1870–1900	3.24	3.70
1900–13	3.75	4.20
1913–29	0.72	2.70
1929–38	−1.15	2.00
1938–48	0.00	4.10
1948–71	7.27	5.60
1971–4	8.31	6.84
1974–80	4.15	3.60
1980–6	2.94	2.65
1990–2000	6.80	2.30

Source: Holtfrerich, 1989: p. 2 Table 1.1; WTO, *Annual Report*, 2001: Chart II.1.

ratio, measured either by exports or by exports plus imports as a percentage of GDP. I prefer the former, as exports and imports are two sides of a coin (though not necessarily equal sides), so the use of both is a sort of double-counting which arguably doubles the apparent importance of trade. Even measured just as exports to GDP there is a range of estimates depending on the way the indices are compiled. The World Bank (*WDR*, 2000/2001: Table 13) estimates the world trade ratio to have been 19 per cent in 1990 (22 per cent in 1999) while Maddison (see Table 4.3) has

Table 4.3 Trade ratios: merchandise exports as % of GDP (exports and GDP at 1990 prices)

	1820	1870	1913	1929	1950	1973	1992
Western Europe	n.a.	10.0	16.3	13.3	9.4	20.9	29.7
France	1.3	4.9	8.2	8.6	7.7	15.4	22.9
Germany	n.a.	9.5	15.6	12.8	6.2	23.8	32.6
Netherlands	n.a.	17.5	17.8	17.2	12.5	41.7	55.3
UK	3.1	12.0	17.7	13.3	11.4	14.0	21.4
USSR/Russia	n.a.	n.a.	2.9	1.6	1.3	3.8	5.1
Australia	n.a.	7.4	12.8	11.2	9.1	11.2	16.9
Canada	n.a.	12.0	12.2	15.8	13.0	19.9	27.2
USA	2.0	2.5	3.7	3.6	3.0	5.0	8.2
Latin America	n.a.	9.0	9.5	9.7	6.2	4.6	6.2
Brazil	n.a.	11.8	9.5	7.1	4.0	2.6	4.7
Mexico	n.a.	3.7	10.8	14.8	3.5	2.2	6.4
Asia	n.a.	1.3	2.6	2.8	2.3	4.4	7.2
China	n.a.	0.7	1.4	1.7	1.9	1.1	2.3
India	n.a.	2.5	4.7	3.7	2.6	2.0	1.7
Indonesia	n.a.	0.9	2.2	3.6	3.3	5.0	7.4
Japan	n.a.	0.2	2.4	3.5	2.3	7.9	12.4
Korea	0.0	0.0	1.0	4.5	1.0	8.2	17.8
Taiwan	–	–	2.5	5.2	2.5	10.2	34.4
World	1.0	5.0	8.7	9.0	7.0	11.2	13.5

Source: Maddison, 1995: p. 38, Table 2.4.

put it at only 13.5 per cent in 1992 and less than 10 per cent until the post-war era.

Economists have identified a long list of possible causes of increased trade, including technological innovations in transport, communications and finance; rising IIT (see above); trade liberalisation; growing numbers of TNCs; business out-sourcing to foreign partners within supply-chains (see above); growing links between

TNCs, FDI and trade; oligopolistic strategies of overseas expansion (see Chapter 3); splitting and outsourcing overseas of newly privatised or corporatised former public enterprises; and changing national borders when nations split up. Clearly many of these are discretionary political factors rather than evidence of 'unstoppable' globalism. One study (cited in Pryor, 2000: 7) attributes two-thirds of recent trade increases to IIT and most of the remainder to discretionary trade liberalisation by government, with only a minimal share attributed to technology, while Krugman (1995) mainly credits trade liberalisation. The two main periods in which trade expansion exceeded GDP growth, 1840–70 and since about 1970 (Table 4.2), were both eras of major cuts in protection (Holtfrerich, 1989: 3), which suggests a causal role for liberalisation.

Whatever the causes of apparent trade increases, questions remain about how much the trade ratio really tells regarding the importance of trade. First, the numerator of the ratio, trade volumes, can be overstated in three ways: the commonly used constant price (inflation-adjusted) data tend to overvalue traded goods, whose prices usually rise more slowly than those of domestic goods; there is some double-counting of intermediate goods as they cross national boundaries, and of reexported goods from entrepôt states like Singapore; TNC transfer pricing creates artificial trade values, though with uncertain effects.

Second, the denominator, GDP, is a notoriously narrow indicator which tends to over-estimate real output by counting environmental 'bads' as 'goods', or when subsistence production in developing countries is marketised and reclassified as formal GDP. On the other hand, GDP underestimates real output by omitting the 'hidden economy' (crime, drugs, barter etc.), the 'informal sector' (small, unregistered enterprises) and the 'household economy' (domestic work), as well as by inaccurately measuring consumer price levels, the alternative indicator being known as 'purchasing power parity' (PPP) GDP (see below).

The effects of these three omissions cannot be reliably measured and they doubtless overlap. The 'hidden economy' is often estimated to be 10–20 per cent of official GDP in the West, more in poorer countries, and the 'informal sector' more than 50 per cent (Chapter 7). The UN (UNDP, 1995: ch. 4) has estimated the 'household economy' (probably including many 'informal sector' activities) to be some 70 per cent of official world GDP, or $16 trillion on top of the official $23 trillion. Of the extra $16 trillion, $11 trillion is women's work, which, added to their share of official GDP, indicates that women do more of the world's work than men! Thus, allowing for all three omissions so as to estimate what could be called a 'real people' GDP would increase GDP in all countries by margins probably ranging from 50 per cent in First World countries to 100 per cent or more in the rest. Not enough is known about such factors over time to assess how they affect longer-term trends in trade ratios, but I suggest that, on balance, at any one time conventionally measured GDP understates real output. Underestimates of GDP may be partly countered by the above-mentioned overestimates (due to pollution and marketisation), but on balance it is likely to be greatly under-measured for most countries.

The effects of PPP GDP are better known. Standard GDP compares country GDPs using current exchange rates, but in an era of massive financial speculation these no longer accurately reflect the real economy. PPP systems use a single index, often based on US price levels, for comparison, this greatly increasing the GDP of poorer countries with large, low-price, non-traded goods or services sectors which are otherwise undervalued. The use of PPPs remains controversial, but the differences can be startling. World Bank data (*WDR*, various: Table 1) show world turn-of-the-millennium PPP GDP to be 32.7 per cent higher than conventional GDP, and 200–300 per cent higher for some Third World countries! Even some richer countries like Australia and Canada have higher PPP GDPs.

Now, the point about all this is that if GDP is underestimated by up to 100 per cent through omissions and up to 300 per cent through lack of PPP adjustments, then the usual trade ratio estimates (exports to standard GDP) are up to four times higher than they should be, and probably at least double for most countries. Thus, trade is less than half as significant as the usual trade ratios imply. The same applies to FDI, the late 1990s world investment ratio (FDI to GDP) being 5.7 times larger for standard GDP than for PPP GDP and over 16 times for Third World countries.[13] Together these adjustments, to both trade and FDI ratios, suggest that the quantitative importance of globalisation is greatly overstated in the mainstream literature.

Conclusion

The five Free Trade myths examined in this chapter, which broadly state that free trade, free markets and free enterprise trading are ancient, natural propensities (what I call the 'Smithian Propensity'), that free trade is highly beneficial and that trading is increasingly important in the life of nations, are overstated or untrue. Trading is an ancient activity, but one which, through what I call the 'Gandhian Propensity', was traditionally controlled, 'embedded' in social norms, made subservient to cultural values and sometimes frowned upon as well as having its occasional seamy side and its own vested interest groups. Claims of measurably large benefits from freer trade are open to question, while statistical assertions regarding the large and increasing importance of trade in the life of nations are oversimplified and overstated. In particular, if a number of arguably quite justifiable adjustments are made to standard GDP, then most countries' trade ratios, the usual method of gauging the importance of trade, are only a half to a quarter of what is usually claimed, thus suggesting that the degree and inevitability of globalisation are greatly overrated. This also calls into question the insistence by Free Traders and the WTO (Chapter 8) that nations will languish in dire poverty without trade 'reform', a claim which is grossly overstated and probably nonsense! However, the ultimate claim made for Free Trade is that it leads to economic growth and longer-term beneficial development, assertions which the next two chapters will challenge.

Notes

1. See Malinowski, 1921; Thurnwald, 1932; Viljoen, 1936.
2. Polanyi, 1977; Finley, 1973; Garnsey et al., 1983; Duncan and Tandy, 1994; 'Industry' and 'Trade' in Peake, 1995; Sahlins, 1974.
3. Simkin, 1968: esp. 257; Norberg-Hodge, 1991: 91; 139; Elvin, 1973; Howe, 1996.
4. Bairoch, 1993: Part 2; Thomas, 1997; Blackburn, 1997; 'Economics' and 'Slave Trade' in Drescher and Engerman, 1998; Klein, 1999.
5. Sediri, 1970; Braudel, 1982: 211ff; 1984: 48.
6, List, 1841; Judd, 1996: ch. 6; Chang, 2002.
7. Kravis, 1970; Crouzet, 1980; Riedel, 1984; Evans, 1989: ch. 9.
8. See McCloskey, 1992; Cain, 1982; Irwin, 1991b; Bhagwati, 1958.
9. Also see Arndt, 1967: 271; Broadberry, 1986; Kitson and Solomou, 1990; others cited in Dunkley, 2000b: 117.
10. See Irwin, 1998 and sources cited there.
11. Trade percentages calculated by the author from recent WTO *Annual Reports* (Statistical Supplement) and output data from World Bank *World Development Report* (various).
12. Bloc shares calculated by the author from WTO statistics (Ibid), Section IV, appropriate tables.
13. Calculated by the author from UNCTAD, *World Investment Report 2000*: Annex Table B6 (Standard GDP basis) and World Bank, *World Development Indicators 1999*: Table 6.1 (PPP GDP basis).

CHAPTER 5

DEVELOPMENT, MYTHS AND ALTERNATIVES: A CRITIQUE OF GLOBALISING GROWTH

[W]e must embark on a bold new program for making the benefits of our scientific advances and industrial progress available for the improvement and growth of underdeveloped areas.... [People of these areas] are victims of disease. Their economic life is primitive and stagnant. Their poverty is a handicap and a threat both to them and to more prosperous areas.

US President Harry Truman
pledging the first US aid programme
(cited in Rist, 1997: 71)

We all aspire to Cadillacs and would be concerned about any tribe wishing to remain in the bush communing with flora and fauna.

Mompati S. Merafhe, Foreign Minister of Botswana,
justifying his government's policy of expelling the
Kalahari Bushmen from their ancestral homes
(Survival International pamphlet, 2001)

I do not believe that industrialisation is necessary in any case for any country. It is much less so for India. Indeed, I believe that Independent India can only discharge her duty towards a groaning world by adopting a simple but ennobled life by developing her thousands of cottage industries and living at peace with the world.

Mahatma Gandhi, 1946 (CW, 85: 205–6)

In previous chapters I have explained how the case for Free Trade rests on claims that it is supposedly able to improve the specialisation and efficiency of an economy, and raise consumption or 'psychic income' through a mechanism known as 'consumer

97

surplus', thus leading to higher economic growth. Under assumption 15 (Chapter 2) maximisation of income growth is the almost exclusive goal of Free Trade theory, and of mainstream economics, although this is supposed to flow into 'welfare gains' such as higher living standards, longer life expectancy and overall social development. I have queried the assumptions, corollaries and general mechanisms of this doctrine, showing how the benefits of free trade are probably overstated, both in theory and practice, as well as outlining some alternative 'heretical' perspectives. In this and the next chapter I question whether free trade is the best way to achieve economic growth and longer-term development, as well as whether or not these concepts, as conventionally defined, are desirable goals. I suggest that an alternative view of development and goals greatly weakens the validity of free trade and globalisation.

Inventing Development

Some commentators have quipped that concepts such as 'development' and 'underdevelopment' were 'invented' on 20 January 1949 in US President Truman's inaugural speech pledging a new form of massive aid programme for poor countries (quoted above). This quip makes a good story, but the US sociologist Robert Nisbet (1969) has traced development thinking back to the Greeks' belief in cyclical descent from a Golden Age and the Enlightenment notion of perpetual, linear progress through knowledge and action in pursuit of perfection. Amartya Sen has attributed the first known piece of development advice to the pioneer English economist Sir William Petty, who in 1676 told the French they were growing *too fast*! Systematic development theory is usually traced back to Smith (see Chapter 2) or to the early Industrial Revolution (Cowen and Shenton, 1996: ch. 1), with the Darwinian era introducing the ominous idea that the most economically advanced societies are superior (Nisbet, 1969: Part 2; Rist, 1997: ch. 2).

By 1949 Truman was expressing this entrenched belief in inevitable evolutionary progress, his new slants being the claim that 'underdevelopment' was a threat to everyone (tribesmen don't consume Cadillacs – above – and peasants support communism), plus the policy of throwing money or technology at the 'problem'. This was the heyday of 'modernisation' theory, which saw progress as evolution from primordial societies and traditional values, such as status, ascription, religiosity, localism and inward orientation, to modern (Western) values of achievement motivation, rationality, universalism and outward orientation. The US sociologist Daniel Lerner wrote about the supposedly inevitable passing of traditional society in favour of the modern, American 'rationalist and positivist spirit', against which Islam (or any other tradition) 'is absolutely defenseless' – 'old ways must go because they no longer satisfy the new wants'. Others wrote of worldwide convergence upon Western managerial, industrial, rational values and institutions, leading to four great transformations – modernisation, industrialisation, urbanisation and globalisation (Lerner, 1958: esp. ch. 2; Kerr et al., 1971).

Blatantly deterministic views of this sort are reflected in Western definitions of development such as that of former OECD official Rutherford M. Poats, who described development as 'the social transformation of traditional stagnant economies to a structure compatible with progressive modernisation, growth and constantly improving standards of living'. This staggeringly presumptuous definition prejudges the 'need' to demolish traditions, and the alleged desirability of Western living standards, as well as confusing 'growth', which is narrow and quantitative, with 'development', which is broad, longer-term and qualitative. Such a definition also precludes any notion that people should have some say in development, just as I have already argued that Free Trade brings 'nonconsensual' change, and just as Bill Gates (1996: 11) has admitted that people cannot vote on technological innovation.

The great economist Joseph Schumpeter, who saw economic history as driven by innovation and entrepreneurship, described development as a process of 'creative destruction'. He failed to point out, however, that few have any say in what gets created or destroyed, although he did warn that the emergence of dissenting values would be the Achilles heel of capitalism. At present, elites 'invent' development and people must accept the course chosen, but this situation is now being challenged. For reasons explained in due course, I prefer to define development as the appropriate evolution or consolidation, through participatory methods, of a society's agricultural, industrial, social, cultural and belief systems so as to meet basic needs, maintain social stability and justice, provide educational, intellectual and spiritual stimuli, protect vital ecosystems and preserve cultural integrity.

There Are Alternatives!

As discussed in previous chapters, the Free Market Economic Rationalist view of history sees trade as a key initiator of growth and development – not the only one, although some globalisers imply it is the main and indispensable one (Legrain, 2002: 21ff). The connection is through the 'gains from trade' (Chapter 2), with trade liberalisation leading to specialisation, efficiency, higher consumption and 'psychic' income, or 'static gains', thence to 'dynamic gains' through investment and productivity increases. The implied sequence is as follows:

Static gains				Dynamic gains
trade ♦	specialisation, structural efficiency ♦	consumption and income growth ♦	exports ♦	skills, technology, productivity, investment
				⌡
		general development, modernisation, industrialisation, urbanisation, globalisation	ℜ	economic growth

However, there are several problems with this story. First, it is a direct, linear, simplistic, trade-determinist mechanism, with reality likely to be much more complex. Second, it suggests one-way causality from trade to development, whereas reverse causality (from development and growth to trade – see Chapter 6), or at least bicausality (both directions), is possible. Third, other factors besides trade (e.g. investment) are involved in initiating the above processes and this will complicate the picture. Fourth, there can be other causal factors within the sequence – consumption is affected by 'autonomous' savings behaviour, exports by exchange rates, investment or technology by entrepreneurship and so forth, which in aggregate may be more important than trade. Fifth, as outlined in Chapter 2, the concepts of static and dynamic gains from trade are uncertain, with likely social costs frequently counted as benefits. Finally, the sequence implies 'development' as a single, agreed upon goal, whereas there are many different visions of desirable development goals. It also implies the 'one size fits all' notion relentlessly pursued by the IMF/World Bank and WTO in their respective policy areas. By contrast, I shall advocate, in this and later chapters, a 'horses for courses' principle that each society has differing traditions, needs and desirable trajectories, the development of which requires national autonomy.

Indeed, all three alternative approaches covered in this book would challenge some aspect of this sequence and propose alternatives which in some way question free trade, or even globalisation in general. Most Interventionists follow Keynes in seeing the growth 'motorboat' as driven by 'aggregate demand', of which consumption is the largest component, investment the most strategically important and trade (exports minus imports) a relatively minor one. Many also see the need for 'infant industry' protection or industry policy to stimulate and direct development, although Thurowians (Chapter 3) may otherwise agree with much of the sequence, including the goal of globalisation, and some have questioned the direction of causality, suggesting it is at least partly from growth to trade.

Human Development theorists raise similar queries about the sequence, but they particularly propose alternative goals which focus on social indicators of development. To this end Drèze and Sen (1989: Part 3) propose a mild interventionist strategy of 'growth mediated security' as opposed to the 'unaimed opulence' of free markets. Some Marxists and Gandhians have long held that excessive trade or other dependence can inhibit development. Community-Sovereignty theorists question most aspects of the above sequence, offering radically alternative goals or even questioning industrial development itself, as did Gandhi (quoted above). Such views have become sufficiently common for the World Bank (2002: 18) to bemoan 'the nationalism, protectionism and anti-industrial romanticism that [are] all too prominent'.

As with trade (Chapter 4), development has also historically been embedded in social norms and traditions. Reflecting what I call the 'Gandhian Propensity', some scholars find that traditional societies are viable and change only unwillingly in response to external pressures such as population growth or invasion, thus being 'conscripts of civilisation, not volunteers' (Diamond, 1964: Introduction; Johnson and Earle, 1987). Nisbet (1969: ch. 8) argues that historical-anthropological evidence does not support claims of linear, directional social evolution, nor of inevitability and irreversibility, there being in most societies a widespread fundamental desire for stability, social preservation and maintenance of values.

Smith (1776, 1: 402) surmised that people would remain attached to rural life, and many pre-industrial philosophers thought traditional institutions should not be destroyed in the name of progress, Edmund Burke even using this as an argument against British colonial occupation of India, Ireland and America (Cowen and Shenton, 1996: 33, 434). Mill (1848: 287) preferred a stationary state (no growth) to destruction of nature and cautiously endorsed Carey's theories of community (Chapter 3). Marshall (1920: 207) thought development should be gradual and mindful of the impact on nature, while Keynes (cited in Dunkley, 2000b:

xiv) wanted preservation of rural society and warned against striv-ing without enjoyment (1930: 368). Today there is a wide range of alternative views about development and its goals, including specifically African, Middle Eastern and Indian (mostly Gandhian) visions (Ayittey, 1991; Wiarda, 1999). All of this suggests that development is non-directional, non-inevitable and often non-consensual, being driven by discretionary political forces towards both economic and non-economic ends. Below I will propose some alternative, less exclusively economic, goals.

Trading Development

Smith and other early economists saw trade as just one factor in development, 'trade determinism' arising in the late nineteenth century with the notion of trade as the 'engine of growth', until it was reduced to 'handmaiden' status a century later (see Chapter 4). Early post-war mainstream economists often based their development advice on a theory of 'gaps', claiming that poor countries had gaps such as between imports and exports, savings and investment or technological requirements and capacities, thence prescribing mixes of trade, FDI and aid, with moderate Protectionism occasionally accepted.

A dissident circuit of 'development economics' theorists, such as Prebisch, Singer, Myrdal, Nurkse and Rosenstein-Rodan, advocated an inward-looking, state-led 'big push' for growth to overcome 'vicious circles of poverty', 'backwash effects' from imports or other 'blockages' to development. These theorists have often been condemned as 'export pessimists' because they thought that poor countries could export little and would suffer declining 'terms of trade' (see below), a not unreasonable view in the 1940s. However, all such theorists presumed the Smithian Propensity (Chapter 1) and the supposed imperative of rapid growth/development. But in the Thatcher/Reagan-inspired 1980s all such dissidence was brushed aside in the epoch-making Neo-classical, Free Market, Free Trade revival which declared that 'government failures' outweighed market failures, that regulation led to 'rent-seeking' (individual profiteering), that public enterprises were almost always less efficient than private business, that planning distorted market 'signals' and that free, outward-oriented trade policies maximised growth and poverty reduction. The result was a so-called 'Washington Consensus' between the US Treasury, the IMF and the World Bank that the policies of Free Markets, Free Trade, small government and privatisation would be pressed upon all countries under the influence of these three bodies and would be generally trumpeted in global fora.

Today the consensus of opinion has eased slightly from the Free Market extremities, the IMF and World Bank reluctantly acknowledging global instabilities from speculation (after the late-1990s Asian Crisis) and new market failures such as 'asymmetric information' raised by the US Nobel laureate Joseph Stiglitz, a former World Bank chief economist, turned globalisation critic. Respected economists such as Lance Taylor (1993), Dani Rodrik (1995; 1999) and Keith Griffin (1999) have produced evidence critical of the Washington Consensus, Free Trade and trade determinism, particularly questioning the much-proclaimed link between trade and growth (see Chapter 6). Even former WTO director general Renato Ruggiero, and UNCTAD head Reubens Ricupero, have admitted that 'trade is not enough' for requisite development (WTO, 2000a), while some mainstream economists now concede that history, institutions, distributional issues and the like are at least as important as trade and 'getting the prices right', a policy perpetually urged by Free Marketeers (e.g. Hoff and Stiglitz, 2001).

The rest of this chapter examines a selection of issues, including structural, distributional, environmental, human development and sociocultural questions of the sort raised by the three alternative schools of thought discussed in this book. The nature of, and preferred solutions to, these matters call into question the validity of arguments for Free Trade and globalisation.

Of Ladders, Lock-in and Scale Economies

Drawing on earlier historical stage theories, a currently popular development metaphor is that of a ladder with successive sectoral 'rungs' such as agriculture, mining, crafts, light industry, heavy industry, 'elaborately transformed manufacturers' (ETMs), high technology and super-high tech. Free Marketeers say countries should seek to ascend the ladder as rapidly as seems appropriate and that this is best done through markets and trade. But, following List (Chapter 3), many Interventionist theorists fear that a country with initial comparative advantage at a low 'rung' could, via 'path dependence' (see Chapter 7; Arthur, 1994; Chang, 2002), be locked on to that rung if Free Trade policies preclude governments from directing the ascent, as some think happened with Portugal (Chapter 4).

Free Marketeers base their growth analysis on assumptions similar to those for Free Trade (see Chapter 2): constant or diminishing returns; natural comparative advantage; growth driven by resource inputs through the market; 'exogenous' technology (random inventions external to the system); supply-side driven development; growth equally effectively led by any sectors with comparative advantage. By contrast, Interventionists in the Keynes/Kaldor mould (see Chapter 1) make virtually the polar opposite assumptions: increasing returns; dynamic comparative advantage; growth driven primarily by 'endogenous' (within the system) investment; endogenous technology (generated within the system from public and private research); demand-driven development; and the view that manufacturing and technology, which have greater multiplier linkages to the rest of the economy, present more growth potential than other sectors.

The Interventionists' assumptions clearly imply that development is non-automatic, non-directional, vulnerable to disruption or stagnation and needs nurturing, including by state planning, to encourage appropriate industries and avoid lock-in on low rungs. There is evidence to support this view (see Chapter 6), although emphasis on the role of education and research may be over-stated, the importance of scale economies overestimated and the need for industrial development overrated (see below). Overall, however, the very concepts of ladders and 'lock-ins', if valid, suggest the need for Protection rather than Free Trade.[1]

Two Steps Backwards: The Terms-of-Trade Problem

Early 'export pessimists' (discussed above) claimed to have found a major flaw in Free Trade theory, related to the 'lock-in' prob-lem, that not all sectors were the same for development and that free trade could make a country worse off if its comparative advantage proved to be in a product whose export prices grew more slowly than the country's import prices. Known as the 'declining terms of trade' problem, early post-war research by UNCTAD founder, Raoul Prebisch, and British economist (now Sir) Hans Singer, seemed to suggest this was the fate of nations which exported primary commodities and imported manufactures. Proposed solutions included world price support schemes, more market access into the First World, export diversification, 'import substitution' for more self-reliance (see next chapters) and even the banning of luxury imports.

Ever since, an avalanche of statistical studies has brought conflicting results, a standard mainstream conclusion being that the terms of trade were only a problem for certain periods, com-modities or countries, not a long-term trend; that First World protectionism was not a major problem; and that export diversi-fication may not help because poor countries have declining terms of trade for their (meagre) manufactured exports as well. The problem was said to be poor organisation, low skills, inflexibility of Third World states and the unavoidable volatility of primary commodity prices in world markets (Michaely, 1984; Hansson, 1993). One survey of the literature concluded, from data for 1900–1991 period, that the terms of trade for primary compared with manufactured goods declined 'marginally' by about 0.5 per cent per annum, that short-term price fluctuations are a greater problem, and that countries should not necessarily abandon primary exports on the basis of aggregate trends (Bleaney and Greenaway, 1993).

Yet the ghosts remain. A 'marginal' 0.5 per cent per annum is a 45 per cent decline in poor countries' prices throughout last century! NGO studies from IMF/World Bank data show most commodity prices declining over the past two decades, some by over 50 per cent – sugar by 76 per cent, cocoa by 71 per cent and coffee by 64 per cent, for instance (Oxfam, 2002: ch. 6, esp. Table 6.1; Curtis, 2001). Over 1,000 million people worldwide rely on such products for their livelihoods, some people's incomes having been halved since 1980; this is often a factor in many countries' debt crisis. Moreover, for a time the IMF/World Bank, in one of the world's great policymaking fallacies, advised most countries to pay off debt by increasing primary exports, which simply resulted in glutted markets and lower prices (Barratt Brown, 1995: 79ff).

Prebisch and Singer attributed the terms-of-trade problem to low income elasticity of demand (slow demand growth) in rich countries, to First World wage–profit bargaining systems which boost manufacturing prices, and to natural resource-displacing technological developments. Today we could add factors such as oversupply due to the above-mentioned World Bank-supported export scramble, widespread dependence on TNC-led supply-chains (Chapter 4) and TNC transfer pricing. So the terms of trade problem remains a major flaw in Free Trade doctrine, presenting a case for more interventionist policies, fair price trading schemes (see Chapter 8) and more self-reliant development, as well as perhaps a new look at international commodity agreements for price stabilisation, even though these have not been very successful to date. Indeed, some studies have found that commodity prices hold up better in a regulated than in a free-market, deregulated environment (Akyüz and Gore, 2001: 278ff).

Two Cheers for the Poor:
Globalisation, Poverty and Inequality

During the 1970s Human Development theorists such as Streeten
(Chapter 3) and Seers proposed alternative development goals
such as reduction of unemployment, poverty and inequality. In
response the ILO advocated targeting 'basic needs', while the
World Bank, under mild Interventionists like Robert McNamara
and Hollis Chenery, declared for 'redistribution with growth',
policies which have since slipped into the background without
totally disappearing. By the 1980s rampant Economic Rationalism
was claiming that free markets, FDI and some trade liberalisation
under GATT were fixing most problems through accelerated
growth, 'technology transfer', 'convergence' of national growth
rates and the so-called Kuznets Curve, which predicts that economic growth at first worsens inequality as profits rise, then eases
it as these 'trickle down' and incomes of the poor catch up.
Through such mechanisms globalisation is supposedly able to
stimulate growth, raise all incomes, eliminate poverty and reduce
excessive inequality, if given the chance (World Bank, 2002).

However, there are many complications to this question. First,
it is complex enough analysing growth and distributional trends,
let alone trying to correlate these trends with trade or wider
globalisation (see Chapter 6). Thus, experts come up with many
differing results, one globalist citing contradictory evidence in the
one book (Legrain, 2002: 22 cf. 51). Second, parameters can be
uncertain – for example, poverty lines are rubbery, cross-country
comparisons are notoriously difficult and the use of PPP GDP
(see Chapter 4) indicates much smaller income gaps between
countries than conventional GDP. Third, the largest income gaps
between rich and poor countries are due to different levels of
development, but these levels have complex historical origins and
countries value development in various ways. Fourth, trends in
one major country can affect comparative statistics and mask other
trends. Fifth, many factors, both international and domestic, can

affect growth and distribution, so single correlations such as between trade and growth are unreliable (see Chapter 6). Finally, GDP levels and gaps are not necessarily ideal indicators of real living standards (see below).

Bearing in mind such complications, the overall evidence is unclear, but is not as favourable to globalisation as globo-euphorists claim, for the following reasons:

1. Historical studies indicate that nineteenth-century globalis-ation increased domestic inequality and 'divergence' between countries because migration reduced wages in some countries, capital flows benefited the rich and trade had many social costs. Inequality then *declined* during the inter-war period when globalisation was reversed and rose again after the mid-1970s with renewed globalisation, although this trend is not as marked as some anti-globalists claim.[2]

2. IMF/World Bank studies in the 1990s claimed that world inequality had markedly declined since around 1980, sup-posedly due to globalisation. However, more recent studies incorporating more countries and new methods (notably Milanovic's household income survey) show increasing in-equality over that time. Other evidence suggests that, whilst absolute poverty has declined worldwide and in many countries, gaps remain huge and have worsened since the 1970s as globalisation accelerated. Divergence and rising inequality is occurring between countries, within countries and between certain groups, notably between rural and urban areas, in terms of growth rates, living standards and produc-tivity, although some convergence has occurred between the richer OECD countries. Rapid growth in China may be concealing the rate at which other countries are falling behind.[3]

3. Many specific gaps are widening: World Bank data (*WDR*, 2001: Table 4) show poverty worsening in many countries; the gap between countries with the highest and lowest per

capital GDP has grown continuously from 4:1 in 1820, 10:1 in 1913 and 26:1 in 1950 to 39:1 in 1989 (Maddison, 1994: 23), apparently worsening with globalisation; and the world's three richest men own more wealth than the poorest 600 million people (UNDP: various), many of these fortunes being made in very globalised and globalising high-tech sectors.

4. Much evidence now suggests that IMF/World Bank SAPs inhibit growth and worsen inequality;[4] a suppressed World Bank report has found that the Bank's anti-poverty approaches are not working and should be more interventionist (Denny, 2000: 14); some speakers at one WTO conference have admitted that trade liberalisation could reduce income and equality (Ben David et al., 2000, esp. Winters); and studies by Lance Taylor and associates (2001) confirm much of the above.

5. To the (questionable – see Chapter 6) extent that globalisation does enhance growth, this is seldom enough to reduce poverty, as policies such as targeted public programmes or employment generation are required and market-led development has not provided these, especially where trade liberalisation has left Third World exporters dependent on global supply-chains (Kaplinsky, 2001; Curtis, 2001; Oxfam, 2002). Some Indian scholars point out that India's acclaimed recent growth has mainly benefited the rich and that foreign or privatised companies seldom observe state affirmative action requirements for poor and tribal peoples.[5] In one of the World Bank's own tables (2002: 35, Table 1.1) purporting to show the superior performances of 'more globalised' countries over the 'less globalised', the latter actually display rather similar indicators, showing continuing improvements and equal or better performances on some items!

6. One remarkable study has found that in some cases trade liberalisation appears to promote growth, but only because new imports and competition reduce employment and welfare for poor farmers or labourers, thus making them work harder and raise output (Barrett, 1998).

7. Over time FDI has provided only about 10 per cent of Third World investment and has been on a downward trend since 1960 *despite* accelerated globalisation; thus, FDI has not greatly helped development (Griffin, 1999: 84), even in countries which have liberalised capital flows (Helleiner, 1994: 22–3).

8. An Oxfam study (cited in Curtis, 2001: 116) has claimed that governments lose up to $200 billion per annum through TNC transfer pricing, revenue which may have been available for social purposes if the same amount of trading had been done by more controlled local firms.

9. Anecdotal evidence from NGOs (e.g. Oxfam, 2002: 135ff) reveals many cases where trade or FDI liberalisation has destroyed traditional jobs, created new ones only in exploitative sectors and in a myriad of ways forced wages downwards. Much of this would occur in the informal sector (see Chapter 7), most of which does not enter the aggregate statistics upon which the World Bank or other global optimists base their studies.

10. Many Third World countries that have sought to industrialise, globalise and export manufactured products have found their export prices and income shares stagnating or declining, possibly because much of their trade is through TNC-controlled 'supply-chains' (see Chapter 4) in which their value-added share is constantly squeezed (Kaplinsky, 2001).

11. Globalisation appears to be having complex effects on labour markets as the types of technologies and development it induces in both rich and poor countries stretch the gap between skilled and non-skilled incomes (see below).

12. Overall, one former top OECD official (Emmerij, 2000) has expressed the opinion that not only does globalisation fail to solve old social problems like unemployment, poverty or inequity, it also generates new ones such as increased crime, 'urban dualism', drug cultures and social marginalisation via excessive cut-throat competition or other adverse social change.

Conclusions cannot be definite, but it appears that models of development which rely on free trade and globalisation exacerbate inequalities between people and countries, do not markedly alleviate poverty and have no special claim to be able to stimulate economic growth. This suggests that more interventionist models of development might do better (see below).

Belaboured Playing Fields

Probably the most hotly debated issue in the history of globalisation has been the 'pauper labour' or 'cheap labour' argument against free trade, the crudest version of which claims that rich nations will always be out-competed by low-wage countries whose workers live on 'a bowl of rice a day', thus threatening the hard-earned living standards of the former. Free Traders have always passionately denied this, quite correctly in my view. Low wages are normally the result of low skill, low productivity and low development, which give such countries a comparative advantage in unskilled labour-intensive industries, there being little evidence that TNCs migrate to these countries simply because of low wages or that those countries reap an unfair trading advantage as a direct result of low-wage labour.

However, there is evidence for a more sophisticated version of the case. This holds that there will be a trading advantage and an attraction for TNCs when higher technology plants are combined with wages which are much lower than the levels warranted given the productivity of those plants. I call this the 'exploited labour' case, which arises when there are what I call substantial 'unit cost gaps' between countries – that is, unit labour costs, or wages per unit of output, will be much lower in the exploiting country and it is this, not the *absolute* low-wage level, that counts. In this context, 'exploitation' simply refers to workers being paid much less than is justified by the productivity of their plants, although ill-treatment may occur as well. There is plenty of evidence for this case, the much-discussed 'sweatshop' phenomenon, the free-trade-zone strategy, the 'Nike syndrome' and so forth being due to exploited labour rather than to cheap labour per se. Even mainstream economists accept that exploited labour does occur but believe it is only temporary until development increases, a faith which the evidence does not really justify (see Dunkley, 1996; 2000b: 161ff).

There are various implications of 'exploited labour', none of which is easy to identify or quantify. First, unit cost gaps make it possible for many Third World workers to be paid at well below plant productivity levels while some skilled employees are paid at rates close to these levels, though well above local standards; such disparities can distort local labour markets and cause large income inequalities. Second, TNC capital will be attracted to such countries for their relatively, rather than absolutely, low-cost labour, though only if the skill levels are adequate. Fourth, much of the technology thus imported will be inappropriate for the country concerned and thence distort development. Fifth, the resultant exports will displace some labour-intensive production in First World countries, reducing unskilled employment and cutting wages of those workers.

There is evidence for all of these implications, but the effect on world trading is hard to assess. Mainstream economists now admit to, and have extensively debated, the fifth point, most claiming that the impact of lower-cost imports on rich countries is rather small and that most First World unskilled labour displacement is due to technology. However, some economists see this impact as a more significant factor in First World unemployment, especially former World Bank economist Adrian Wood, who also points out that trade and technology are closely linked, so that imports can both displace unskilled labour and induce further labour-displacing technology (see Dunkley, 2000b: 165).

Even some mainstream economists partly concur, Bhagwati (1998: 20–21) conceding that rising Third World import competition is creating volatile comparative advantage and First World job insecurity, especially for older and unskilled workers. Indeed, the famed Stolper–Samuelson theorem (Chapter 2) forecasts that free trade will help workers in poor countries but hurt those in rich nations, as appears to have happened. More recently Samuelson (1996, 1999) has warned that such import competition can reduce incomes, while new technologies may boost them but not necessarily to pre-free trade levels, and he has declared (1996: 8) that we must 'stop prattling that free trade helps everybody all the time'. 'Cheap labour' can be fair if the low wages are related to low productivity, appropriate indigenous technology and adequate job creation, but 'exploited labour' can be unfair, especially if accompanied by bad working conditions, deprivation of rights, inhuman treatment of workers and so forth, in which case Protection against imports from such countries may be justified.

Human Development and the r-Curve

Over the years dissatisfaction with the limitations of GDP/GNP per capita as an indicator of development led to the construction of alternative indices, though most were simply material enumerations – housing, cars, telephones, radios, televisions, schools, doctors per capita – which did not rank countries very differently from GDP (Todaro, 2000: 69ff). Then in 1990, influenced by Sen's notion of development as capacity expansion (Chapter 1), the UN began a report (UNDP, annual) based on three conceptual indicators: life chances, knowledge and income, these specifically measured as life expectancy, adult literacy, years of schooling and adjusted PPP GDP per capita. Though subject to criticism and still somewhat materialist, the HD index produces country rankings which can differ considerably from those based on levels of GDP per capita.

Using this index, plus related human indicators such as health, infant mortality, position of women and water quality, Sen and other Human Development (HD) scholars have noted strikingly little correlation with GNP growth (Drèze and Sen, 1989; Sen, 1999). This clearly contradicts the still common mythology that we need rapid economic growth in order to increase life expectancy or reduce infant mortality. Individual indicators tend to correlate with growth via what I call an r-curve graph (Figure 5.1), which implies that the crucial improvements can be made at low income levels with simple developments such as better sanitation. One study found that, when allowing for poverty reduction and public health expenditure, the correlation between life expectancy and income (GNP) disappeared altogether (Anand and Ravallion, 1993). This does not mean that economic growth is irrelevant, but that it mostly benefits life expectancy when it gives priority to reducing poverty and boosting public health spending, which can usually be done without high GNP per capita or rapid growth.

A number of countries, such as China, Sri Lanka, Cuba, Zimbabwe and Botswana, some twenty-five in all, have achieved much better HD indicators for their income levels than the rest of the world. The Indian state of Kerala has achieved the best HD indicators in India, despite being one of the poorest and least industrialised states in that country, while World Bank head James Wolfensohn has startlingly conceded that socialist, self-reliant, non-globalised Cuba has attained the best HD record in Latin America despite ignoring his Bank's advice![6] By contrast, black people in the USA have a lower life expectancy than citizens of the above countries and of Kerala, despite a far higher per capita GNP in the USA as a whole (Sen, 1999: 21ff). These better than average HD records appear to derive primarily from an active state, non-reliance upon 'trickle-down', early and extensive investment in education, health and basic infrastructure, good nutritional and food security standards, and targeted programmes for women, the poor or other needy groups (see Mehrotra and Jolly, 1997).

Similarly, cross-country surveys of 'happiness' also display the r-curve pattern and show only a marginal link with growth or absolute income level. Richer countries are only slightly happier than the poorer, with happiness levelling off or even declining (as in the USA) over the post-war, globalising era despite a trebling

Figure 5.1   The r-curve

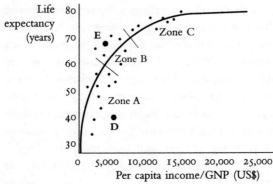

Notes

1. This diagram is schematic, and not based on actual data. Each dot represents a country and the curve (graph) a general trend. Its crucial feature is the way it flattens out rapidly from a relatively low income level.

2. The shape of the r-curve suggests that the greatest HD improvements occur at relatively low income levels (Zones A and B), that improvements at high income levels (Zone C) are gradual and minimal, that a variety of HD results are possible at any given income level (e.g. Country E compared with Country D at $5,000) and that some countries (Zone B) can achieve HD levels comparable to high income countries at modest income levels, mainly by active state-led HD policies.

3. The r-curve also applies to other indicators such as infant mortality rates, literacy levels and even happiness.

of per capita GDP. Other research results suggest that poorer people and countries seem more easily satisfied than the affluent, that relative income inequality, democratic participation and trust bring greater happiness, while happiness may cause growth rather than the reverse.[7]

I have some qualms about Sen's (1999) 'capacities and freedom' view of development, which, whilst refreshing, remains narrow, partly growth-oriented and uncritical of globalisation. Sen never mentions the environment and analyses the role of culture only minimally (see below). The UNDP's Human Development Index, partly developed by Sen, is an improvement on GDP but is still narrower than the widely proposed Index of Sustainable Economic Welfare (ISEW), which adjusts GDP for various social and environmental costs, thence showing 'progress' in First World countries levelling off since the mid-1970s (Cobb and Cobb, 1994). Nevertheless, the HD approach is a clear rebuttal of the myth that rapid economic growth and globalisation are essential to life on Earth. It also demonstrates that alternative development models based on well-targeted government policies may be socially better than narrow free-trade-led growth.

Greening Trade or Trading the Green?

Perhaps the most audacious claims made by a world body in recent times are those by the World Trade Organisation (WTO) that its key goal is 'sustainable development' and that trade helps the environment. Trade supposedly does this by encouraging new export industries which are 'cleaner' than traditional sectors like forestry or tanning, by facilitating the importation of pollution-reduction technologies, by inducing more efficient production and (believe it or not) by stimulating economic growth, which, apart from initial pollution increases, supposedly makes people environmentally aware and provides more resources for clean-up. Known as the 'environmental Kuznets curve', this last-mentioned mechanism is widely touted by Free Marketeers as making economic growth environment-friendly, but I have questioned this claim elsewhere (Dunkley, 1999).

This story is oversimplified, if not fatuous. First, it relies heavily on governments and firms sincerely endeavouring to 'internalise the externalities' with effective environmental protection policies, but Third World politicians and businessmen do not have much of a reputation for being green! Second, the idea of trade bringing cleaner industries is unduly optimistic, as many poor countries have comparative advantage in rural and resource activities which are potentially damaging unless strongly regulated, the World Bank frequently funding major development projects in such sectors. Third, although the idea of poor countries creating 'pollution havens' to attract TNC investment in 'dirty' industries seems overstated, there is evidence that it is true to some extent (Dunkley, 1999: 78). Fourth, export-oriented development of the sort pushed heavily by the World Bank and the WTO creates huge pressures for environmental risk, forestry and prawn farming being particularly notorious. One UN study of mining in Chile, cars in India and prawns in Bangladesh has found environmental or other costs considerably eating into the export benefits, while in many countries villagers have resisted, sometimes violently, the encroachment of such industries onto their agricultural or communal lands (UN, 1999; Lockwood and Madden, 1997).

A fifth criticism of the 'green trade' story is that trade directly damages the environment in various ways, including through pollution from, and energy used by, transportation, by the spreading of exotic micro-organisms on the hulls or in the ballast water of ships (Dunkley, 1999; 2000b: ch. 10) and through rich nations' overall 'footprints', or the total ecological impact of all resource imports and pollution 'exports'. Finally, although the claim that trade can be a key 'engine for growth' is dubious (see Chapter 6), to the extent that it does spark growth this may damage the environment more than Free Traders claim because carbon dioxide and various pollutants directly increase with growth, as does energy and resource depletion (Dunkley, 1999; 2000: ch. 10).

In sum, trade is not assuredly green. Free Traders accept 'externalities' as a legitimate basis for trade intervention but say that environmental problems are mostly domestic, and so should be tackled primarily through local or national regulation rather than trade intervention. However, the above suggests that this simplistic separation cannot always be made, so that some trade intervention, along with a less globalising development model, may be required to manage the world's worsening ecological crisis (see also Dunkley, 1992).

Don't Forget the Ladies!
Development, Globalisation and Women

It was not until 1970, almost two centuries after Smith, that anyone bothered to write a book specifically on women in development, the author, of course, being a woman – the Danish mainstream economist Ester Boserup. In *Women's Role in Economic Development*, Boserup pointed to the crucial economic role women played in most traditional societies, others later noting that what the German eco-feminist Maria Mies has called 'housewifeisation' (confinement of women to domestic roles) is mainly limited to advanced Western capitalism. Historically the protection of women's rights variedly greatly between societies and was seldom adequate, but traditionally women were active as workers and sometimes entrepreneurs, especially in agriculture, often also being a key repository of knowledge, both esoteric and practical. This is still widely misunderstood, one prominent sociologist, Inglehart (2000: 223), asserting that women's historic role was largely confined to child-bearing and -rearing.

In time, economists, and even the World Bank, 'discovered' the key role of women, the latter (e.g. 2002) proclaiming education, employment and 'inclusion' for women as key development goals, the benefits of such goals including a growing but flexible workforce and a lower birth rate. There is some validity in this, but the globo-euphorists' claim that globalisation is good for women via new job opportunities and (particularly low-skilled electronic) skill formation is dubious. Boserup long ago observed that modernisation and urbanisation disproportionately create jobs for men, who thenceforth benefit from the ensuing industry-specific skill formation and political influence, while women's traditional roles, skills or knowledge are sidelined. She pointed out that modern urban industrial society is historically the only one which so greatly polarised male–female economic roles. Moreover, as noted earlier (Chapter 4), more than half the world's production is not counted in official GDP, much of this – in fact

80–90 per cent of it in the Third World – being women's work (Pietilä, 1997; Wichterich, 2000: ch. 4).

Today much evidence suggests that the present integrative form of globalisation does indeed tend to destroy traditional female roles, creating instead mass, urban, low-skilled, often insecure, part-time jobs under exploitative conditions, or else menial, sometimes degrading or unsafe employment in the mass assembly and service sectors. According to the UN this picture applies to possibly three-quarters of all globalised female work in all parts of the world (see Dunkley, 2000b: 158–9; Wichterich, 2000).

Globalists often retort that such work is better than nothing, but many women writers and activists claim that plenty of empowering work still exists for women in areas such as small-scale or subsistence agriculture, crafts, small local industry, community-related services and so forth, although an alternative, more locally focused and less globalising development model would be required to develop such opportunities properly. In fact throughout the world women's movements and NGOs are reasserting traditional activities or creating new, economic, social or political roles through self-empowerment by methods which include communes, co-ops, credit systems, companies and the seeking of political office, as well as by a plethora of social activism, including some delightful cases I encountered in India where women burnt down (illegal) sly-grog shops which had been distracting their menfolk.[8]

Yet all of this is domestic and does not require trade or globalisation, many women fearing that competition, privatisation and foreign ownership would harm their cause because local companies and local branches of state-owned banks have often helped them (Dunkley, 1993). The jobs most likely to be destroyed by import liberalisation are those rural and craft-based activities which traditionally have been within the women's sphere (Wichterich, 2000: 4, 73, 80ff). So it is clear that truly women-friendly development would require a much less globalising development model than is being enforced at present, and a more female-centred development model could be a more self-reliant one (Pietila, 1997).

A Poor Relation: The Neglect of Agriculture

Development economists have long debated whether agriculture or industry should lead development, and whether the two should grow in balance. The debate was initiated by two branches of the mild Interventionist stream, notably Rosenstein-Rodan's idea of a 'big push' for rapid industrialisation and Kaldor's notion that 'manufacturing is special', although Kaldor himself advocated an initial focus on agriculture. Free Marketeers, who think that any sector can lead so long as it has comparative advantage, did not enter the debate much, although they thought development likely to begin with traditional, thenceforth 'non-traditional, agricultural exports. 'Agriculture-first' Interventionists argued only for rural development as a means for surplus-generation and long-term industrialisation (Mellor, 1986), but many Gandhians and some eco-feminists advocate rural improvement and a more agrarian society as a long-term *goal*. Another variant of the 'agriculture first' argument (Seavoy, 2000) argues that there is a systemic bias against commercial agriculture in favour of subsistence, until political coercion is used to suppress the latter.

Before long, however, politics took over from academia, with Second and Third World governments everywhere planning manic industrialisation, trying to do in a decade or two what had taken the First World a century. Clouds of pollution were taken as prestigious signs of industrial development. Reasons for this industrial mania ranged from the consumerist 'demonstration effect' or Western copyism, the importing of Western 'experts' and burgeoning 'progressivist' ideologies, to the practice of 'urban bias', whereby town workers and urban elites sought to hold food prices down at the expense of farmers. Forms of discrimination against agriculture have included overvalued exchange rates, urban-centred infrastructure, pro-industry administrative or credit bias suppression of traditional crops and seizure of traditional lands for development. Free Marketeers often blame inward-looking protectionist policies for the neglect of agriculture, but one such group (Little et al., 1970) has also blamed excessive emphasis on industrial development, a policy failing which is rectifiable.

The effects of agricultural neglect have included rural stagnation, massive food import dependence, pollution of waterways used by farmers, the decline of traditional and indigenous communities (MacAndrews and Chia, 1982) and generally distorted development (Barrett Brown, 1995: 32ff). Even a 'successful' country like South Korea has suffered much more rural, social, cultural and ecological disruption, as well as excessive dependence on food imports, than is generally acknowledged (Bello and Rosenfeld, 1990; Park, 1992). Most First World countries face a variant of this problem: agriculture remains important but is now so 'industrial' (capital- and technology-intensive) that traditional farming communities have become insignificant and perhaps face extinction. The much-maligned rural subsidies of the West are actually aimed not at a sector so much as at a class, which arguably deserves to exist but is being exterminated by 'overdevelopment'.

Pro-agriculture theorists argue that farming is 'multi-functional', providing labour, materials and finance (rural areas tend to have higher savings than cities), as well as communal, cultural and ecological resources or knowledge. Even the World Bank now claims to agree that agriculture has been neglected, but advocates the Free Market solutions of world parity pricing (supposedly to raise farmers' incomes), internal deregulation, abolition of marketing boards, the construction of 'proper' markets and the conversion of traditional, communal or family land tenure systems into Western-style individual titled holdings, often now funding projects to do this (Cornia, 1994).

Yet the World Bank's 'global market' approach is questionable. Critics of world parity pricing say that it can induce volatility, that local markets are often underdeveloped or unreliable, and that market prices do not reflect the multiple functions of farming (noted above). Marketing boards often provide resources or training for farmers and, when these are abolished, prices often fall, making farmers worse off (Oxfam, 2002: 163ff), the problem probably being the inefficiency and pro-urban bias of boards, not their existence per se. As regards tenure systems, the evidence suggests that land redistribution improves equity and productivity, but individual tenure, which the World Bank pushes, does not necessarily do so and can even disrupt production or reduce incomes (Cornia, 1994). In their textbook *Rural Development and the State*, Lea and Chaudhri (1983: 337–8) observed that the need for modern inputs has been exaggerated, the main developmental requirement being local participation and the 'skilful use of historical experience'. In short, traditional systems do work, and development requires, not free trade or globalisation, but equity, appropriate adaptation, a fair go for farmers and respect for people's knowledge and traditions, of which more below.

Small Farms Are Beautiful

Notwithstanding Schumacher's fame, globalisers still parrot clichés, especially regarding farms, such as 'big is better' and 'get big or get out'. Yet the historical and statistical evidence says the opposite! Adam Smith thought the small yeoman farmer 'who knows every part of his little territory' much more likely to make improvements than large proprietors (1776, 1: 441, 410, 418). J.S. Mill claimed that European peasant tenures had proved more productive than larger-scale English holdings, and in Parliament he backed the restoration of peasant proprietorship in Ireland, subject to fair regulation, for both economic and social reasons (Koot, 1987: 44).

Contemporary research has confirmed this historical view by showing small farms to be lower cost and more efficient for a range of reasons, including lower marginal labour costs; higher family labour retention; higher unit capital and land costs, which lead to saving these resources; higher land or other resource utilisation rates; a stable family ethic; and better ecological awareness. One mainstream study found small farms so superior that

land redistribution towards smaller holdings would raise agricultural output by 20 per cent or more in the countries studied,
and by 80 per cent in parts of Brazil.[9] This does not mean there
are no economies of scale for large units, capital intensity often
resulting in higher labour productivity and wages (Cornia, 1994:
238–9). Even large farm co-ops in the old socialist countries
achieved some efficiencies for this reason (Griffin, 1999: 212ff),
but generally small farms have higher land productivity, or yields
per acre, as well as being more likely to maintain community
structures (Dunkley, 2000b: 169–70) and to use ecologically sound
polycultural methods. Also, traditional land tenure systems do
work, can be efficient and are adaptive (Richards, 1985; Cornia,
1994).

Another sector in which small can be beautiful is fishing, where
long-standing battles have occurred between small, traditional
artisanal fishing communities and large, often TNC-backed, trawling fleets. The latter can catch more fish and pay higher wages to
their sparse workforces, but traditional fishing employs far more
people, reinforces the community and has multiple roles for
women, especially in marketing (Dunkley, 1993). Moreover,
traditional methods are ecologically sensitive, whereas trawling
can be catastrophic in tropical waters where species mingle closely
and target schools are hard to pinpoint, so that small-scale fishing
will always be much more sustainable. It is a story little known in
the West that this battle is being won by the small people, with
countries like Indonesia and India now protecting the artisanal
sector (Dunkley, 1993). It is a story which proves that big and
global are not the only, or best, ways to develop.

Re-greening My Valley:
The Organic Agriculture Revolution

In globalisers' parlance, small, traditional, organic systems have a
ring of unrealistic, 'anti-industrial romanticism' (e.g. World Bank,
2002: 18). There is nothing inherently wrong with romanticism,

but today evidence is mounting for the massively destructive effects of large-scale, Western 'industrial' agriculture and Third World 'Green Revolutions' in terms of pollution, biodiversity reduction, resource depletion, adverse impacts on small farmers and even nutritional crises as bread and (globalised) junk foods displace traditional, varied diets in many societies (Thaman, 1982). Evidence is also mounting that organic farming, in its many forms, is far more ecologically, socially and nutritionally beneficial.

Organic agriculture is not simply a restoration of traditional methods, but draws on and experiments with non-chemical systems, both customary and new, for fertilisation, pest control and so forth. It is based on concepts such as species diversity, natural fertilisation (manures and compost), biological or physical pest control, intercropping and numerous other features, many of which are capable of *increasing* the productivity of traditional systems. Some countries are now experimenting with such systems on a growing scale, notably Cuba; this potentially presents the quietest, greenest and most far-reaching revolution of the century, but one which requires little globalisation, and in fact has a massive potential for 're-localisation' (see Chapter 7).

The Four Lost Causes:
Culture, Community, Values and Tradition

I once attended an economic seminar on the relation between culture and trade, and all non-economists to whom I mentioned this assumed that it was about the impact of trade on culture; in fact the seminar was about whether attention to cultural issues could boost Australian trade! Surely only economists and trade officials would bother about that link. The attitude of many Free Traders to culture is perhaps reflected in Bhagwati's ire, expressed through a letter to the *Financial Times* (27 September 1999), at the World Bank's recent (minimal) funding of some cultural preservation projects rather than continuing with its prime focus on economic growth. There is a minor economic literature, and a substantial anthropological one, on culture and development, but this is largely utilitarian, mostly asking how traditions, cultures and values must change to induce development. Generally these literatures find that achievement motivation, secularism, rationality, mobility and the like – that is, materialism and modernity – are good for development, these being thenceforth recommended. Some hold that high-income societies eventually shift to less materialist 'post-modern' or 'post-materialist' values, but these bear little relation to traditional values.[10]

This approach thus sees the four 'lost causes' of culture, community, values and tradition as largely instrumental, to be manipulated in favour of change, although religion or other 'harmless' traditions are not necessarily discouraged. Free Market economists regularly recommend getting rid of institutions unfriendly to markets, one study urging 'rationality unconstrained by tradition' and materialist values as a stimulus to greater production (cited in Todaro, 2000: 642), although the World Bank (e.g. 2002) shows some sporadic concern about the cultural impacts of development. Interventionist and Human Development theorists have not been unsympathetic to this instrumentalism. Marx decried India's 'undignified, stagnatory and vegetative life', seeing Britain's role, though based on 'the vilest interests', as an ultimately beneficial one – that is, 'the annihilation of old Asiatic society, and the laying of the material foundations of Western society in India' (cited in Fieldhouse, 1999: 423). Sen (1999: 312, 240ff) agrees that culture and development needs may clash, so that some people might want to preserve the former, but in near-Darwinian vein he hints that certain old cultures, like less-fit species, may not be missed; any trade-off between culture and development should be decided by democratic participation. I agree with Sen's participatory solution but not his rather social-Darwinist analysis.

These four 'causes' are complex and interrelated, so I will not analyse them in detail. Culture is the overall framework for a society's norms, expression and identity; values are the attitudes which shape behaviour; community entails the locational and relational structure of society; tradition is the evolving legacy of the other three. Together these make up the 'non-economic' core of society, shaping the ultimate goals and way of life which a society seeks. Beyond the narrow circles of Economic Rationalist globalisers or Cadillac-seeking elites, both 'right' and 'left', there is a widespread view that culture or other 'non-economic' mechanisms should lead development, that Western models have unacceptable costs and that, in accordance with the Gandhian Propensity, development should seek to maintain indigenous traditions.[11]

The historical evidence regarding development imperatives is mixed. Some say wants grow from the earliest times (Herskovits, 1952), while Sahlins (1974: ch. 1) says that traditional hunter–gather societies could feed themselves with less than half a day's work and did not seek change much beyond modest variety or marginal improvements. In fact, wealth is an encumbrance to nomads, many societies resisting accumulation and often having no word for 'development' (Rist, 1997: ch. 6). Braudel found evidence, in the sixteenth-century Mediterranean, of people living satisfactorily autarkic lifestyles and resistant to change. In fact, he suggests (1982: 255ff) that everywhere the peasantry was remarkably stable and tolerably satisfied with modest enterprise or other minor changes until the Industrial Revolution.

In Russia the Bolsheviks were initially frustrated when, after the Revolution, many poorer peasants wanted no more than consolidation of their traditional *volia*, or self-reliant agrarian communal system (Figes, 1996: 519, 788). Helena Norberg-Hodge's (1991) work in the Ladakh region of India has shown that traditional peoples do not seem to desire change while they have modest but reasonable living standards, cooperative communal security and strong spiritual traditions, although self-reliant values can be undermined by external materialist forces. One US sociologist was surprised when his fieldwork revealed that for many societies 'the wisdom of tradition still carries weight' and that 'the urge for development and the willingness to change are not equally present in all peoples'.[12] Such evidence confirms my view (Chapter 1) that societies tend to be ambivalent between the Smithian and Gandhian Propensities, or between material change and preservation of tradition.

A World Bank report on the Pacific Islands once noted much slower growth than should have been occurring with the investment levels and SAPs the region had received. The Bank labelled this a 'Pacific Paradox', but the better Pacific scholars easily explained it. Traditional Pacific life was good, many older people still remember it, and everyone has seen the destructive effects of Western media, tourism, technology and fast food on traditions, cultures, communities, health, nutrition and so forth. One economist describes this as a massive 'market failure' of development, giving rise to rationally based 'socio-cultural resistance' (Poirine, 1993: esp. 40ff; Thaman, 1982). There has always been Pacific scepticism about Western-style development. After a historic world tour in 1881 the last king of Hawaii, Kalakaua, observed that his subjects were better off than most peoples he had seen, being better fed, clothed and entertained, never being robbed and having no dyspepsia (indigestion), which 'was common in America' (Armstrong, 1995: 276).

Confirmation of traditionalism has come from a curious source. The US economist, Ronald Seavoy (2000) argues that subsistence agriculture becomes culturally entrenched, that commercial farming is necessary for development, that market incentives cannot overcome subsistence traditions and that all forms of social, legal, political and even military coercion should be used to suppress subsistence. With staggering irresponsibility, Seavoy (2000: 112–13) urges recruitment of the police and army from pro-development urban and farming elites, decreeing that armed forces should be allowed 'to enforce commercial policies on peasants with the maximum amount of violence if necessary'. Although some surplus production is required for development, not only is non-consensual coercion immoral, it usually does not work unless applied murderously, as Stalin and Mao found, and it ignores the evidence that traditional systems can be effective for both subsistence and surplus generation (see Cornia, 1994).

Around the world there are now many proposals for, or actual experiments with, development models which use, without precisely duplicating, appropriate traditional institutions. For Africa, the US-based Ghanian writer George Ayittey (1991) proposes using as a basis for development indigenous institutions such as kinship-based cooperative communalism (as opposed to tribalism), community democracy and traditional rights, which have been neglected since the colonial era, rather than Western individualism. Ayittey (1991: 16) discusses a traditional African value system he describes as 'I am because we are', as opposed to the Western system of 'I am because I am and I want', which could form the basis of communally-oriented development. Indeed, one study has found that African co-ops often fail *because* they are based on profit and economic rationalism, as advocated by the World Bank and Free Marketeers, rather than on traditional communal mutual aid (cited in Verhelst, 1990: 27), whereas traditional-style co-ops do work (Richards, 1985: 154). In Burkina Faso the Mossi people have restored their traditional *naam*, or age-grade cooperative system, for a range of development tasks, though against the opposition of many modernising bureaucrats. Such ideas are not confined to the Third World but can also be found throughout Europe and in Scotland, where a project to revive crofting and Gaelic culture is under way.[13]

A key motive for such experiments is to prevent or reverse the destructive impacts integrative globalising development has been having on communities, cultures and languages (see Box 5.1). An Indian scholar told a 1998 international conference that over three hundred Indian farmers had recently committed suicide under pressure from World Bank- and World Economic Forum-backed development policies. He reported that many people worldwide were rejecting 'this engine of destruction called development' and 'reviving ancient practices and traditions that may inspire hope' (Swamy in Aga Khan 1998: 64–5).

Of particular concern is the widespread physical and cultural erosion of traditional indigenous peoples, one Indonesian leader having advocated ethnic assimilation until there is only 'one kind of man' (Hancock, 1989: 134). Indigenous peoples are not quaint relics of the past, but sophisticated communities which are different from the modernised majorities and from the social models required for globalisation or growth. They are said to number some 250 million, and double that figure if premodern African groups (who are usually the majority in their own societies) are counted. These 500 million wholly or partly traditional peoples would, together, be the third largest country on Earth. Advocates for such peoples are often accused of romanticising that which should really be brought 'into the mainstream'. But many, perhaps most, indigenous or other premodern peoples generally want to retain their lifestyles and traditions, with appropriate adaptations and modest living standard improvements. Often they eat and live better than the urban poor. Their cultures are seldom static, but do not change in linear, modernising, globalising directions. Their agricultural, botanical, ecological and other knowledge systems are often so profound and extensive that Western research scientists rely heavily upon them.[14] Many now argue that indigenous knowledge, with its own forms of rationality, provides a feasible basis for alternative local development, conservation and bio-diversity projects, the search for medical species and alternative sustainable agriculture, this idea now even being promoted to a minor extent by the World Bank.[15]

One study of export-oriented agricultural cash crop development in Malaysia found that the modernisation process has reduced national forest cover from 74 to 55 per cent in just twenty years, caused massive soil erosion or other ecological damage and displaced many indigenous peoples. The author surmises that a modest adaptation to surplus production of traditional, high-diversity systems could have provided better overall returns, a sounder ecological basis and a better quality of life than offered by the plantations and artificial commercial farms which the government has created (Rambo, 1982). A brilliant piece of research in West Africa by the British economic anthropologist, Paul Richards (1985) has shown that extreme agricultural modernisation has not worked, that traditional agrarian ecological knowledge is profound and reliable, that local people are capable of generating their own 'indigenous agricultural revolution' and that this is best based on modest, appropriate adaptations of traditional knowledge.

In sum, the 'four lost causes' of community, culture, values and tradition have been neglected by mainstream theorists, both as factors in development and as factors affected by orthodox development, or else have been merely conscripted for assistance in modernising and globalising everyone. Even a brief examination of these issues makes evident the huge variety of traditions, needs and values embraced by the world's societies, clearly suggesting the desirability of a 'horses for courses' approach with each society deciding its own development path. This requires autonomy and self-reliance rather than globalisation. Of the four streams of thought considered in this book, only the Community-Sovereignty or Gandhi–Schumacher approach affords them a high priority in setting development goals.

I suggest that economic growth should be replaced as a core development target with three alternative goals of social justice, environmental sustainability and cultural integrity. Social justice would consist of adequate sustenance and general welfare for all, elimination of absolute poverty, non-discrimination against women or minorities, and so forth. Environmental sustainability would require what I have called 'sustainably organised systems' (Dunkley, 1992) or the restructuring of all agricultural, industrial, service, energy, transport or other core systems to sustainable principles of the sort now prolifically outlined by environmental organisations worldwide. Cultural integrity means the general preservation, rather than exact replication, of worthwhile traditions so as to ensure that each society maintains the character and identity it, preferably democratically, chooses. 'Worthwhile traditions' should

Box 5.1 Some costs of development

The benefits of development and growth, as heavily emphasised in orthodox texts, include large increases in material living standards; greater availability of goods and services; greatly improved health and life expectancy; and a wide range of economic opportunities. Possible costs of Western-style, high-consumption, high-growth globalising development are much less emphasised, and include:

- extensive adverse social change, most of this non-consensual;
- disruptive inter-regional and rural–urban population shifts;
- disruption caused by water, transport or general urban development projects, with up to 30 million people displaced in the Third World and many more affected in some way;
- decline of certain regions and communities;
- erosion of some cultures, traditions and languages (see below);
- weakening sense of place, community, norms and trust;
- displacement of spiritual traditions by materialistic outlooks;
- possible concomitant increase in crime, drug abuse and general social marginalisation processes;
- replacement of direct, communal interaction with indirect, less face-to-face, more alienating interaction;
- rising socioeconomic inequality and class resentments;
- burgeoning environmental pollution, including UN estimates of 10,000 Third World deaths per annum from pesticide poisoning and 150,000 deaths a day worldwide from all pollutants (Dunkley, 1992: 30);
- depletion of natural resources;
- destruction of biodiversity;
- increasing foreign control and erosion of local or national sovereignty;
- reliance on increasingly complex technologies and rising social costs of these (see Chapter 7).

One of the least publicised of these costs is a massive attrition of the world's languages (Dixon, 1997; Nettle and Romaine, 2000; Crystal, 2000). Some commentators, whom I call 'linguistic Darwinists', insist that this is of no concern because languages are 'dynamic' and 'obsolescence' has been common historically. Others disagree, however, arguing that, in fact, historically, when most language groups were of a comparably small scale, there was a 'linguistic equilibrium' with dying languages being replaced by new ones (Dixon, 1997).

Yet since the Middle Ages, especially following the Industrial Revolution, some languages have gained the ascendency, displacing or marginalising others and disrupting the equilibrium in an eerie parallel to the erosion of biodiversity. Where this has occurred through destruction of a community's habitat, the connection between erosion of linguistic and biological diversity is direct and clearly related to development. In other cases, such as where people shift from their local tongue to a national or global language for occupational or advancement reasons, then the connection between linguistic decline and development or globalisation is less direct but nonetheless real.

Today we are on the brink of a holocaust of language death, half the world's known languages in *c.* 1500 having now died out and at least half of the present 5,000 to 6,700 tongues being in extreme danger because few children are learning them. These fateful figures do not include threatened dialects or varieties of major languages like Australian English, which is also dying because most children are abandoning characteristic Australian words, terms and expressions, mostly replacing them with US equivalents. Causes of decline range from population contraction, invasion, discrimination, geographic marginalisation and habitat destruction to out-and-out genocide, but also include globalisation, especially via globally dominant languages, inequitable development and the increasingly dominant role of English in business, education, travel and the Internet. Attempts at rescue are occurring and seem feasible, but may require a new form of relocalising development of a sort implied in the above quotation from Gandhi (p. 97).

be identified on the basis of what I have called 'adaptive traditionalism' (see Chapter 1), with those practices which are incompatible with other goals, such as discrimination against women or inimical to the environment, being phased out, as Gandhi advocated, although often such practices are not genuinely established traditions. Such goals would suggest a much less globalising model of development than those which prevail today.

Conclusion

This chapter questions the widely proclaimed myth that what the world needs now is the maximum possible Western-style economic development and growth, with all-out free trade and globalisation being the best way to achieve this. Earlier chapters pointed out that the Free Traders' ultimate claim for their doctrine is that free trade will always be the best policy for achieving economic growth and development. This chapter poses the question, 'what is development?', suggesting that the materialist, growth-oriented model embraced by Western mainstream economists tends to lock countries into undesirable, inequitable, unsustainable growth paths, to underemphasise human development, to neglect agriculture, to devalue women and largely to ignore non-economic goals such as community, values, culture and tradition. If these were to become the prime focus of development, as I propose they should be, then a much less integrative globalising model of development, one which allows each country to determine its own development path, would be possible. I suggest that such an alternative is feasible because the key benefits claimed for growth tend to accrue at relatively low levels of per capita GDP, according to what I call the r-curve (Figure 5.1). Throughout the world many people and organisations are now advocating, even creating, such alternative approaches to development.

Notes

1. See Kaldor, 1977, 1989; Hudson, 1992; Taylor, 1993; Kitson and Michie, 2000; Thirlwall, 2002.
2. Williamson, 1997; O'Rourke and Williamson, 1999: ch. 14; Rodriguez and Rodrik, 1999: 32ff.
3. Between countries: Pritchett, 1997; Milanovic, 2002; UNCTAD, 1997: ch. 2; Rodriguez and Rodrik, 1999; Mosley, 2000. Within countries: Galbraith and Berner, 2001; Taylor, 2001. General: UN *HDR*, various; Ackerman et al., 2000; Sutcliffe, 2003.
4. Stewart, 1995; de Mello et al., 1999; Vreeland, 2003.
5. *The Hindu*, 6 December 1999: 3.
6. Kerala: *New Internationalist*, 241, March 1993; Cuba: Reuters Report, *The Age*, 2 May 2001: 12.
7. Kenny, 1999; Frey and Stutzer, 2000; Lane, 2000; Inglehart, 2000.
8. Dunkley, 1993: 30; Kaino, 1995; Mies and Bennholdt-Thomsen, 1999; Wichterich, 2000; Bennholdt-Thomsen et al., 2001.
9. Berry and Cline, 1979: esp 130ff; Ellis, 1988: ch. 10; Francis, 1994; Cornia, 1994: 233ff; Griffin, 1999: 141ff; Rosset, 1999.
10. See Adelman and Morris, 1971; Granto et al., 1996; Inglehart, 2000.
11. Clark, 1987; Dove, 1988; Verhelst, 1990; Apffel Marglin and Marglin, 1999.
12. Foster, 1973: 5; also, Verhelst, 1990; Rist, 1997: ch. 6 and *passim*.
13. See Rajan, 1993; Apffel Marglin, 1997; Rahnema and Bawtree, 1997; Pietila, 1997. On the Mossi, see Skinner, 1996; on Scotland, see Womersley, 1998.
14. Brokensha et al., 1980; Richards, 1985; Dove, 1988; Warren et al., 1995.
15. MacAndrews and Chia, 1982; Hancock, 1989; Davis and Partridge, 1994; general: Burger, 1990; Jamison, 2000.

CHAPTER 6

THE EXPORT CULT:
THE IMPORT-SUBSTITUTION VERSUS
EXPORT-ORIENTATION DEBATE

It is now widely accepted that growth prospects for developing
countries are greatly enhanced through an outer-oriented trade
regime and fairly uniform incentives ... there is no question of
'going back' to the earlier thinking.

Krueger (1997: 1–2)

[I]n every case where a poor country has significantly overcome its
poverty this has been achieved while engaging in production for
export markets and opening itself to the influx of foreign goods,
investment and technology: that is by participating in globalization.

former Mexican president Ernesto Zedillo
(quoted in Rodrik, 2001: 57)

[T]he nature of the relationship between trade policy and economic growth remains very much an open question ... We are in
fact sceptical that there is a general, unambiguous relationship
between trade openness and growth waiting to be discovered. We
suspect that the relationship is a contingent one, dependent on a
host of country and external characteristics.

Rodriguez and Rodrik (1999: 4)

The much more disquieting possibility is that liberalization can
unleash dynamic forces leading not only to an unimpressive
aggregate economic performance but also to long-term slow
employment expansion and increasing income concentration.

Berg and Taylor (Taylor, 2001: 54)

It has been one of the biggest debates in the history of economics.
It is known by various terminology but mostly as 'import-

substitution (IS) versus 'export-orientation' (EO), often with 'industrialisation' (ISI vs EOI) tagged on. As not all IS or EO seeks immediate industrialisation I will use the 'I' tag only where appropriate. Effectively the debate is about Protection versus Free Trade as a growth-development strategy and entails two assertions. One of these assertions is that trading and free trade are better for growth than trade intervention, the other holding that non-interventionist policies which give free rein to exports are better for Third World development than restricting imports. Both issues have long been contentious, the latter since the early 1970s, but the World Bank, the WTO, Free Market scholars like Anne Krueger (quoted above) and most governments now proclaim the debate to be over – trade is best for growth, and EO via trade liberalisation has been proven best for everyone, the Global Free Trade Project being heavily posited upon this alleged 'victory'.

However, in this chapter I dispute such claims as misleading, perhaps dishonest. I argue, contrary to Free Market assertions and parallel claims regarding nineteenth-century development (see Chapter 4), that EO and trade liberalisation do not clearly produce better growth rates or other superior outcomes; that IS can work, though it is often bungled; and that state-led industrial policy is effective. The two core issues, trade–growth links and IS versus EO, are integrally connected and are generally discussed together in this chapter. In a 1987 book, *The Export Cult*, economist Alex Rubner questioned the fashion of export subsidisation on the grounds that the value of exports is overestimated, that an export push can undermine itself by generating imports, and that the IS alternative has been neglected. I argue here that today's Free Market version of the export cult or trade obsession, led primarily by the WTO, is equally questionable, for these and other reasons.

An Elite Consensus

For much of the first three post-war decades some First World, most Third World and all Second World countries used extensive

ISI under a sort of Keynesian consensus based on the notions of 'export pessimism' (Chapter 5) and rapid development, on a belief in the need to generate effective demand through 'infant industry' assistance, on the assumed efficacy of state-led development and on a supreme faith in the industrialisation imperative.

Actually, Free Marketeers have always accepted that the early stages of development afford an 'easy' ISI option where a country has comparative advantages in resources, agriculture or light consumer goods, pots and pans for instance, so that IS can be effective at this time. But further stages of ISI were said to require substantial protection, which Free Marketeers claimed would cause an anti-export bias, distorted price signals and overvalued exchange rates. ISI critics, beginning with a much-quoted study for the OECD by Little et al. (1970), rejected most arguments for IS and began hunting for evidence of its failure. Thereafter Free Market scholars like Krueger and Bhagwati, along with bodies such as the World Bank, claimed to have compiled irrefutable proof for IS failures and EO successes.[1] On the other hand, many Market Interventionists favour ISI and some argue that it was a necessary strategy in the recessed pre-war and wartime environment when global markets were limited, EOI only being feasible in the more buoyant post-war conditions, which arguably ended in the mid-1970s, making ISI again more feasible.

By the late-1980s the Thatcher–Reagan Free Market revolution was well under way, the Washington Consensus (see Chapter 5) regarding Free Market development was established and the Geneva Consensus (Dunkley, 2000b: 17 and *passim*) about global Free Trade was under construction. By the 1990s the supposed clinching of the IS–EO debate in the latter's favour was also used to hustle laggard nations into globally oriented modernisation. The EO 'victory' has thus been crucial to the globalisation project (see Krueger, 1997: 10), so if the pro-EO arguments could be invalidated, the case for global free trade would be heavily undermined. Below I will indeed challenge those arguments.

Models, Numbers and Export Cults

The IS–EO debate is so complex as to defy brief summation, but I will do my best. The now-standard mainstream view is that ISI works only in the 'easy' or 'pots and pans' phase (above), beyond which protection distorts prices and exchange rates, discriminates against exports, hampers the development of natural comparative advantage, especially in agriculture, encourages excessively capital-intensive enterprises, produces longer-term dependence on imported inputs or FDI by TNCs (thus defeating its own self-reliance purpose), induces inequality as some industries and classes are favoured over others, and markedly reduces the growth prospects of the nation.

EO allegedly extirpates these sins, although Free Marketeers are divided over whether EO policy should simply aim to remove discrimination against exporting or actively promote exports. Most favour non-discrimination, but either way exporting is seen as the saviour of poor countries, through comparative advantage-based development, enhanced competition, more efficient governance, greater foreign exchange generation and maximisation of productivity or economic growth. This is allegedly now so clearly proven that most countries are rushing to liberalise. By contrast, many commentators still advocate some form of IS policy, but now do so less on the earlier 'export pessimist' grounds, discussed above, than on Kaldorian-style advocacy of infant industry protection, learning processes and inducement of scale economies (see Chapter 3). Such Interventionists have often supported export subsidies and promotion of the sort criticised by Rubner (1987), whereas most Free Traders oppose direct export assistance just as much as import controls. Nevertheless, Free Traders are 'export-oriented' in the sense that they believe exports can be an 'engine for growth', given the chance, and should thus lead development.

Before assessing the debate a few preliminary comments are required. First, the 'rush of enlightenment' explanation for recent widespread liberalisation is, like the parallel claim regarding the nineteenth-century shift to free trade (see Chapter 4), grossly oversimplified. Some countries have unilaterally liberalised, partly on the assumption of ISI failure. Probably more commonly, however, liberalisation has been adopted through domestic pressure from pro-global business interests and US-trained Free Market Economic Rationalist bureaucrats, or through arm-twisting by the IMF/World Bank, most of whose SAPs contain trade and capital liberalisation requirements.[2] Second, IS and EO are not mutually exclusive but can be combined in various ways. Third, advocates of both approaches have varying versions, some ISI theorists admitting to IS failures, some EOI supporters (e.g. Little et al., 1970) conceding that it is not a panacea and accepting a degree of infant industry protection for industrial development. Pioneer critics of ISI, Little et al. (1970: 1), stated their main concern as being that 'industry has been over-encouraged in relation to agriculture', a genuine problem (see Chapter 5) which many Interventionists ignore. Fourth, it is quite possible for IS to be a valid strategy which is often misapplied in practice, and I will cite evidence for this. Fifth, the outcome of the IS–EO debate is extremely sensitive to factors such as modelling assumptions, data selection and definitions of key concepts (such as 'openness').

A final comment on complications in the trade-growth debate is that the ultimate causes of economic growth are unclear, disputed and will probably never be agreed upon. One survey of mainstream growth studies (Kenny and Williams, 2001) has found that nothing, including 'fashionable' factors like research, education and literacy, or the 'Washington Consensus' factors such as small governments, financial deregulation, macroeconomic stabilisation, privatisation and trade liberalisation, causally correlate with growth. Thurowian and 'New Growth' Interventionists have often nominated 'research and development' (R&D) as a key cause of dynamic growth, but one study for the World Bank has shown only a loose correlation at higher income levels, likely reverse causality (i.e. economic growth *leads to* more R&D) and no correlation for Third World countries (Birdsall and Rhee, 1993; also Gittleman and Wolff, 1995). Likewise with trade, prominent economist Gerald Helleiner (1994: 2) has observed that 'the historical record seems to offer remarkably few recent cases of rapid industrialisation or development that can be associated with the currently recommended (free) trade policies'.

So, no one cause of growth is apparent in the literature, the closest being investment and its embodied technology (Sen, 1983; Helleiner, 1994; Griffin, 1999: ch. 4), although even in that case there can be multiple causes and reverse causality. All this uncertainty does not mean that the above-mentioned factors are unimportant in growth, only that cross-correlations are too complex for highly reliable modelling or causality conclusions. It does mean that we have to be cautious about assertions regarding exports or trade directly causing growth. Certainly, as noted in previous chapters, there is historical evidence of protection sparking economic growth and development, from the late-nineteenth-century European 'take-off' (see Chapter 4) to post-war reconstruction, the Asian 'miracle' and a successful Australian import restriction policy in the 1950s (Dunkley, 1995).

Assertion by the World Bank or other Free Marketeers that the IS–EO debate has been 'clinched' in their favour can only be made by ignoring extensive evidence to the contrary and is misleading, if not downright dishonest. Contrary evidence is provided, not only by many credible non-mainstream commentators but also by fairly mainstream or sub-mainstream Interventionists such as Dani Rodrik, Lance Taylor, Gerald Helleiner and David Greenaway, as well as by Human Development-oriented scholars like Paul Streeten (1982, 1990, 1998) and Keith Griffin (1999). There is even an entire UN-related research group, the Helsinki-based World Institute for Development Economics Research (WIDER), whose work, including that by Taylor and Helleiner, to be cited below, has been critical of EO. This work, largely ignored by Free Marketeers, clearly shows, as Rodriguez and

Rodrik (quoted above, p. 136) state, that the debate is far from closed. Many mainstream textbooks (e.g. Todaro, 1997: ch. 13) point to deficiencies in ISI but still identify a legitimate role for protection in development.

A major problem with the IS–EO debate is that the methods of analysis are complex, the issues are not as straightforward as EO theorists claim, the criteria for assessment are variable, usually being based on subjective assumptions, and all inferences drawn by Free Marketeers are contested, though they rarely admit this. Three broad groupings of analytical methods have been used in the IS–EO debate and for related issues such as the relationship between trade and growth. I will term these the welfare, modelling and case study methods, which I outline in turn.

Welfare Methods

The earliest approach to trade analysis involved various methods for measuring the so-called 'deadweight loss' from protection – the 'Harberger triangles' explained earlier in Figure 2.1. As noted in Chapter 4, historical applications of these methods found, embarrassingly, that Britain and some European countries may have lost from free trade, that pre-1914 protection actually increased *both* trade *and* growth, and that trading may be a 'handmaiden' rather than an 'engine' for growth – that is, trade is helpful but not miraculous. Static gains from trade were found to be very minor and supplementary 'dynamic' gains very uncertain (see Chapter 4).

Then in 1974 a leading EO advocate, US economist Anne Krueger, proposed the seminal but controversial idea that wasteful protection-induced lobbying and corruption added further 'political' deadweight losses to those allegedly deriving from tariff or quota protection. She called this 'rent-seeking', Bhagwati labelling it 'directly unproductive profit-seeking activity' (DUP), and she deemed it much greater than protection losses, amounting to 7.3 per cent of GDP for India (in 1964), for instance, and

15 per cent for Turkey in 1968 (Krueger, 1974). The supposed danger of DUP under regulatory regimes is now one of the key arguments regularly employed by Free Traders for free markets and EO.

Undoubtedly corruption and shady influences are widespread, but there are problems with the DUP story. First, Krueger's loss figures seem improbably high, being based on some sketchy local studies and arbitrary assumptions. Second, DUP is not strictly comparable with the concept of 'deadweight loss' from protection (Figure 2.1), the latter deriving from higher production costs while DUP is a service or transfer payment of sorts which accrues to someone, albeit undeservedly, and has associated social costs. Third, DUP mainly occurs in relation to competition for quotas or import licences, which are not the most efficient form of protection anyway and are avoidable. Fourth, waste also occurs in lobbying for freer trade or for EO-related export subsidies, though Free Traders do not usually approve of the latter. Fifth, there is evidence that liberalisation does not necessarily prevent DUP, while actual *increases* in corruption have been associated with (though not necessarily caused by) liberalisation in India, Turkey and elsewhere (Chandra, 1997: 179ff). Finally, the above suggests that influence and corruption are matters of political will, so that with good governance it is surely possible to minimise DUP, at least over time (Shapiro and Taylor, 1990). Overall, the welfare methods of analysis and related historical evidence do not seem to demonstrate convincingly the superiority of EO over IS.

Modelling Methods

Modelling involves the mathematical treatment of economic data, with two broad methods commonly used – 'econometric' models and 'computable general equilibrium' (CGE) models. Econometric models use correlation and regression analysis to examine possible links between trade and output or productivity growth, usually in one industry at a time, variously using cross-national, single country, cross-section or time-series bases. CGE models endeavour to model all key elements of an entire economy in order to gauge trade-growth links (see Box 6.1). Most of the studies cited below use econometric methods, but CGE models are becoming more common, especially to forecast the aggregate impacts of trade liberalisation agreements, most claims regarding the supposed overall benefits of free trade deriving from such models, which have been widely criticised (see Box 6.1).

Early results from both approaches suggested that trade liberalisation improved at least some indicators (World Bank, *WDR*, 1983, 1987), although *not* for the poorer nations, according to one World Bank study (Michaely, 1977). Soon, however, studies appeared which found no clear link between trade openness and growth, or else found the links to be dependent on the method used.[3]

Both modelling systems have a number of problems, a few regarding CGE models being noted in Box 6.1, those discussed below particularly applying to econometric methods. Five concerns stand out. First, specification of the variables can be problematic and largely judgemental, many different definitions of 'openness' being used, for instance, and results vary with the definitions employed. Second, results are sensitive to how countries are classified – most pro-EO studies, for instance, ranking South Korea and Taiwan as very 'open', whereas models by Taylor and others, which rate them as more closed, obtain results that make openness seem much less conducive to growth. Third, apparent links between variables are not always 'robust' (reliable), one study finding some fifty factors partly linked to growth, but most, including trade, were found not to be 'robust'.[4] All modelling methods are notoriously unreliable at projecting growth rates or causes thereof, and no one factor can explain all growth, so a range of factors, including non-economic ones, appear to be involved (Dowrick, 1994, 1997; Kenny and Williams, 2001: 5ff).

Fourth, misspecification of behavioural or causal links between variables is common, some studies critical of EO finding, for instance, that trade influences growth only indirectly via invest-

Box 6.1   CGE models

'Computable general equilibrium' (CGE) models are complex, computerised mathematical systems used for measuring the impacts of policy changes on an economy. Most quantitative claims about benefits arising from trade liberalisation are now derived from CGE model results, particularly the widely used General Trade Analysis Project, or GTAP (see Hertel, 1997). CGE models use thousands of mathematical equations to represent key relationships within an economy.

Many CGE models simply use Neo-classical 'perfect competition' assumptions (I call these 'Neo-classical models') outlined in Chapter 2 (e.g. Hertel, 1997), but some 'Imperfect Competition' models (as I call them) follow NIET assumptions (Chapter 3) such as oligopoly, increasing returns or learning effects (e.g. François et al., 1997). Others again are 'Structural' models (e.g. Taylor, 1990) using even more structural imperfection assumptions such as 'mark-up' pricing and unemployment, often encompassing a 'social accounting matrix' (SAM) system which measures more dimensions than the other models, including employment, regional and distributional impacts of changes.

Differences in results between the three types of model are unclear, and, as a rule, the more complex the modelling the less reliable the results. One difference between the first two types is that Imperfect Competition models claim markedly higher benefits from trade liberalisation, particularly because economies of scale generate more output per unit of input than the constant returns assumed by Neo-classical models.

For instance, François et al. (1997) found that under Neo-classical assumptions the Uruguay Round liberalisations would actually *reduce* Second and Third World GDP by 0.01 per cent and increase world GDP by just 0.52 per cent, whereas Imperfect Competition assumptions would result in increases of 1.29 per cent and 1.36 per cent respectively – i.e. 2–3 times more benefits. Needless to say, the WTO and other globalisers emphasise the latter types of results!

However, it is not clear that 'Imperfect Competition' assumptions are the more valid, many economists still believing that perfect competition assumptions remain good approximations for the Third World and the world as a whole. Some also think that the importance of economies of scale or increasing returns is overstated (Chapter 7). In short, conventional modelling shows the 'static' gains from trade to be very small, but larger on more disputed assumptions (Chapter 2), all of which confirms the main thesis of this book that benefits from free trade are contingent, not assured.

It is not clear whether or not Structural models are directly comparable with the other CGE types, but structural models usually indicate the need for government macro-intervention (Taylor, 1990, 1993), and CGE pioneer, Lance Taylor, holds that standard CGE models are structurally biased towards pro-market, pro-liberalisation, pro-EO results (Shapiro and Taylor, 1990; Ocampo and Taylor, 1998).

One ILO-commissioned model using a SAM system (above) found that, for Indonesia, established domestic industries using indigenous technology can produce more employment, distributional or other localised benefits than those using imports and foreign techniques (Khan and Thorbecke, 1988), thus confirming standard Gandhi/Schumacher views. Yet this remarkable study has been largely ignored.

Some possible pro-free-trade biases in standard CGE models include the following issues: the commonly used full employment assumption will understate the structural costs of free trade; the common assumption of 'exogenous' (external) technological change may understate the possibility of 'endogenous' (policy-induced) generation of indigenous firms or ideas; the frequent assumption of Say's Law (supply creates its own demand) may exaggerate the chances of new firms or sectors emerging after trade liberalisation.

In sum, CGE model results are widely quoted to justify trade liberalisation, but are complex, controversial and questionable, some versions in any case finding minimal, even negative, benefits from trade liberalisation.

ment or macroeconomic stability (Taylor, 1993; Rodrik, 1999a).
Some studies suggest that EO success may be due primarily to its
rectifying the adverse impacts on agriculture of badly applied ISI
(see Mellor, 1986: 74), rather than EO being a virtue in itself.
The fifth concern with econometric methods is that standard
regressions do not reveal the direction of causality, though certain
statistical tests help. Some commentators suggest reverse causality
– that is, growth leads to trade, probably because strongly growing countries have the confidence to liberalise and because it is
efficient firms which seek to export, rather than exports boosting
efficiency, as EO mythology has it.[5] Also, one study suggests that
EO and freer trade may increase output by squeezing rural
incomes and forcing people to work harder rather than by improving efficiency as Free Trade theory claims (Barrett, 1998).
These problems do not invalidate modelling systems, but they do
suggest the need for caution and a critical understanding of the
approaches.

   Overall, modelling results are much less favourable to EO than
Free Traders claim, many such studies finding, not unexpectedly,
that only import and export growth are linked to trade liberalisation, with other indices such as productivity and GDP growth
less clearly so. In the case of productivity, whilst some studies find
a positive link to trade, many, including those of Free Trade
champions Krueger and Bhagwati (see above), have found little
sign of a linkage to trade liberalisation, one study finding reverse
causality – that is, larger, higher productivity firms with expanding investment plans are the most likely to export.[6] Rodrik (1999a:
70–71) found that, until the mid-1970s oil shock, most ISI
countries were reasonably efficient and had productivity growth
rates comparable to those of East Asia.

   As already noted, attempts to identify the link between trade
and economic growth have been uncertain and the overall data
unclear, those for 1960 to 1990 showing no meaningful pattern,
especially if the few 'outliers' like Singapore and Hong Kong are
excluded as exceptions – see Figure 6.1. Most countries are either

Figure 6.1   The relationship between trade and economic growth

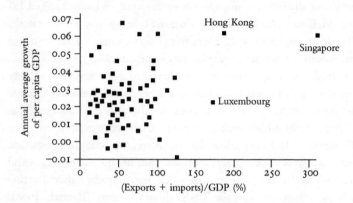

Notes

1. The three 'outlier' countries are in many ways exceptional, with Hong Kong and Singapore being 'entrepôts' with extensive re-exporting and Luxembourg being very small.
2. The unlabelled dots represent many other countries and, if the three outliers are excluded, these dots show no discernible relation between trade ratio (horizontal axis) and economic growth (vertical axis).

Source: Dowrick, 1997: 119, Figure 7.1.

weakly IS or weakly EO and there is no clear difference in growth performance between the two (Evans, 1989; Dowrick, 1994: 24). Also, EOI may be more successful in countries with a higher initial income level and a strong manufacturing base.[7] Rodriguez and Rodrik (1999) have critically analysed some of the main pro-EO studies with respect to their assumptions, definitions and robustness. They found, for instance, that of the various criteria for openness used in Sachs and Warner's much quoted pro-EO study, only two minor indices – currency black market premia and state trade monopoly – seemed linked to economic growth. Tariff and non-tariff barriers did not appear to affect growth adversely.

In general, Rodrik (2001: 60) concludes that there is no firm evidence for a positive relationship between trade liberalisation and growth, and in fact for the 1990s there was a slight *positive* link between *protection* and growth! He sees most countries as beginning with ISI, then liberalising as they grow, so that *growth* causes *trade* and general development causes globalisation. Rodrik also finds that social conflict and governance problems, rather than ISI or 'closed' borders, have held back growth (Rodrik, 1999b).

Growth is too complex and variable a phenomenon to be caused by a single factor like trade. Macroeconomic policies, exchange rates, social forces and so forth also play crucial roles in the growth–development process (Rodrik, 1999a, 1999b; Kenny and Williams, 2001). As noted in previous chapters, growth and development are multi-causal concepts whose worth needs to be evaluated critically, while the gains from trade are, as Rodriguez and Rodrik (quoted above, p. 136) also confirm, non-automatic and contingent upon many country-specific conditions (see Chapter 2).

Case Study Methods

These entail detailed country-by-country studies of policies and their impacts on performance, with several approaches possible, notably studies 'before-and-after' liberalisation; cases of 'countries-with, compared to countries-without' liberalisation and a variety of industry- or theme-specific issues. The advantage of case studies is that a wide range of non-quantifiable country-specific factors can be considered in an integrated way, the disadvantage being that these factors may not be fully comparable with other countries. No method is perfect. 'Before–after' studies of a country suffer from the difficulty of distinguishing between policy and non-policy causes of a particular outcome, while 'with–without' studies across countries may be affected by country-specific factors (see Clark and Kirkpatrick, 1992).

For the sorts of reasons discussed above, Free Trade doyen Jagdish Bhagwati mistrusts cross-country regressions, preferring single-country case studies of the sort he pioneered, and which the World Bank has continued, culminating in 1991 with a mammoth seven-volume series. Such studies claim that EO is more beneficial for growth, employment and equality than IS.[8] But other scholars disagree. For two decades the WIDER group (see above), which has been conducting country surveys led by local experts and based on modelling by Lance Taylor and others, has been obtaining polar opposite results to the World Bank. The WIDER surveys have concluded that country experiences are complex and variable, that macro and debt problems, not ISI, cause slow growth, that ISI can work, that EOI is overrated and that, in any case, the two strategies are interlinked.[9]

Another critic (Buffie, 2001: 189ff) argues that the methodology used by the World Bank in the above-mentioned studies was 'too crude to isolate the impact of trade reform from that of other policies and shocks'. Buffie also points out that in some cases pledged liberalisations did not eventuate or were very limited, a possible inference being that some success indicators may have actually been due to continuing intervention. Indeed, on a number of occasions WTO trade policy reviews have revealed that trade liberalisation has not led to growth as expected (e.g. WTO, *AR* 2001: 121 re Bangladesh), and reviewers once agreed that Japan should focus more on domestic demand stimuli than exports for recovery (1999: 114–15).

Another WIDER study (Helleiner, 1994: esp 25) found that even where exports did rise after liberalisation, this was mainly due to factors such as favourable exchange rate changes, improved macroeconomic management, wage restraint, export incentives and a range of direct assistance to firms of the sort which the WTO has now outlawed. Recent WIDER surveys have concluded that, while trade liberalisation can raise exports, these are often outweighed by imports, thus reducing demand, growth, employment, state revenue and equality, contrary to World Bank claims (Ganuza et al., 2000; Taylor, 2001). Surveys by UNCTAD (1997: ch. 3) and Oxfam (2002: ch. 3 and 5) have confirmed the tendency for EO to exacerbate inequality. Case studies by many other scholars (e.g. Fontaine, 1992; Kofman, 1997) have reached similar conclusions and confirm my argument (Chapter 2) that countries differ in their capacities to gain from trade, depending on country-specific factors.

This does not mean that EO is always malign, nor IS invariably beneficial. Frequent IS mistakes have included a disastrous neglect of agriculture (see Chapter 5); the pushing of inappropriate, excessively capital-intensive industries; excessive wage escalation and urbanisation; overdependence on imported, inappropriate technology and TNC supplies thereof; the overvaluation of exchange rates to cheapen capital imports, but which also boosts imports and discourages exports; excessive elite consumerism; and under-exportation, resulting in foreign-exchange shortages.[10] Thus, ISI was often badly applied, resulting in overzealous destruction of agriculture, communities or cultures. One study of inter-war Eastern European ISI (Kofman, 1997) found that, though reasonably successful, its design was narrowly nationalistic, often discriminating against Jews or other minorities. But these IS failings have not been universal; they are avoidable, with sensible policy design, and EOI has made some of these mistakes too (Streeten, 1982: 162ff; Akyüz and Gore, 2001).

Rodrik (1999a: 68ff; 1999b) argues that IS policies worked effectively until the mid-1970s' oil crisis, after which they performed less well, not due to the exhaustion of 'easy' ISI, as Free Marketeers tend to claim, but because of macro-instability and social conflicts, these often resulting from IMF/World Bank austerity measures. The most successful countries were those which best handled these problems, and democracy often helped.

Innumerable other studies have demonstrated benefits from IS and problems with EO, an early focus being on the East Asian 'Tigers', whose success, Free Marketeers insisted, was due to market incentives and EOI. But critics soon produced ample evidence that, apart from Hong Kong, the Tigers had initially used a strategic mix of ISI and EOI, along with a swag of social, redistributive, educational, training and industrial policies for strong state-led development. The World Bank eventually occupied the middle ground, conceding only that the Tigers' success derived from limited, selective 'market-friendly' intervention, but critics have shown that some Tigers were relatively IS almost until the 1990s, with particular emphasis on government policies for technological and skill development.[11]

In fact, Rodrik (1995) argues reverse causality: Tiger growth stemmed from factors such as domestic investment, government resource coordination and sensible ISI, which led to exports, though these were initially from too small a base to provide the growth or technological dynamism attributed to them by EO theorists. Some research (Hayami, 1998) has attributed much Asian development impetus to small-scale rural enterprises or networks of the sort which could benefit from ISI (see next chapter), although critics say the Tiger model has come with severe social and environmental costs (Bello and Rosenfeld, 1990).

A central theme emerging from many studies is that, despite its faults, ISI has often established efficient, viable industries, beyond just pots and pans, or generated new areas of skill and technology, some of these thenceforth laying export foundations for which later EOI may have been accorded the undeserved credit.[12] Studies of Zimbabwe, for instance, show that industry policy and ISI, along with historical advantages such as enforced self-reliance during the sanctions period, successfully established many efficient industries, some even being internationally competitive. Many have now declined with the trade liberalisation of the 1990s, not due to non-viability but because of import 'floods', macroeconomic problems and social instability.[13]

IS can play varying roles in different countries. A three-nation study by Sridharan (1996) found that, despite their faults, ISI policies variously created 'strategic capacity' for industrial development in South Korea, established new skills and industries in

Brazil and facilitated an unusual degree of technological self-reliance in India (see also Bruton, 1989: 1632–3). It has additionally been noted that IS is more effective for small-scale, localised enterprises than for capital-intensive sectors based on imported technologies (Cracknell, 1992; Peters, 1996).

Where trade liberalisation and EO do appear to have had some exporting or growth successes, various costs and qualifications have been observed, including the following:

- Exports generated via EO are often outweighed by 'floods' of imports, these having adverse impacts because 'cold winds of competition can wither, as well as strengthen, tender plants' (Streeten, 1982: 163).[14]
- Throughout the Third World the results of trade or other liberalisations since the mid-1980s have now become clear and for many countries, especially in Africa, these show devastating losses of industries and manufacturing employment as hitherto successful new enterprises were wiped out by import competition (see Buffie, 2001: ch. 6).
- Although there have been many EOI successes, such as in Sri Lanka, these have frequently relied heavily on FDI and the exports generated have often had only limited 'spread' effects or 'linkages' to local industries, as documented for Sri Lanka and Mexico for instance,[15] 'export processing zones' being particularly notorious for this failing.
- A study of the Ivory Coast found EOI no more successful than earlier, misapplied, ISI because the benefits were confined to urban elites (Mytelka, 1983).
- Studies in Chile, Mexico and elsewhere found that EOI mainly generated small, fragile micro-enterprises and cash crop variants of traditional agriculture, along with just a few 'non-traditional' export lines which the World Bank urges, rather than innovative new industries.[16]
- Many studies show that, even if EOI creates new firms, it may not improve employment because of excessive capital intensity

in practice (though it is supposed to avoid this in theory), damage to existing industries, production for elite exports and limited spread effects.[17]

- In practice EOI tends to increase technological dependence, as documented for Brazil and other countries, due to discouragement of local technologies, to cost reductions which stem from foreign takeovers rather than from real innovation, and to demands by world markets for input standards which only imported equipment can meet (Sridharan, 1996; Amann, 2000).

- EOI may 'crowd out' local investors, resulting in a net reduction in investment, as documented for Ghana (Fontaine, 1992: ch. 10).

- World Bank SAPs have often dismantled earlier, arguably successful, ISI systems but thence did not substitute adequate mechanisms for viable EOI, presuming this to be somehow automatic, and failed to grasp that many countries have market structures which are too poorly developed for workable Free Market, Free Trade policies (Akyüz and Gore, 2001).

- There is anecdotal evidence that EO or other foreign contacts often create vested interests in importation, which thence favour imports even where there are cheaper or more appropriate local substitutes.

- Some suggest that EO mainly works when world demand for a country's exports is expanding and not too many countries are competing for the same export markets – one estimate is that only 10 of the world's 150 Third World states could benefit extensively from large-scale labour-intensive exporting into any one glutted market.[18]

- Recent evidence suggests that EO-led import competition squeezes many people's incomes and increases inequalities (Taylor, 2001; Oxfam, 2002: ch. 5), which may thence force people to work harder, thus increasing growth, but in a pressured, undesirable way (Barrett, 1998).

- Free Traders have always argued that protection creates jobs at the expense of other countries, but Keynes (1936: 338ff) said it was also possible to have 'beggar-thy-neighbour exports' (my term) if EO policies of some countries caused others to incur large, chronic trade deficits (which many countries now have); Keynes wanted macroeconomic stabilisation and employment generation via active interest rate, investment and public spending policies, with international coordination of these, rather than an export cult.

- Some Christian Aid case studies (Curtis, 2001: 153ff) show massive hidden costs of EO-led exporting – for example, many EO 'non-traditional' exports, which the World Bank advocates, are artificially created for exporting and are inappropriate to the societies concerned (for example, flowers in Kenya or asparagus in Peru), such industries often having adverse community or ecological impacts; many EO exports depend heavily on imported technologies, insecticide-intensive cash crops and the like; some resource-based export projects entail large-scale environmental damage or community disruption – for instance, to facilitate an oil project in Sudan the government displaced or killed thousands of people and razed entire villages or communities (Curtis, 2001: 176ff; generally, see Dunkley, 1999).

In sum, the IS–EO debate remains wide open: IS arguably provides more benefits and EO clearly inflicts more costs or problems than Free Traders will admit.

Industry Policy Does Work!

It is hard to imagine a greater ideological gulf than that outlined above, with Free Marketeers and Interventionists or other critics reaching virtually polar opposite conclusions regarding the IS–EO debate, and even about the supporting evidence. The differences are part of the Free Trade versus Protection divide. Several factors may account for the gulf. First, as noted earlier, Free Marketeers see the economy as a yacht whose sails must be trimmed to market winds by 'getting the prices right', while most critics follow Keynes in seeing the economy as a motor boat powered by investment and are more likely to perceive the failures of EO. Most Interventionists are sceptical about the need to 'get the prices right' in any precise sense, and some even advocate 'getting the prices wrong', or selectively influencing prices, with a view to changing the boat's direction.

Second, Free Marketeers see the economy as pushed by supply-side breezes, and so are likely to believe that exports will stimulate growth. Interventionists believe in demand-side powering and hence are more likely to advocate deliberate stimuli for domestic investment, to perceive the adverse 'backwash' effects of an export focus or to be concerned about consequent import 'floods'. Third, Free Marketeers tend to see comparative advantage as a natural evolution, while most other schools see it as developmental and amenable to shaping by conscious policymaking (see Chapter 4). Fourth, Free Marketeers take a narrow view of what is important, so they are less likely than other schools, especially Community-Sovereignty theorists, to see the wider non-economic impacts of EO and trade liberalisation, seemingly believing that the markets will take care of these in the long run. Fifth, the puzzling differences in interpretations of evidence revealed in this chapter may perhaps be explained by the varying methodologies available, as discussed in this chapter, and the possibility of inadvertently building certain results into the models used (see Box 6.1). Finally, advocates of EO palpably ignore contrary evidence. They claim that case studies prove the superiority of EO in practice, but I have never seen Free Marketeers cite the WIDER surveys, noted above, which clearly contradict their results.

Not all the critics of EOI cited above support 'hard line' ISI, but most advocate some degree of government intervention for development via at least initial infant industry ISI and systematic industrial policy (see Shapiro and Taylor, 1990; Prasch, 1996), a policy which was common historically (Chang, 2002) and which recent trade theory is increasingly justifying (see Chapter 3). US scholar Michael Rock has critically examined World Bank reports on Indonesia and Thailand which dismissed industry policy as irrelevant to development, finding, to the contrary, that such policies are quite effective in establishing both new IS industries and export sectors, even well beyond the 'easy' pots-and-pans phase. Indonesia's policies also successfully created self-sufficiency in rice. Likewise for India, industry policy has generated sectors and products which, if not always up to world standards, are usually specifically designed for local needs and are quite satisfactory for these.[19]

Thus, most Interventionists or other EO critics now accept some form of early IS, preferably strategically combined with an element of EO as each country's resource base permits, in a sequence described as 'import substitution, then export' (ISTE). EO theorists hold that East Asian ISI models cannot be duplicated because of their special circumstances, but I am not proposing such models, the ideas outlined below being more Gandhian and less reliant on high growth or consumption. In any case, mainstream economists fail to understand that East Asia ISI models made extensive use of very decentralised, community-focused systems centred around close personal relationships, an approach which one research group (Hayami, 1998) believes could be used by many other countries. Indian ISI is often criticised as being high-cost and failing to export extensively, but this reflects the trade- obsessed export cult and misses the point about ISI. Many Indian industries have become highly self-reliant, with extensive R&D directed at *local* needs and domestic infrastructure (Sahu, 1998) so exports are not essential, although India does export a good deal of 'alternative' technology (see Chapter 7). Some question the frequent claim that Indian industry is inefficient, arguing that ISI has generally been successful (e.g. Chandra, 1997).

From the above literature and my own assessment, I suggest that countries should begin their development with IS, and that the model used should:

- avoid adverse impacts on agriculture and traditional industries, using these wherever possible as a base for new development;

- ensure that any consumer goods industries encouraged are aimed primarily at modest local needs, including HD requirements, rather than at elite wants, and restrict consumption where reasonable savings–investment targets require this;
- avoid the use of excessively capital-intensive or imported technologies, where possible, so as to maximise the use of local resources, and so as to make local capital goods and research sectors more feasible;
- promote appropriate, locally focused education, training and technological development systems;
- conduct regular economic and social efficiency audits on assisted firms or industries;
- maintain relatively modest wage levels, especially to assist the previous aims, but also have laws enforcing fair labour rights and conditions;
- use cautious 'infant industry' protection, along with more direct assistance for training, finance, research or the like, but avoid very high levels of protection, making all IS assistance conditional upon observation of the above requirements, environmental laws or other social obligations;
- link IS policies to at least some export generation, via incentives such as credit or tariff exemptions, and encourage promising export sectors, so as to ensure a requisite supply of foreign exchange;
- seek to maintain stable macroeconomic policy settings, including a downwardly-biased exchange rate, develop policies to encourage savings, and design tax or other measures for equitable income redistribution.[20]

Conclusion

Free Marketeers claim that the IS–EO debate, one of the most extensive and contentious in the history of economics, has been resolved in favour of openness, liberalisation and free trade, with advocates of globalisation regularly basing their case on this supposed outcome. But the claim is disingenuous if not dishonest! No debate can be closed in favour of one side when there is so much evidence in favour of the other, even if it is not entirely conclusive, and I have provided extensive documentation to make this point.

The Free Marketeers misleadingly overstate their case because of their strong ideological bias towards EO; because they have chosen methods and models which do not tell the full story and are not always accurate; because they ignore evidence which contradicts their case; and because they tend to oversimplify the issues. The IS and EO concepts are not mutually exclusive, most studies are subject to many uncertainties and qualifications, various alternative strategies are possible and policy outcomes are highly contingent upon a wide range of country-specific circumstances. If some form of IS approach is more valid than Free Traders allow, then self-reliant trading and development is feasible, as I will argue in the next chapter.

Notes

1. The key studies were Little et al., 1970; Bhagwati, 1978; Krueger, 1978; Balassa and Associates, 1982. For a fuller list and overviews: Sodersten, 1980: ch. 16; Kruger, 1997.
2. Thacker, 2000; Bowie and Unger, 1997; Dunkley, 2000b: 278.
3. Helleiner, 1986; Clark and Kilpatrick, 1992; Greenaway and Sapsford, 1994.
4. Levine and Renelt, 1992. Also, Pritchett, 1996; Harrison and Hanson, 1999; Rodrik, 1999a.
5. Bruton, 1989; Rodrik, 1995, 1999; Rodriguez and Rodrik, 1999; Clerides et al., 1998. Also, Senghass, 1985; Bairoch, 1993; Kofman, 1997.
6. Liu, 1999. Also see: Kirkpatrick and Maharaj in Fontaine, 1992; Helleiner, 1994: 28ff; Edwards, 1998.
7. E.g. Bruton, 1989; Dodaro, 1991; Clark and Kirkpatrick, 1992; UNCTAD, 1997; Buffie, 2001.
8. Papageorgiou, Michaely and Choksi, 1991. For a recent defence of pro-EO studies, Srinivasan and Bhagwati, 2001.
9. Taylor, 1988, 1993 2001; Helleiner, 1994.
10. Bruton, 1989; Fontaine, 1992; Barratt Brown, 1995: 195ff, 306; Todaro,

2000: ch. 13; Dunkley, 2000b: 247ff.

11. World Bank, *WDR*, 1991; World Bank, 1993. Interventionist view: Amsden, 1989; Wade, 1990; Lall, 1996, Dunkley, 2000b: 248; Rodrik, 1995.

12. Teital and Thoumi, 1986; Sachs, 1988; Singer and Alizadeh, 1988; Bruton, 1989; Shapiro and Taylor, 1990; Edelman and Oviedo, 1993; Teitel, 1993; Stein, 1994.

13. Riddell, 1990; Ndlovu, 1994; Rattso and Torvik, 1998; Wood and Jordan, 2001; Buffie, 2001: ch. 6.

14. Cracknell, 1992: 88; Sridharan, 1996. On Chile: Ffrench-Davis et al., 1993; on China: Breslin, 1999.

15. Peters, 1996; Wignaraja, 1998; Athukorala and Rajapatirana, 2000.

16. Schneider, 1993; Green, 1995; Peters, 1996; Buffie, 2001: 190.

17. Peters, 1996; Harrison and Hanson, 1999.

18. Kavoussi, 1985; Singer, 1998: 128ff; Shapiro and Taylor, 1990: 866; Hong in WTO, 2000: 191.

19. Rock, 1995, 1999. On India, Chandra, 1997; Sahu, 1998.

20. For some ISI policy discussion see Bruton, 1989; Shapiro and Taylor, 1990; Taylor, 1993; 2001; Zagler, 1999; Rodrik, 1999a, 2001; Dunkley, 2000b: ch. 12; Amann, 2000; Buffie, 2001, and other references cited above.

CHAPTER 7

THE SELF-RELIANCE OPTION: GLOBAL MYTHS AND ALTERNATIVE DEVELOPMENT

> In place of the old local and national seclusion and self-sufficiency, we have intercourse in every direction, universal inter-dependence of nations.
>
> Marx and Engels in the *Communist Manifesto*,
> on earlier capitalist globalisation
> (Marx and Engels, 1967: 84)

> Globalisation is now inevitable due to economies of scale and the nature of technology.
>
> Kaspar Villiger, president of Switzerland
> (*Public Eye on Davos* Conference,
> New York, January 2002)

> [Under free trade] poor countries slip – and are pushed – into the adoption of production methods and consumption standards which destroy the possibilities of self-reliance and self-help. The results are unintentional neo-colonialism and hopelessness for the poor.
>
> E.F. Schumacher (1973: 163)

The most fundamental item of mythology in today's techno-global theory is that no country aspiring to reasonable growth rates or living standards can any longer be self-reliant. The world is presumed to be now so interlinked and dependent upon globalised technologies that self-reliance supposedly must be displaced by comparative advantage-based, export-led, market-funded development, as Marx and Engels (above) once presciently observed. Economies of scale and ever higher technology are allegedly so imperative that the eternal pursuit of global competitiveness is said to be unavoidable, and small, simple economies non-viable. In previous chapters I have queried some of these suppositions, and in the present chapter I take this further, particularly questioning the nature of technology, economies of scale and competitiveness, as well as the inevitable globalisation they allegedly induce and the 'one size fits all' approach to development which many economists and global bodies adopt.

Self-Reliance: A Respectable Lineage

Self-reliance is widely seen as a non-mainstream, even quirky, notion and certainly it was integral to the ideas of 'heretical' theorists from List and Carey (see Chapter 3) to Galtung (1980), Senghaas (1985), Amin (1990), Schumacher (1973, quoted above) and Gandhi. But, in addition, some mainstream theorists have been less hostile than is generally realised.

Smith (1776, 1: 475) and Ricardo (1817: 155) favoured trade but thought entrepreneurs would invest as close to home as possible. Mill (1848: 287) sympathised with Carey's model of community-based self-reliance (see Chapter 3), but this was to be achieved through education rather than Protectionism. Marshall (1920) thought that nations contained inherent localising mechanisms (see below). Bhagwati has seriously theorised about, though does not approve of, non-economic-based self-reliance policies, and Krugman has said the world would not collapse if global trade was halved (see Dunkley, 2000b: 256). Rubner (1987: 252) once adjudged most countries' trade ratios to be *too high*, so that national welfare would be *increased* by fewer exports and imports. The British development economist Paul Streeten (1998) says that intra-industry trade (IIT – see Chapter 4) now makes most trading non-essential and moderate self-reliance feasible. Around the mid-twentieth century detailed models for self-reliant industrial development were constructed by Romanian minister/economist Manoïlescu (Irwin, 1996: ch. 10) and Indian planner Mahalanobis

(Chandra, 1997: 174ff). In the mid-1970s a Cambridge-based, Keynesian-oriented modelling group proposed a self-reliant industry policy with 30–70 per cent tariff levels to prevent burgeoning unemployment (Dunkley, 1995), an eventuality which has now occurred, whether for the reasons they anticipated or not.

Yet the most spectacular imprimaturs for self-reliance have come from no lesser figures than Samuelson and Keynes. Samuelson (1999: 2) says that, given current technology levels, most First World countries could autarkically produce at a 'respectable level of comfort and affluence', perhaps with slower growth over time. Although Keynes's pronouncements on the matter (quoted above) are not always taken seriously, he clearly considered partial 'self-sufficiency' (as he called it) a discretionary but viable option. His case rested variously on grounds of security, defence and avoidance of capital flight, as well as on the perceptive points that because, over time, development reduces comparative advantage gaps between countries and raises the share of non-traded services in GDP, trading becomes less necessary.

However, Keynes's main argument was that controlled domestic investment could adequately substitute for exports in generating full employment, and he once described international trade as 'a desperate expedient to maintain employment at home by forcing sales on foreign markets' (1936: 382). During the war he rejected US pressure for post-war trade liberalisation on grounds that Britain could self-reliantly produce most of her pre-war manufactured requirements. Keynes admitted that self-reliance could be misapplied and may have costs, but memorably declared it to be not 'a matter of tearing up roots but of slowly training a plant to grow in a different direction' (1933: 236).

Defining Self-Reliance

No society is totally autarkic, but many could be deemed highly self-reliant, so the issue is what degree of delinking from other societies constitutes self-reliance. Senghaas (1985) says that most

European countries have had an 'autocentric' (self-controlling) phase, but so have most countries. Some claim that the EU is self-reliant because three-quarters of its trade is internal, but most countries have a trade ratio of less than 25 per cent and a FDI ratio of less than 10 per cent (Chapter 4), thus fitting this criterion. The USA is often called autarkic due to its 10 per cent trade ratio, but it is heavily dependent externally for crucial resources, export markets and capital flows.

Clearly each country has a different international linkage pattern, so both quantitative and qualitative criteria are required. Up to ten linkages can be identified: (1) trade for key consumption goods or services; (2) trade for capital goods; (3) trade for energy and resources; (4) trade for export markets; (5) inward FDI and finance; (6) outward FDI and profit repatriation; (7) transfer of technology, knowledge or skills; (8) aid; (9) migration and income repatriation of nationals; (10) flows of culture and values, or what some US commentators call 'soft power'. I do not insist that all these should be avoided, but the more of them a country relies upon the less self-reliant it is. A nation's degree of linkage is not preordained but depends upon the gap between its requirements and its capacities. Requirements are partly subjective and capacities can be developed through discretionary policy-making.

Most mainstream economists accept a degree of self-provisioning, especially for basic needs, but self-reliance is surely more than this. Galtung (1980: 23) links it with power, seeing self-reliance as 'a pattern of regeneration through one's own efforts, [and] of fighting dominance'. Others link it to capacity for fairly autonomous development (Olaniyan, 1996: 20) or with transition to socialism (Amin, 1990), while Gandhi saw self-reliance as the autonomy necessary for national self-respect, non-exploitation and moral development. I would define self-reliance as the degree of political, economic, cultural or other autonomy required for adequate national sovereignty in seeking to achieve a society's legitimate aspirations, especially with regard to social justice, environmental sustainability and cultural integrity, for all people and groups both domestically and internationally. This definition does not imply mechanistic formulas, total autarky or hostility to the outside world, but entails a right to reasonable sovereignty in relation to the ten above-mentioned linkages for purposes of attaining goals which reasonable people would deem acceptable. Sen's notion of capacity expansion (see Chapter 1) is important but not enough. Specific goals like the three I propose in the above definition are required to ensure that self-reliance does not become an exclusive end in itself. Reference to the rights of other societies in the above definition is included so as not to legitimise one state increasing its resource or other self-reliance by reducing the self-reliance of another state. Self-reliance should not entail dogmatic adherence to existing national boundaries, especially where these were unjustly created, but should include multicultural tolerance of pre-existing subnational groups.

A country's capacity for self-reliance varies with population (the more populous a country the lower its trade ratio – see Dowrick, 1997: 120, Fig. 7.2), with the level of development sought (some say high technology makes self-reliance impossible) and with resource or other geographical endowments. Thus, a society aspiring to self-reliance must ultimately decide its own preferred degree and pattern of delinking on a 'horses for courses' basis.

The Case for Self-Reliance

Over the years self-reliance has particularly been advocated by Dependency Marxists (e.g. Amin, 1990), who claim that rich country dominance inhibits development; by nationalist activists or commentators (e.g. Olaniyan, 1996), who seek a renewal of national sovereignty; and by Gandhi/Schumacher-style theorists (e.g. Galtung, 1980), who see many political, social or cultural costs of dependence. The inhibitory effects of international linkages can be exaggerated, but dependency can variously involve excessive reliance on other countries politically, administratively, financially (via aid or capital), technologically and culturally. The results can include subservience, indebtedness, inappropriate technologies or development models, and subversion by exotic diets, foreign films, emulatory tastes, language attrition (see Box 5.1 above) or inappropriate social change.

Global pressures through dependency links are common. For instance, various US leaders have promoted aid as creating markets and inducing free enterprise among recipients, have described trade agreements as 'vehicles for the spread of democracy and American values', have harangued Japan about reducing manufacturing self-reliance in the interests of imports, and have urged India to privatise public enterprises. The World Bank regularly forces countries to sacrifice food production for non-food exports or to export food even as people go hungry. Indian food activist Anuradha Mittal reports that three-quarters of countries with child malnutrition export food. Many cases have been noted of technically, socially or culturally inappropriate imported products 'invading' countries through heavy promotion by TNCs or domestic importing interests.[1]

Consistent with what I have called the Gandhian Propensity (see previous chapters), self-reliance is normally aimed at minimising these forms of dependency and avoiding such pressures rather than at total autarky, so that a country should seek to maintain requisite foreign exchange, access to emergency supplies and commitments to appropriate international cooperation. I advocate greater self-reliance on the basis of the following broad principles:

1. 'subsidiarity', or the principle that decisions should be made at a level as close as possible to the people affected (see Dunkley, 2000b: 130–31);
2. the Buddhist principle, of 'priority to locals' (as I call it), that serving local needs from local resources should take precedence over, but not preclude, more distant relationships (see Schumacher, 1973: 49);

3. the right to national or other group sovereignty;
4. the right to cultural and community *integrity*, as opposed to exclusiveness;
5. the moral obligation to limit a nation's 'ecological footprint', or external resource usage – First World countries use resource volumes many times their own land area, ranging from 8 times for Japan to 19 times for the USA;
6. greater self-reliance at all levels from village to nation, in interlinked, cooperative 'oceanic circles', as Gandhi picturesquely described this (*CW*, 85: 33), which would make overall self-reliance more feasible (see also Womersley, 1998; Hines, 2000);
7. 'alternative development' or the principle that if societies pursue development models which differ from large-scale, consumerist, high-tech, centralised Western patterns, then self-reliance is much more feasible than conventionally admitted;
8. 'horses for courses', or the principle advocated in Chapter 5 that societies are highly diverse and should thus have the autonomy to determine their own development paths; Gandhi (*CW*, 13: 315) said in 1916 that India could not have American wealth while avoiding its (undesirable) methods, and Womersley (1998: 267) has observed that an indigenous Scottish development model could not emerge until the recent abandonment of centralised, modernising English approaches; but this requires self-reliance rather than the World Bank–WTO 'one size fits all' mania.

The Feasibility of Self-Reliance

The feasibility of self-reliance depends significantly upon the degree of autonomy desired, the criteria used and the goals sought, self-reliance being more practicable at modest income levels (see Rosecrance, 1986: 144), and the adjustment time allowed for Keynes's dictum of 'training a plant to grow in a different direction'. The more modest the goals and the more time allowed, the more feasible is a moderate self-reliance policy.

Critics of self-reliance stress four main grounds for scepticism. First, they point to the supposedly 'natural' Smithian Propensity to 'truck, barter and exchange' (see Chapters 1 and 4), but against this I counterpose the 'Gandhian Propensity' for people to want reasonable autonomy. Second, they cite the 'law' of comparative advantage which proclaims specialisation to be more efficient than autarky, but if I am right that the gains from trade are small and contingent (in Chapters 2 and 4), then as Keynes and Samuelson also hinted (above), the sacrifice may be small and worthwhile. Third, small nations are often declared 'non-viable', but Schumacher (1973: 59) denied this concept, arguing that it depends upon goals, of which more below. Fourth, critics often claim that industrialisation is impossible in isolation, but many First World countries industrialised substantially autonomously (Senghaas, 1985; Chang, 2002), as did most Second World countries later (Galtung, 1980; Kofman, 1997), while ISI has had some success (see Chapter 6) and, as already noted, modest development goals are more feasible. Finally, self-reliance sceptics usually cite the allegedly disastrous isolationist experiments of Albania, North Korea or Burma, but I do not hold these up as ideals, and in any case the criteria for assessment can be complex, as illustrated by the case of North Korea.

Seeking to resist Western development models and US cultural imperialism, North Korea's extensive, but not total, self-reliance (*Juche*) in sectors such as food, energy, defence, machine tools, consumer goods and savings was initially successful. From 1955 to about 1990 *Juche* brought dramatic reconstruction after the Korean War devastation, growth rates similar to other Third World countries and human development indicators equal to those for South Korea, a performance which induced the British Human Development economist, Keith Griffin (1999: 210) to conclude that 'self-reliance in a medium-sized country is possible'.

North Korea's subsequent deterioration has been widely attributed to the alleged follies of communism and isolation, but the story is more complex, especially considering the early successes. Arguably North Korea is a case of mismanaged ISI (see Chapter 6), having persistently emphasised industry over agriculture, heavy over light industry and military (including a manic nuclear weapons programme) over civilian production, regularly spending a staggering 25 per cent of GDP on defence compared with 3 per cent in South Korea. In particular, agriculture has suffered underinvestment, heavy-handed collectivisation, ecological mismanagement and inappropriate, excessively capital-intensive technology, which may account for much of the recent starvation. Furthermore, for a time North Korea was partly dependent upon Soviet administrative, industrial and technological models, which arguably has not served North Koreans well. Thus, in this sense, perhaps North Korea was not self-reliant enough! So the North Korean experience suggests that self-reliance can probably work if handled more efficiently, insightfully and democratically using a Gandhian alternative development model.[2]

Africa's current, seemingly intractable, problems are often loosely attributed by globalisers to inadequate global integration. This is a massive oversimplification. In the best-known self-reliance experiment, Tanzania nationalised trading companies, reduced trade, restricted luxury imports (cars, televisions, etc.), raised domestic savings and increased growth, many commentators thus declaring it a success. However, two avoidable mistakes limited this success. First, some businesses, exporters and bureaucrats ignored the self-reliance policy and imported inappropriate technologies, despite local alternatives being available. Second, the government's famed new communal *Ujamaa* villages were artificial creations, were bureaucratically run, often uprooted people from traditional communities and were resisted, so they did not produce as well as traditional villages or tenure systems, and food self-reliance was never achieved. With better enforcement and more adherence to traditions, the self-reliance experiment may have been more successful.[3]

In other African cases, Botswana, supposedly successful because it has obeyed the World Bank, has actually used extensive state and local ownership, state-led ISI, local content policies (which the WTO now restricts), decentralised projects, support for women entrepreneurs and leadership by progressive traditional groups, thus being more autonomous than is usually acknowledged.[4] Early industrial development in the Ivory Coast petered out substantially because over-dependence upon foreign capital, technology management and ideas constrained the use of traditional social structures and available local techniques (Mytelka, 1983). In Zimbabwe, promising ISI-led development appears to have been cut off at least partly by surges of imports after trade liberalisation (see Chapter 6 above). Cameroon's self-reliant development has been fairly successful due to sensible regulation, price control, state-provided training, appropriate agricultural development measures and policies to limit displacement of local crops by wheat imports (De Lancey, 1986). In Nigeria and elsewhere, indigenous farming improvements have proved capable of providing locally led development (Richards, 1985), but to date self-reliance policies have been badly managed (Olaniyan, 1996: ch. 4). The concepts of national and 'collective' self-reliance have been widely advocated in Africa (Barratt Brown, 1995; Olaniyan, 1996), many countries being forced to abandon autonomy and ISI only reluctantly, as a result of IMF/World Bank/WTO pressure.

Africa's much-discussed problems are multi-causal, but three factors have been underestimated: the destruction of indigenous African institutions,[5] the neglect of agriculture or crafts in the rush to Western-style industrialism (Barratt Brown, 1995), and the stifling of local opportunities through excessive food, technology or general industrial imports, some modelling suggesting that Africa is overdependent on trade relative to its resource structure (Akyüz and Gore, 2001: 277). These deficiencies could have been greatly alleviated by sensible self-reliance policies, especially if people and NGOs had much more say in policy-making. As the British economic anthropologist Paul Richards (1985) has put it, attempts at Western-style 'dramatic modernisation' in Africa 'has a track record so poor that a return to slower and more incremental approaches' is required (160). He proposes building on what he calls Africa's 'inventively self-reliant' traditions (16), on indigenous co-operatives which 'thrive because they reflect local needs and circumstances' (154) and on the fact that small-scale farmers are capable of generating their own styles of development (16–17).

Overall, I argue that the record of self-reliance experiments is better than generally realised, the apparent failure of repressive regimes like Albania or Burma not being particularly relevant. North Korea and African countries have had some success but made avoidable errors. Latin America has had some success with ISI, despite much (avoidable) mismanagement (see Chapter 6). China remains more self-reliant than most comparable countries. Despite persistent poverty and maladministration, India, highly autonomous until the 1990s and still substantially so, sustains reasonable growth, has abolished starvation and many injustices (Drèze and Sen, 1995), and is largely self-reliant in sectors such as food, consumer goods, defence, information technology, machine tools and entertainment, extensively developing and exporting alternative technologies. Major industry policy programmes in areas such as machine tools, pharmaceuticals and computers have been criticised as high cost, but have left Indians with their own appropriate designs, with some of the cheapest medicines in the world, both for Western and traditional Ayurvedic products, and with many other social benefits (Chandra, 1997; Sahu, 1998). In addition, India has improved the environment, is passably democratic with a free, active NGO sector, boasts very high cultural integrity and is said to be the Third World country least dependent upon TNCs (Sahu, 1998: 177).

Self-reliance proposals abound, including for Africa (Olaniyan, 1996), the Caribbean (McAfee, 1991), India (Chandra, 1997) and the Middle East (Sayigh, 1991), while NGOs regularly advocate local or national self-reliance based on traditional cultures, sustainable agriculture and alternative technologies – see below (e.g. Womersley, 1998). The above evidence and experiences suggest that national self-reliance is far more feasible than mainstream theorists grasp and than globalisers will ever concede, particularly if methods and goals alternative to Western models are pursued. This evidence also clearly indicates that societies are extremely diverse, traditionally, and hence require self-reliance to determine their own suitable development models.

Ten Reasons Why Self-Reliance
Is More Feasible than Globalisers Admit

I have argued in previous chapters that trade and globalisation, along with the type of economic growth they supposedly stimulate, are less beneficial than claimed and that more self-reliant, IS-led development is possible, especially if alternative, more human, less materialistic goals and development models are pursued. Below I argue that for a range of technical reasons a more decentralised, multi-level, self-reliant model of development is possible and is preferable to high-growth, high-tech integrative techno-globalism.

1. *Path dependence*   As noted in previous chapters, although Free Market economics regards the economy as malleable under competitive conditions, other schools believe economic and technological development can be shaped by historical, political or social forces, as well as by discretionary government decisions, thence becoming established or 'locked-in' for the long term. Apparent examples range from the familiar QWERTY keyboard, which is inefficient but accepted as satisfactory, to various automotive and nuclear technologies (see Pool, 1997). As a result, no one technology or development path is inevitable. Development paths can be politically or socially determined, including by more democratic, consensual means than in the past, and self-reliant paths could almost certainly be fostered. Indeed, the far-reaching implications of the 'path dependence' concept is perhaps one of the great untold stories of economics (Kaldor, 1989; Arthur, 1994; Krugman, 1991), of which more below.

2. *Local development*   This is the principle that development should centre around regions, communities or localities, and the more self-reliant these units the more feasible is national self-reliance. Most governments have some localisation policies and acknowledge the benefits thereof, even if these policies only involve minor decentralisation or attraction of TNCs to outlying regions. More radical proposals for local self-reliance entail centring many industrial, technological, financial, ecological and community development activities in decentralised localities, of which some examples below.[6]

3. *The informal sector and rural-based development*   Peruvian business economist Hernando de Soto was once widely quoted for his finding that half Peru's population, 60 per cent of its working hours and 40 per cent of its GDP were in the 'informal', unregistered sector, a sector which Gandhians and development economists had long ago discovered in other countries. UN and other research now suggests that this 'informal' sector, plus household work (mainly by women), are at least equal to the known GDP in most countries (see Chapter 4 above).[7] De Soto attributed the predominance of the informal sector to over-regulation and lack of free-market incentives, while Marxist critics often see it as pathological or due to lack of development. But Gandhians and others depict this sector as a reaction to large-scale centralised, excessively industrialised development and the neglect of agriculture (Chapter 5), seeing it as a movement to regenerate traditional rural or craft livelihoods and employment.

Much research shows that small-scale rural industries, ranging from food, crafts and consumer goods to traditional equipment or simple machinery, currently provide the bulk of Third World employment, and did so historically, in countries like Japan and Korea. These industries best function through traditional networking systems, providing much higher local employment and community-maintenance effects than larger, centralised enterprises.[8] Thus, small, localised, informal activities, if appropriately regulated and formalised, could be the basis of extensive local and national self-reliance.

4. *Over-estimation of scale economies*   The president of Switzerland (quoted above, p. 161) is not alone in claiming that economies of scale make globalisation inevitable; this concept is regularly invoked to explain large firms, to justify TNCs and even to rationalise the occupation of small states by larger neighbours. Scale economies or 'increasing returns' (see Chapter 2) entail, for technical reasons, declining unit production costs as output rises, thus making larger, centralised, even globalised, activities more economical and self-reliance less viable. However, if the value of scale economies is overestimated, as I claim it is, then the reverse applies.

Textbooks still regard scale economies as primarily the preserve of heavy and technology industries, with 'decreasing returns' (rising unit costs) in agriculture, crafts and light industries. Various economists say that the evidence for scale economies is exaggerated (Maddison, 1994: 50ff), that plants in most industries could be efficient at one-third their current size and that scale economies do not apply to small, labour-intensive, custom-made enterprises of the Third World, so that large-scale mechanisation is not inevitable and appropriate small-scale production is efficient.[9]

Since about 1960 both the proportion of small firms and their productivity have increased in most First World countries, implying that small is still beautiful. There is also a widespread view that new 'flexible' technologies are enhancing this trend, energy expert Amory Lovins arguing that newly emerging small, decentralised, alternative energy systems will soon reduce power distribution costs by a factor of ten! It is generally held that scale economies tend to prevail in mass production, in the early stages of an industry's development (Samuelson, 1999) or where research and marketing overheads can be spread over a larger output, but that small firms have advantages in management, industrial relations, internal organisation, product development and services, where 'diseconomies of scale' may apply. The latter, or what I call 'tyrannies of scale', include factors external to the firm such as pollution, transport costs, urban disamenities (Schumacher, 1973), the waste generated when scale factors make new products cheaper than parts or repairs, and even the non-democratic nature of giant firms, first noted by Marshall (1929: 254). Scale expert Brian Arthur lists some features of scale economies as including market instability, unpredictability, market lock-ins, possible inferior products and large profits for 'winners', all of which sound more like tyrannies than benefits![10]

Also, economists readily acknowledge that some apparent scale economies are actually 'pecuniary economies' where large units can, through market clout, wangle discounts which are disproportionate to any real resource savings, or else are 'external' economies which derive from inter-plant cooperation rather than from internal plant size. Many giant firms use only small or average-sized plants, but derive their advantages from these more 'political' pecuniary and external economies of scale. Thus, the benefits of scale economies are probably exaggerated, which suggests the feasibility of smaller-scale, more decentralised, self-reliant activities now and in the near future.

5. *Industrial districts*   Another reason why small firms are increasing is a worldwide trend for 'agglomeration' or 'clustering' of small complementary units in 'industrial districts'. This was first noted by Marshall (1920: 222ff; 1923: 599ff), who attributed it to accidents of geography or history and to 'external economies' (inter-firm benefits) regarding cooperative specialisation, labour or other resource procurement, information sharing, even education and training. Marshall (1923: 599–600) described agglomeration as 'automatic co-operation of many industries' in an 'organic whole', and, anticipating 'path dependence' (above), he observed that, once established, industries stay put due to 'advantages which people following the same skilled trade get from near neighbourhood to one another' (1920: 225).

Particularly associated with the famed 'Third Italy', but also found in many other countries worldwide,[11] industrial districts are still analysed in Marshallian terms, along with new concepts such as 'economies of agglomeration', 'joint action for shared ends' and 'collective efficiency' (Krugman, 1991; Schmitz, 1999). New versions of the industrial district are often seen in terms of the Silicon Valley-style 'knowledge economy' and high-tech exports, but this is overstated. Krugman (1991: 64–5) notes that high-tech clustering is mostly for low-tech (Marshallian) reasons like labour- or skill sharing, others observing that high-tech may use cheap micro-chips but also needs costly hardware, software, advertising and marketing, which entail scale economies and centralisation (Alcorta, 1994: 755ff). In *The Second Industrial Divide* (1984) Piore and Sabel famously advocated 'flexible specialisation' for small-scale (but not exclusively high-tech) clustering, noting that this may strengthen regional or national self-reliance.

Indeed, the Italian model is based partly on traditions, farm and craft heritage, family networks, communal solidarity and so forth, which some left-wing critics scorn as romantic or exploitative, but which many unions and radicals support. One Italian Keynesian economist advocates industrial districts as a development model and the use of 'local traditions as much as possible, especially if they are old and therefore deeply rooted' (Sylos-Labini, 2001: 164ff, 176). Undoubtedly industrial districts could be fostered for alternative, more self-reliant development, though government needs to help. In India, home to fifteen major clusters and some sixty smaller ones in New Delhi alone, municipal authorities often abolish small clusters in favour of up-market, export-oriented TNCs, even though the former generate far more jobs for the poor and better meet local needs, this surely being a major cost of globalisation (S. Benjamin in TWNF, April 2002).

6. *Technology and the chimera of global competitiveness* One of the great myths of globalisation theory is that a nation must seek perpetual global competitiveness to accelerate growth, balance its

trade or even 'survive'. Most schools of thought accept this supposed imperative and advocate methods for achieving it, especially the maximisation of total factor productivity (TFP) and the growth thereof. However, some Community-Sovereignty theorists question the competitiveness imperative (see Hines, 2000), while I argue that its importance is overrated, its causes oversimplified and the role of technology misunderstood.

Certainly a country needs some competitive products to sell in world markets, with technology playing a role in this, and certainly technology is closely linked to globalisation, but there is more to the story. First, not all studies link technology and performance. Marin, for instance, has found productivity growth correlating with exports in only one country (Japan), and Daniels has found that technology-intensive trade does not markedly correlate with GDP growth. Other studies find that technology helps First but not Third World exports, and that there is some reverse causality – that is, exporting leads to more R&D or technological development. Second, many studies show that FDI is not correlated with exports, suggesting that globalisation via TNCs may not help trade, while other studies show that technology imports can sometimes damage local technological capacity.[12]

Third, many studies find that a firm's ability to sell in world markets is determined, not primarily by price/cost competitiveness, but by an ability to produce and deliver the desired goods or services (Fagerberg, 1988; Kitson and Mitchie, 2000). Technology plays a role in creating this ability, but other key factors include product quality, reliability, attention to client needs, reputation, managerial capacity, harmonious industrial relations and trust, or general co-operation under regulated conditions rather than cut-throat competition (Kitson and Michie, 2000: ch. 9). 'Cheap labour' provides a competitive advantage only for very low-skill, labour intensive products, and even then these other factors can be important.

Fourth, a nation's trade balance is not normally governed by competitiveness, even according to mainstream economists, but by macroeconomic factors, particularly savings and investment. Indeed, the competitiveness of one sector can reduce that of another by inducing a higher exchange rate and a higher wage level, so the process is about trade-offs, not absolute global competitiveness (Dluhosch et al., 1996). Thus, whilst 'cutting edge' technology may be central to the competitiveness of certain individual products, for a country as a whole trade balance entails a mix of macroeconomic conditions, quality local industries and a reputation as a reliable trader.

A fifth complication in the competitiveness story is that, whilst technology and research are crucial for the competitiveness of some (not all) products, the cost of R&D is rising and product life cycles are shortening (Group of Lisbon, 1995: 66), so that technology is a double-edged sword for competitiveness, increasing in both importance *and* cost. Recoupment of these high costs requires world-scale markets, and high-tech TNCs are demanding free trade or global 'market access' for this purpose (Dunkley, 2000b: 43–4). But I suggest it is ethically dubious that nations be pressured to open up and surrender autonomy just to oblige such companies.

Sixth, many leading mainstream economists do not attribute to competitiveness the importance that dogmatic globalisers do, Krugman describing it as a 'dangerous obsession' because national living standards are, in reality, shaped by comparative advantage and domestic productivity. A country whose productivity growth falls behind world rates will *not* collapse, but, as Baumol, Corden and others point out, will structurally adjust to different activities and possibly to slower growth rates or lower relative wages.[13] This need not matter if good, equitable living standards are maintained or if appropriate alternative technologies are developed (see below). Some Interventionist economists argue that 'competitiveness does matter' and that nations with lagging productivity could cumulatively fall behind. However, I suggest that with strong policies for the maintenance of adequate savings and investment levels, this fate can be avoided.

Finally, global competitiveness is not necessarily desirable, economists variously depicting it, some favourably, others unfavourably, as a 'head to head' rat race (Thurow, 1993) for 'thinning margins' of 'kaleidoscopic comparative advantage' which create chronic job insecurity (Bhagwati, 1998: 22–3), as a 'battle without mercy' (Emmerij, 2000: 134) all in the name of an 'endless race' for innovation (see Dunkley, 2000: 244). The competitiveness obsession is also probably responsible for many wage-cutting, labour-displacing strategies by TNCs. Indeed, Keynes once (1936: 381–2) surmised that 'the competitive struggle for markets' was a major cause of wars, but one which could be banished by more self-reliant, domestic job-generation through his proposed macro-economic policies.

In short, global competitiveness is somewhat chimerical – meaningful, but not what it is claimed to be, and it should not become the basis of all policymaking or global governance (see Group of Lisbon, 1995, Emmerij, 2000: 134). Alternative, more self-reliant, forms of development are feasible without unduly sacrificing living standards or trade balance.

7. *The Gatesian nightmare*   There is a widespread view that high technology and the omnipresent computers of Bill Gates's vision (nightmare?) are desirable, inevitable and preclude self-reliance due to necessary global specialisation. I reject this prognosis for several reasons. First, alternative technologies are possible (below). Second, 'path dependence' (above) means that technological development has discretionary social origins rather than a predetermined trajectory (see Pool, 1997). Third, new technologies like nuclear power, biotechnology and information technology (IT) have higher costs than previous innovations, these arguably outweighing the benefits (e.g. see Emmerij, 2000: 135). Costs of IT include unemployment, deskilling, privacy incursions, cultural erosion, Internet addiction, information overload, crime, fraud, balance of trade imposts, compulsory computerisation, or what I call the 'Gatesian Nightmare', and most IT is not essential to

basic human needs despite the claims of Gates, Negroponte or other advocates of 'being digital'. Even Gates himself (1996) admits to concerns about the privacy implications of digital cameras and artificial intelligence, although he claims that technology will not become dehumanising.

Fourth, the high-tech 'new economy' is growing but has limits. It is dependent upon the traditional agricultural and industrial 'old economy'; the proportion of IT in total investment is still low; until recently economists doubted that IT helped productivity and some still foresee diminishing returns to technology (Gimpel, 1994); the 'tech wreck' share collapse was a reaction to persistently poor IT profits, which would have been 40 per cent lower still if executives' share options were counted as costs;[14] an Australian survey of e-commerce users found over a third dissatisfied with the concept;[15] Internet disillusion has left 28 million ex-users in the USA alone.[16] Many observers now see the overall impact of burgeoning technology as, on balance, negative, while electronic learning by TV, video and computer is being proven greatly inferior to traditional oral methods for basic education, perception and the development of critical thinking.[17]

In sum, I suggest that the benefits of new technologies are overstated, the costs underestimated and the alternatives neglected, so that the supposed imperative of techno-globalism is largely mythological and self-reliant alternatives are feasible.

8. *Alternative technology (AT)* The concepts of 'alternative', 'appropriate' and 'intermediate' technology, popularised by Schumacher (1973), have often been attacked as likely to lock poor countries into low levels of development. But such criticisms are overdrawn and misunderstand Schumacher's key points, which were that technologies are not predetermined, are adaptable and can be tailored to each society's needs, resources or circumstances. Some Third World critics have actually attacked Schumacher for downplaying as outdated (1973: 156) various traditional indigenous technologies in favour of new small-scale systems intermediate

between local and modern Western modes – that is, they accuse him of not being alternative enough!

Numerous studies worldwide have now identified countless cases where either traditional or new intermediate technologies are more appropriate and efficient than those imported via TNCs, aid projects or foreign 'experts', especially where broader criteria such as local employment, reduced transportation, local resource use or community maintenance are considered.[18] Alternative research centres and regular displays, a few of which I have visited, now proliferate throughout the Third World, especially in India and China. Such research in Africa has designed simple agro-processing equipment for women and in the Caribbean local research has identified alternative farm and craft products, including 360 new uses for coconuts and 135 for sugar cane (ILO/WEP, 1984; McAfee, 1991: 163ff). One neglected ILO study of Indonesia found traditional technologies performing better, even for local income and employment generation, than imported Western systems (Khan and Thorbecke, 1988).

A similar picture occurs in the West, where studies now confirm the notions of 'decentralising technologies' and 'flexible specialisation' techniques. For instance, decentralised, small-batch production has been successful throughout Europe for long periods and British engineering declined *despite* adopting US-style centralised specialisation, possibly *because* it abandoned its traditional smaller-scale methods (Mariti, 1993; Sabel and Zeitlin, 1997). Alternative energy systems such as solar, wind and hydrogen promise much greater self-reliance in a burgeoning 'post-oil' era. Thus, if home-grown systems are more suitable, on wider criteria, than imported techniques, then self-reliance is much more feasible than global fatalists allow.

9. *Organic agriculture* The most crucial alternative technology sector, organic or 'sustainable' agriculture, is often criticised as idealistic and inadequate to feed growing populations, hence the alleged need for genetic engineering technologies. But such

criticisms ignore widespread evidence for the efficiency of organic alternatives and the past neglect of agricultural development (Chapter 5 above), rectification of which could massively raise production and food self-reliance. The British ecologist Jules Pretty calculates that low-input organic methods, both traditional and new, would increase crop yields in poor countries, maintain or slightly improve these in 'green revolution' countries and slightly reduce them in the First World, where food is overproduced anyway (Pretty, 2002; Madeley, 2002).

Many experiments around the world now confirm the ability of organic methods to cut inputs, raise output, generate local employment, stimulate new locally supplied inputs, increase local resource usage and greatly improve the environment. In the most far-reaching experiment, Cuba is seeking completely organic farming for food self-reliance via conversion incentives, research, urban gardens, information sharing and use of traditional knowledge.[19] Such systems present massive potential for self-reliance in both inputs and food output.

10. *Alternative or Green development* The 'green' tag is now widely used to presage an alternative economy or society based on principles of ecological sustainability. Many versions have been proposed, including my own (Dunkley, 1992), but the main elements of most models include population restraint, pollution control, resource and energy conservation systems, materials recycling, nature preservation and renewable energy technologies. Some models extend to more far-reaching Schumacherian alternatives such as decentralised settlements, self-reliant cities, bioregional planning, 'soft' technologies, organic farming, sustainable communities, new forms of household-based subsistence, and so forth.[20] In the First World such models are often associated with radical democratisation and could be called 'green social democracy'. In the Third World they are often associated with Gandhian-style adaptive traditionalism (see Chapter 5) and could be called 'green Gandhianism'. I suggest that both of these associations are required.

Such proposals are too general to model mathematically at present, but two British left-leaning economists have assessed a 'Green Scenario' as feasible economically but not politically (Rowthorn and Wells, 1987), although new cultural spiritual values incorporating a 'ceiling on desires' (see Chapters 1 and 5) could quickly reverse the latter. Modelling for Mexico has found that an alternative, agriculture-centred, public investment-led, re-distributive scenario is likely to produce better employment and social outcomes, even higher economic growth, than free market policies (Buzaglo, 1984).

Current climate change modelling suggests that greenhouse gas abatement can most easily be achieved by relatively simple means such as reforestation, less energy-intensive production, re-newable energy, energy efficiency, low-input agriculture, better food storage (up to half the national crop is wasted in many countries) and acquaculture, all of which could also enhance national self-reliance. Some models show that such measures could greatly reduce energy-intensive manufacturing and trade for many countries, resulting in massive contractions in global trading, more than counteracting the increase since GATT-led liberalisation be-gan (IPCC, 1995: chs 7–9; Whalley in WTO, 2000: 224). There are innumerable non-quantified but detailed visions for alternative 'green' models of development and socio-economic structures.[21]

In general, alternative 'green' systems are likely to be more labour-intensive, decentralised, tradition-sensitive, local-skill-based and self-reliant than today's techno-global free market models.

Alternative Development and Self-Reliance

The above discussion indicates that self-reliance is more feasible than generally acknowledged, especially if alternative values and development models of the sort outlined are pursued. A sensible self-reliance model might have the following features:

1. broadly defined goals such as social justice, sustainably organised systems and cultural integrity;

2. ethical systems centred around equity, honesty, trust and non-materialism;

3. development to be adaptively set in the context of cultures and worthwhile traditions, with due allowance where a variety of traditions coexist within a nation, and avoidance of unduly rapid changes to these traditions (see Sayigh, 1991: 210; Chapter 5);

4. high levels of democracy and participation in policymaking;

5. reasonable self-reliance in sectors relating to core goals, especially food (within reason), basic consumer items, essential machine tools and capital goods, key technologies, finance, resources and energy (including recycled materials and small-scale energy systems) where feasible, basic medicines, education, entertainment and culture; heavy dependence on any one export item, including tourism, should be avoided, using structural diversification policies where necessary;

6. top priority, at least in the early stages of development, to agriculture, with preference to low-input sustainable forms; this would greatly reduce chemical imports in favour of local organic inputs;

7. an ISI-based industry policy (see Chapter 6) centred around industries and technologies appropriate to the above-defined goals, particularly environmental protection and restoration; some 'infant self-reliance' protection may be required, but if 'collective efficiency' of industrial districts, rural small-scale industries or appropriate technologies do eventuate, this protection need not be excessively high; as I advocate protection only for economic, social, ecological and cultural defence purposes, I believe that protection in the form of export subsidies should not be used for aggressive export promotion, which is often misused, ineffective or aimed at reducing other countries' self-reliance (Krugman, 1998: ch. 1; Rubner, 1987);

8. comprehensive policies for savings at requisite levels via adequate and equitable small-scale financial institutions and through limitations on consumption; in some cases tariffs or

restrictions on consumer goods imports have had the benefits of raising consumer prices, reducing consumption, boosting national savings and thus encouraging investment (O'Rourke, 2000);

9. institutions for appropriate indigenous research and development capacity, or what some mainstream economists call a 'national system of innovation';[22]

10. the development of local resources through conservation, recycling and new indigenous materials (e.g. from sugar cane);

11. planning for decentralised development around traditional bioregions and industrial districts;

12. an outward-looking stance on political, social, legal and environmental matters for cooperative internationalism, and openness to appropriate regional trade agreements, so long as these are not excessively integrative, which many are at present;

13. efforts by neighbouring countries to make their economies more complementary than in the past, so that modest levels of appropriate trade and 'collective self-reliance' are possible (McAfee, 1991; Barrett Brown, 1995: esp ch. 17);

14. modest levels of trade between Third World countries – e.g. India is becoming a major supplier of alternative technologies, services and even English language teaching to other Third World countries.

Conclusion

The widespread claim of inevitable globalism rests on an uncritical, oversimplified understanding of issues such as comparative advantage, gains from trade, economies of scale and technology. In earlier chapters I argued that the benefits of trade are non-automatic, variable and contingent upon a country's circumstances. In this chapter I have argued that country circumstances differ widely and can be designed for greater self-reliance, particularly by using alternative value systems and development models. I suggest that self-reliance is even more feasible when allowing for the overstated benefits of scale economies, high technology and global competitiveness or for the possibilities of informal, local-based development, industrial districts, alternative technologies and planned, redirected 'path dependence'. A closer look at the experience of many countries and the testimonies of some major economists indicates a surprising degree of feasibility for greater self-reliance, especially if it is developed gradually, on a diversified 'horses for courses' basis, or by training a plant to grow in a new direction, as Keynes memorably put it. Self-reliance is, as Keynes (1933) also said, a luxury we *can* afford if we want it.

Notes

1. Respectively: Hancock (1989: 70); Talalay, 2000; Rubner, 1987: 228; Dunkley, 1993: 5; Mittal interviewed in *Chain Reaction* (FOE, Australia) 88, 2002. Inappropriate consumption: McAfee, 1991: 193ff; Stewart, 1993.

2. White, 1982; Hwang, 1993; Chun and Park, 1997; Reese, 1998; Griffin, 1999.

3. Biersteker, 1980; James, 1986; Ayittey, 1991: 428; Forster and Maghimbi, 1995; Barratt Brown, 1995: 38ff; 198ff.

4. Ayittey, 1991: 478ff; Kaplinsky, 1991; Samatar, 1999.

5. Richards, 1985; Ayittey, 1991; Olaniyan, 1996.

6. Krugman, 1991; Demaziere and Wilson, 1995; Douthwaite, 1996; Shuman, 1998; Womersley, 1998; Hines, 2000.

7. De Soto, 1989; Thomas, 1992; UNCTAD, 1995; Pietila, 1997.

8. Chickering and Salahdine, 1991. Marshedi and Setty, 1988; Whatmore et al., 1991; Cracknell, 1992; Bagachwa and Stewart, 1992; Hayami, 1998.

9. Adams and Brock, 1986: esp. ch. 3; Helleiner, 1972: 105; Barratt Brown, 1995: esp. 272; Hayami, 1998: 11.

10. Pratten, 1991; Maddison, 1994: 53; Pearce, 2001: ch. 7 and *passim*; Lovins et al., 2003; Arthur, 1998.

11. See, e.g., Goodman et al., 1989, Pyle and Sengenberger, 1998.

12. Respectively: Marin, 1989; Daniels, 1999; Kumar and Siddharthan, 1997: 114ff.

13. Krugman, 1998: esp. chs 1 and 6. Baumol et al., 1989: ch. 2; Corden, 1994: ch. 15.

14. *The Age* (Melbourne), 18 July 2002: Business 1.

15. *The Age* (Melbourne), 19 February 2002: Business 2.
16. *Guardian Weekly*, 21–27 December 2000: 12.
17. Joy, 2000; Progler, 2001; Gelernter, 2001. Learning: Healy, 1990.
18. Stewart, 1978; Carr, 1988; Thomas et al., 1991; Pedersen et al., 1994.
19. Ching, 2002. Cuba: Rosset and Benjamin, 1994; Funes et al., 2002.
20. For a range, see Dunkley, 1992; Pietila, 1997; Trainer, 1995; Brown, 2003.
21. Brown, 2003; L. Brown, ed., *State of the World*, annual.
22. Freeman, 1996: ch. 2. Also, re Africa see Fabayo et al., 1994; re India, Chandra, 1997; Sahu, 1998.

CHAPTER 8

THE FREE TRADE ADVENTURE: THE WTO, GLOBAL MYTHS AND ALTERNATIVES

The rewards of bringing the world's disaffected and deprived into the global community are manifest. We have seen the ugly alternatives, in the continuing lethal conflicts that rage around the world; and in the haunted faces of the hungry and the homeless.

WTO (*Annual Report*, 2002: 2)

Basically, [trade liberalisation] won't stop until foreigners finally start to think like Americans, act like Americans and – most of all – shop like Americans.

US WTO official
(quoted by Barlow, *The Ecologist* 31(1), 2001: 42)

The WTO is basically the first constitution based on the rule of trade and the rule of commerce. Every other constitution has been based on sovereignty of people and countries. Every constitution has protected life above profits. But WTO protects profits above the right to life of humans and other species.

Vandana Shiva (in Aga Kahn, 1998: 106)

The world is undergoing one of the most far-reaching experiments in human history – the creation of a free-trading, free-investing, deeply integrated, 'liberal' world order enmeshing more nations, people and activities than ever before. This 'Global Free Trade Project', or the Free Trade Adventure, as I have more whimsically called it elsewhere (Dunkley, 2000b), is posited on the theories of free markets and gains from trade, is driven by a business-oriented elite consensus and is being implemented by the IMF/World Bank, the WTO and, with varying degrees of zeal and consistency, by most national governments. These bodies are also endeavouring to 'lock in' trade or other liberalisations to ensure that future governments cannot renege on them. The virtues of this project stand or fall on the validity of its free-market/free-trade assumptions, which in earlier chapters I suggested are part-mythical. In this chapter I briefly examine the WTO, its assumptions, its practices, its myths and some alternatives to the present WTO system. I argue that the WTO is neither ogre nor weakling, as variously claimed, but a non-consensual, non-neutral umpire obsessed with trade above other goals and now having a greater capacity to undermine national sovereignty than most people want.

Foundation Assumptions

The first version of the Global Free Trade Project originated in 1916 with proposals by US statesman Cordell Hull for global free trade through negotiated concessions and 'fair' (non-protectionist) trade rules. Hull argued variously on the grounds of free-trade theory, trade promotion and trade-led world peace, later also citing what I call the 'Legend of the Thirties' (see Chapter 4) – the supposedly destructive 1930s protectionism.

Post-Depression debate divided roughly between Hullian and Keynesian views. Hull sought a free-trade-led, free-market prosperity, while Keynes wanted broadly defined progress, full employment, social equity and a degree of self-reliance (see Chapter 7) through more interventionist policies and less-than-full free trade. The Bretton Woods world order was a compromise, but more Hullian than Keynesian, although the initial world trade model, formed at the 1946 Havana Conference, was fairly Keynesian. Centred on a mooted International Trade Organisation (ITO), the Havana model sought negotiated freer trade but with broader features such as exceptions, safeguards, labour standards, a code of conduct for TNCs and commodity agreements (Aaronson, 1996;

Dunkley, 2000b: ch. 2). This model was ratified by many countries until it was killed off by US hostility, but it significantly influenced the more Hullian GATT of 1947.

The GATT system was loosely based on four core assumptions, which Free Traders have increasingly emphasised over time: (1) that free markets are superior to regulation and planning; (2) that the theories of comparative advantage and gains from trade are more or less universally applicable; (3) that free trade is best for growth and development, and so should be the ultimate goal of the trading system; (4) that free trade is best achieved through unilateral liberalisation by nations, but, short of this, through multilaterally negotiated mutual trade concessions and non-discriminatory international rules. At first liberalisation under GATT was slow, with many countries wavering or backsliding, allegedly due to hypocrisy and vested protectionist interests, but in my view more because of widespread commitment to import substitution strategies for full employment, because of a Gandhian desire for reasonable self-reliance and because of scepticism about these assumptions. Throughout this book I have questioned such assumptions, which is why I argue that the global Free Trade Adventure is extensively based on mythology.

By the Uruguay Round of GATT (1986–93), trade politics were being reshaped and driven by two titanic pro-global forces: the Thatcher/Reagan pro-market revolution and a vast array of goods-, services- and capital-exporting TNCs which were beginning to become aware of their collective capacity for forcing globalisation. One US study identified two categories of pro-global interests: 'industry-specific' lobbies which oppose particular forms of border protection and 'general' interest groups which promote overall trade and capital liberalisation (Destler and Odell, 1987). Industry-specific pro-global interests include industrial users of imports, retailers of traded consumer goods, goods and services exporters to protection-affected countries and governments or companies from those countries. General pro-global interests include TNCs, business coalitions and some consumer groups.

Anti-global forces similarly range from specific domestic industries to an array of community and environmental groups which
have become increasingly active.

From the early 1980s accelerated globalisation was being driven
not by a Free Trade enlightenment as globalists claim (see Chapter
4) but primarily by a conjunction of ascendent Free Market
Economic Rationalism and a burgeoning, complex web of the
above-mentioned pro-global forces. Free Trade Fundamentalists
regularly urge the marshalling of such pro-global forces against
their Protectionist 'enemies' (e.g. Bergsten in WTO, 2000: 169),
and, indeed, such forces were extremely active in initiating the
Uruguay Round, even designing the WTO TRIPs Agreement
itself.[1] Today the WTO is widely seen as frontline artillery in this
'good fight', and its role should be viewed in this context.

The WTO in Principle

The WTO usually states its goals as promoting fair trade, economic growth, 'sustainable development' and 'a system of rules
dedicated to open, fair and undistorted competition' (WTO, 2001:
7). No key WTO document calls for total free trade, and its
present rules allow some protection, safeguards, waivers, exceptions
and various liberalisation exemptions or extensions for Third World
members. However, many WTO officials and supporters want
eventual full free trade in goods and services. The WTO (2001)
describes itself as embracing five working principles: non-
discrimination, transparency, fair trade, 'special and differential'
(S&D) treatment for Third World members and progressive trade
liberalisation. Some brief comment on these principles is in order.

There are two forms of non-discrimination: between WTO
members (Most Favoured Nation or MFN) and between domestic
and foreign traders (National Treatment). MFN simply assures
equal concessions to all members, but National Treatment, which
says that foreign firms seeking trade must be treated the same as
locals, is questionable because it assumes the virtues of globalisation

Box 8.1 The WTO in brief

Based on the original General Agreement on Tariffs and Trade (GATT) of 1947, the 145-member (as of early 2003) WTO was formed in 1995 by the historic 1986–93 Uruguay Round of trade negotiations (signed in 1994), replacing the makeshift GATT Secretariat, although the original GATT agreement still applies.

The WTO's operating basis is a three-legged structure of agreements: GATT (updated to 1994) for goods, the General Agreement on Trade in Services (GATS) for services trade, and the Trade-Related Aspects of Intellectual Property Rights (TRIPs) Agreement for 'knowledge trade'. Under the 'single undertaking' rule WTO members must accept these three plus most other WTO agreements.

Unlike the donation-based voting systems of the IMF and World Bank, the WTO's main decision-making body, the General Council, has one delegate from each country, all having one equal vote, thus making the WTO (theoretically) democratic.

The WTO's main functions include: monitoring trade policies, conducting trade research, assistance and education measures to enhance the 'trade capacity' of members, settling trade disputes, convening trade negotiations and generally promoting trade liberalisation.

There have been eight 'rounds' of trade talks, a ninth having been spectacularly scuttled in Seattle (1999) and then finally convened at Doha, Qatar (2001). Billed as a 'development round', the Doha Round is scheduled for completion by 2005. The Uruguay Round also established continuing 'built-in' negotiation agendas in some areas and 'between-rounds' sectoral negotiations, with agreements already completed in finance, telecommunications and electronic commerce.

The WTO's headquarters is in Geneva. It has a staff of 550, though these often being assisted by members of national delegations at Geneva. Its current director-general is Dr Supachai Panitchpakdi from Thailand.

Sources: Dunkley, 2000: esp. ch. 11; WTO, 2001; 2002.

and ignores the Gandhian principle of 'priority to locals' (see Chapter 7).

The second principle, transparency, means clarity of policy intent and reportage to the WTO of members' trade and protection policies, which seems reasonable, but administration and reporting is costly for poor countries. The World Bank estimates that implementation of the TRIPs, SPS and Customs Valuation Agreements alone costs poor countries over a year's aid funding (ICTSD, February 2002: 4). In fact, disputes can be expensive for any country, especially if many lawyers and scientists have to be flown to Geneva. Also, ironically, the WTO is now being accused of non-transparency in its own internal operations (see below).

By the third principle, 'fair trade', the WTO means avoidance of dirty tricks in trading, such as administrative or other 'non-tariff' barriers, 'unfair' export subsidies, against which 'countervailing duties' are allowed, and dumping (strategic exporting below costs), against which 'anti-dumping duties' are allowed. Fundamentalist Free Traders and some NGOs claim that anti-dumping provisions are being abused by First World countries as protectionism and want these provisions tightened or even abolished, but I have cited contrary evidence (Dunkley, 2000b: 281–2) and the provisions should remain. NGOs say that trade will never be fair while TNCs are unchecked and labour or environmental standards are abused, so they define 'fair trade' as controlling these (see below).

The principle of 'special and differential' (S&D) treatment for poor countries entails MFN-exempt trade concession schemes such as the EU's Lomé Convention, delayed liberalisation and 'trade capacity' assistance, which the WTO claims to be its own contribution to development aid. But critics counter that continuing First World protection, the dilution of trade concessions at today's low tariff levels, and various disadvantages of WTO membership (see below) negate these meagre benefits, while purists protest that free trade is the best development policy anyway. So the WTO's claim to be a development body is rather flimsy, of which more below.

The WTO's final principle, progressive trade liberalisation, means continuing protection reductions (implicitly until full free trade is accomplished), no additional Article XX exceptions (currently trade may be restricted on grounds such as security, morality, health, prison labour, resource conservation, etc.) and 'bound' concessions. 'Binding' means that tariff cuts or other such concessions must be retained, or else compensation be paid to affected trading partners, thus 'locking-in' the concessions forever. However, I argue that binding is undemocratic as it ties the hands of future governments and ignores the costs of globalisation, which later generations may wish to rectify. I also argue that the Article XX exceptions list needs to be extended (see below).

In sum, I am suggesting that the WTO's core principles are poorly formulated, steeped in Free Trade mythology and questionable; hence the many criticisms at present, some of which are discussed below.

The WTO in Practice

The WTO's practical activities now reach into most areas of economic life, thus attracting mounting controversy. Below I outline some of the main areas, debates and problems.

Trade in goods

As the prime early focus of GATT, goods tariffs have now been reduced to an average of about 4 per cent in the First World and around 20 per cent elsewhere, although the WTO still worries about continuing high First World tariff 'peaks' in agriculture, textiles or other labour-intensive industries, tariff 'cascades' (which protect processed products more than semi-processed goods and raw materials) and non-tariff (administrative) barriers. Even some NGOs (e.g. Oxfam, 2002) accuse rich countries of hypocrisy in protecting sectors in which Third World exports are strong, the

Doha Round seeking to tackle such residual protection and have all countries reduce tariffs. Some critical comments are required.

First, evidence suggests that trade liberalisation has seriously damaged emergent industries in poor countries (see Chapter 6) and threatens virtually to eliminate many labour-intensive sectors in rich countries. Theoretically this results in efficient restructuring, but I have argued (Chapter 2) that the benefits of free trade are heavily contingent upon simplifying assumptions, especially that of full employment, whereas, in practice, replacement employment is not guaranteed. Thus, rich countries may be justified in keeping some labour-intensive sectors to cushion employment, to maintain a balance of industries and to observe the Gandhian principle of 'priority to locals'.

Second, it is claimed that elimination of First World farm protection could raise poor countries' incomes by $50–100 billion (Oxfam, 2002: 100), but on my reckoning this represents only 0.3–0.6 per cent of their PPP GDP and these benefits could be negated by a possible 10 per cent rise in food prices due to market adjustments under freer trade (ICTSD, June 2002: 7). At the time of writing the WTO is proposing food tariff cuts of up to 60 per cent, higher minimum food import ratios and gradual elimination of food export subsidies, which sounds reasonable and I agree with eliminating export subsidies which are aggressive rather than socially protectionist. But agriculture is clearly multi-functional (see Chapter 5), yet is in danger of near-extermination in rich countries through overdevelopment of industry and services. I therefore advocate enough protection to maintain a viable sector of small farms (which can be efficient – see Chapter 5), while also cutting aid to agribusiness, abolishing incentives for ecologically damaging practices and encouraging organic agriculture. Furthermore, there is evidence of many First World people wanting a return to the country (Dunkley, 2000b: 170), which suggests that farm assistance may be a popular and democratic measure.

Third, many UN and other studies show that Third World trade liberalisation can massively weaken social and employment structures, raise food import bills and undermine small farms, which tend to be efficient but not highly profitable or politically connected. One NGO study has found that post-Uruguay liberalisation in the Philippines has led to massive food imports, a near-doubling of the food trade deficit and the loss of one in ten rural jobs, yet minimal farm productivity improvement (Aquino, 1998; Shiva, 2000: 40ff).

Overall, I suggest that tariff reductions be ceased until further evaluated and that protection be deemed a legitimate and permanent policy tool, as Keynes once advocated (Dunkley, 1995). Farm protection, except for export subsidies, should be retained where necessary, but be massively redirected towards smaller, more sustainable organic units, while the Third World should refocus research and investment onto agriculture (see Chapter 5 above).

Trade in services

Free Traders claim that services are subject to the same core assumptions (above) as goods, thus being suitable for globalisation and amenable to WTO rules, and that services represent the last great potential for gains from trade. The GATS agreement is compulsory for WTO members and a few sectors must be listed for liberalisation, though further listing is discretionary. In listed sectors alleged discriminatory measures such as protection, FDI restrictions, local content and ownership requirements or immigration limits on foreign providers must be eliminated unless exemptions are expressly listed. Commitments are thence bound (see above) and thus are effectively irreversible. To date, listing has been patchy and exemptions numerous, the Doha Round seeking to rectify this.

GATS is controversial, however, having been largely initiated by US service TNCs. Many poor countries fear service import 'swamping' and some NGOs warn of a 'Trojan Horse' effect for service privatisation. I argue that further services liberalisation is, for the following reasons, not justified. First, the analogy between goods and services is false, the latter being delivered in a range of

Box 8.2   GATS and the water monsters

Claims by globalisers (e.g. Legrain, 2002: 188ff) that NGO fears about privatisation are paranoid and that GATS only helps supplement local service suppliers are wrong, as new research by a team of investigative journalists shows.

- For some years private TNC water utilities, notably the Big Three from Europe – Suez, Vivendi and Thames – have been lobbying world bodies, including the WTO, for 'market access' in water provision. Obligingly, since around 1990 the IMF/World Bank or other global lenders have been forcing countries into water privatisation, via SAPs, most being sold to the Big Three, who had a joint turnover of $267 billion in 2001, about equal to the GNP of Argentina.

- In the name of environmental improvement and free-market scarcity pricing, TNCs (and commercialised national utilities) have been drastically increasing prices and cutting off (poor) users, the World Bank having urged a 'credible threat of cutting services'. Cut-offs cause locals to use (often polluted) waterways, resulting in disease, including (in 2002) the worst cholera epidemic in South Africa's history which infected 250,000 people, killing about 300.

- The Big Three, aided by the EU, have been lobbying the WTO to push for greater market access under GATS and for liberalisation by more countries. Articles 16 and 17 of GATS specifically require countries listing water for liberalisation to allow full National Treatment for foreign service providers, implicitly including access to water resources and infrastructure. In practice this can mean monopoly of a particular water site, some TNCs thence trying to close family wells, or to 'privatise the rain' as one NGO leader has put it.

- TNCs often underbid to win contracts and undercharge at first to impress locals, thereafter more than doubling prices to make up, this leading to the well-known 1999 riots in Brazil which forced local authorities to cancel the private contract.

- In Europe some officers of the Big Three have been charged with bribery and excessive political campaign donations in pursuit of water contracts. Some companies are now also demanding additional compensation for political and exchange rate risks in Third World countries.
- Water is arguably, like agriculture, a 'multi-functional' community asset with resource, ecological, infrastructural, social and equity roles, so should not be treated as a commercial product subject to privatisation, full marketisation or free trade. Many small community-controlled water projects are proving more effective than large privatised ones.

Sources: International Consortium of Investigative Journalists at www.icij.org/dtaweb/water/default.aspx; *New Internationalist* 354, March 2003; 'Background Briefing', *ABC Radio National* (Australia), 12 April 2003.

different ways, having various functional differences, being far more socially or culturally sensitive, and comparative advantage in services is formed through history or tradition in complex ways (see Dunkley, 2000b: ch. 9). Second, many Third World WTO members still feel GATS was foisted upon them, still cannot calculate the full implications of services liberalisation, and could, indeed, be flooded with foreign, often culturally alien, service providers (Raghavan, 2002).

Third, 'Trojan Horse' fears are real, if exaggerated. Officially the WTO allows domestic regulation of services and does not require privatisation, although hints are occasionally dropped and public enterprises are to be WTO-consistent. But the compulsory application of National Treatment (see above) under GATS logically entails granting market access for all foreign service providers including private ones, yet there is no scope in GATS for states to vet or exclude socially or ethically questionable TNCs. NGOs are particularly worried about this in relation to water supply (Box 8.2), and in the infamous Banana Case GATS was invoked in a way which, according to one US legal scholar (Dillon, 1999: 218), provides 'nearly unlimited potential to invalidate national regulations' (see Box 8.3).

The ethics and appropriateness of private and TNC services in areas such as health, education, prisons or social services have been questioned, and one US private health company has vowed to destroy public hospitals. Foreign (mostly US) health TNCs are on track to take over some two-thirds of Australian medical clinics, these being notorious for unnecessary, costly, in-house tests, while drug TNCs regularly pay doctors to provide patients, many of them disabled, for drug testing.[2] TNC retailers like WalMart (from USA) are renowned for their adverse impacts on small shops, townscapes and shopping cultures. US threats (at the TNCs' request) of a WTO case against Japan's small shop laws, which have been crucial to that country's community maintenance and resistance to full-blast Westernisation, were successful in having cabinet agree to repeal these laws, despite the opposition of virtually all parliamentarians (Dillon, 1999).

In sum, the goal of services liberalisation is based on false premises, is being pushed by massive vested interests, entails far more costs than is acknowledged by Free Traders, and the WTO generally refuses to consider such issues (Dillon, 1999). Yet liberalisation by stealth is proceeding as the WTO pressures members, as members pressure each other and as WTO panels expand the purview of GATS (Box 8.3). I argue that further liberalisation should cease until the above issues are adequately studied, and GATS should be made non-compulsory or perhaps even be abolished (see below).

Trade-Related Intellectual Property Rights

The most contentious component of the WTO system, and its possible Achilles heel, the TRIPs Agreement began as an attempt by US TNCs to link intellectual property rights with GATT/ WTO trade sanctions, and the USA forced the issue into the Uruguay Round, once declaring 'No TRIPs, No Round'! The

TNCs were openly targeting intellectual property piracy and cheap Third World generic drug production, with remarkable success, aided by much bilateral US bullying (Dunkley, 2000b: ch. 9; Braithwaite and Drahos, 2000: 194ff).

Critics attack the TRIPs Agreement on grounds such as that it is barely related to trade, that it hurts poor countries, that it encourages 'biopiracy' (the buying or stealing of native plants) and that it damages the WTO, especially after US-backed TNCs tried to prevent South Africa from seeking cheap AIDS drugs, desisting only after expressions of NGO and public outrage. Even Free Traders like Bhagwati (TWN, May/June 2002: 43–4) and Legrain (2002: 330) urge the removal of TRIPs from the WTO. In response the WTO's Doha Ministerial, the meeting which launched the Doha Round, has proposed allowing members to manufacture or import cheap generics (variant products) for public health purposes, but the WTO is divided on the issue, the USA wanting such flexibility confined to poor countries and to AIDS drugs (ICTSD, November/December 2002).

I argue for the abolition, or at least modification, of the TRIPs Agreement on the following grounds: (1) its political origins are biased and amount to the historic 'capture' of a world body; (2) Third World members did not want it and were 'fatigued' or bribed into acceptance as a trade-off for agricultural concessions, as were heavy technology-importing countries like Australia (Braithwaite and Drahos, 2000: 197ff); (3) it has greatly increased royalty and enforcement costs for Third World or other technology-importing countries; (4) its plant patenting requirements largely ignore shared traditional communal knowledge and help agribusiness TNCs; (5) some evidence suggests that intellectual property rights actually inhibit the early stages of development, assisting mainly only in later stages, where national innovation systems are strong, and that some European countries, notably Switzerland, industrialised adequately with minimal intellectual property rights.[3]

Product standards

Posited on a (probably exaggerated) fear that product standards regulation can be used for sneaky trade barriers, the Uruguay Round adopted agreements on Technical Barriers to Trade (TBT) and Sanitary and Phytosanitary (SPS) measures (for food), these requiring product standards to be based on 'scientific' assessments of risk and gradual harmonisation between member countries. These agreements do not officially constrain government regulation of standards or set upper limits, as certain critics claim, but neither do they set lower limits, so that they could theoretically induce competitive reductions, or a 'race to the bottom', as some fear.

There is no clear evidence that these agreements have started either a 'race to the bottom' or a 'race to the top' (higher standards), as some claim can happen (Legrain, 2002: 167ff). Under the WTO's SPS Agreement many First World countries have deregulated and reduced some standards, which they claim were excessive anyway, but Third World countries have tended to raise standards (Braithwaite and Drahos, 2002: 402ff). WTO panels have overturned precautionary, health- or quarantine-based import bans (by Australia on live salmon and by the EU on hormone-grown beef) as being inadequately based on scientific evidence. A panel has also required the EU (Sardines Case, ICTSD, October 2002) to adopt standards set by the WTO's SPS consultative body, Codex Alimentarius, which are claimed to be advisory only.

There are two key problems. First, the term 'scientific' will have to be defined more flexibly, both Australia and the EU presenting plenty of good-quality scientific evidence for their above-mentioned bans. Second, if panels wish to enforce Codex standards more rigorously in a harmonising system, that body will have to be democratised, as at present it is notoriously dominated by business and large countries, one WTO official observing that 'small states do not have a clue what is going on' (Braithwaite and Drahos, 2000: 407ff; Dunkley, 2000b: 208ff). The two agreements should be rewritten to make harmonisation flexible, to define 'scientific' in a way which admits all quality scientific evidence, to democratise the WTO's three standard-setting bodies, and clearly to allow the 'precautionary principle' – that is, the notion that governments should act in anticipation of future problems.

Labour standards

Free Trade theory naively assumes (see Chapters 2 and 3) full employment and non-exploitation of labour, but although main-stream economists admit that trade-enhancing, capital-attracting exploitation can occur in practice, they claim it is temporary and reject trade-union proposals for trade sanctions against labour-exploiting countries as dangerous protectionism. I argue that stra-tegic exploitation can be exaggerated, but does occur, can last for long periods and now often takes the form of 'unit cost gaps' (Dunkley, 2000b: 120–21) where imported high-productivity plants coexist with low wages (see Chapter 5). This suggests a case for both labour standards (though not wage controls – see Dunkley, 1996) and regulation of TNCs to ensure that more ap-propriate technologies are employed.

The most feasible form of labour standards would be the in-clusion of core principles such as labour rights, union recognition, bargaining rights and avoidance of child labour in Article XX, the main exemptions section of GATT. This would enable WTO panels to hear complaints about countries breaching these key conditions, trade concessions thence being withdrawn from those found 'guilty'. But no attempt should be made to force wages up to First World levels, as some unions want, because this distorts development patterns and induces inappropriate technologies.

The environment

As outlined in Chapter 5, Free Traders and the WTO now claim that trade is compatible with the environment, an assertion I have criticised. With the concept of 'sustainable development' now in its platform, the WTO claims to be 'green' and has placed the

environment on the Doha Round agenda, but the green preten-
sion is dubious. Several WTO rulings have held that members
retain the right to make environmental laws and regulations (as
though that should ever have been in doubt!), and a French ban
on asbestos imports has been upheld under GATT's resource conservation exception clause (Article XXg), though in several in-
stances, notoriously the 'tuna/dolphin' and 'shrimp/turtle' cases,
WTO panels have disallowed national laws aimed at restricting
environmentally damaging imports.

These cases have particularly involved two (vague, some say
legally dubious) GATT principles: 'no extraterritorality' (national
laws cannot apply internationally) and 'no processes' (GATT
exceptions cannot apply to the process of production or its impact). Both principles are supposedly designed to prevent the
proliferation of protectionism. I suggest that the WTO could be
'greened' by adding to GATT Article XX three further exceptions
which: (1) facilitate trade sanctions in world environmental agreements; (2) allow Article XX exceptions to apply in cases of environmentally damaging processes as well as products; (3) accord
the environment general priority over trade, including applying
laws beyond borders where required for effectiveness. I propose
these points because trade and the environment can conflict (see
Chapter 5), and nobody outside the global Free Trade elite
seriously thinks that trade should have priority or that undue
protectionism would run rife (see Dunkley, 2000b: ch. 10).

Other issues

The Doha Round has also slated for possible consideration the
key issues of government procurement, competition, investment
and WTO rules, plus a few development-specific topics such as
S&D, technology transfer, and 'trade, debt and finance'. The
WTO's government procurement agreement, which opens state
purchasing processes to TNC suppliers, is voluntary, with only
twenty-eight signatories, a clear indication that members want
the autonomy to favour locally based development. There is little

chance of the number of signatories being greatly raised as the WTO wants.

Likewise, regarding competition and investment, many Third World members oppose their being on the agenda. With competition, only enforcement is to be considered, but the Doha Round may examine most aspects of the OECD's controversial, ill-fated Multilateral Agreement on Investment (MAI), which had sought greatly to liberalise FDI and strengthen the hands of TNCs (Dunkley, 2000b: 231, 286). Many countries oppose an MAI-type system in the WTO and would like to see modification or abolition of the Uruguay Round's Trade-Related Investment Measures (TRIMs) Agreement, which restricts government regulation of TNCs. Indeed there is reason to question the benefits of untrammelled private FDI, which can 'crowd out' local capital, and one expert (Buffie, 2001: ch. 9) has found that most countries can increase their welfare by enforcing local employment, equity and export requirements upon TNCs, which the TRIMs Agreement now disallows (also, above and Dunkley, 2000b: 287). Thus the TRIMs Agreement is based on incorrect theory and information, probably having been adopted during the Uruguay Round at the behest of TNCs wanting to avoid regulation. Most First World countries used such forms of intervention in their earlier development, and the banning of these now, via the WTO, has been likened, in List's words, to 'kicking away the ladder' which they themselves once ascended (Chang, 2002).

Culture is not a major issue in the WTO because most members want cultural sovereignty, but in his book, *The Undeclared War*, British film producer David Puttnam sees an unofficial struggle between Europe and the USA for global cultural ascendency. He documents (1997: 341–4) how the EC almost sank the Uruguay Round over culture until the US desisted from its efforts to place audiovisual liberalisation on the agenda, President Bill Clinton surrendering after a phone call to Hollywood boss Lew Wasserman. GATT allows local film quotas (Article IV) and the

Canadian Magazine Case panel approved cultural protection, though it *still* overturned the Canadian local content law as discriminatory. GATS covers 'culture industries', but few members have listed these for liberalisation. The EU has been unsuccessful in pressing for a 'cultural exception' clause in GATT, although French/Canadian demands for this helped sink the MAI. Despite a staggering domination of world film and television trade, the Americans seek even more 'market access', wanting interventionist measures, box-office taxes, film subsidies and television local content quotas outlawed. Few countries support these US endeavours, but a 'cultural exceptions' clause in GATT Article XX would ensure priority of culture over trade in disputes like the Canadian Magazines case.

Policeman or postman?

While the Doha Round proposes to examine WTO rules and disciplines, the nature of these is debated. Anti-globalists fear the WTO is a disciplinary trade and economic policeman; others scorn it as a weak creature of its strongest members (Rugman, 2000: ch. 2); while moderates and the WTO itself (2002) see a neutral, servicing, mediating, information-collecting, communications-delivering servant of member states, albeit an underresourced one (Dunkley, 2000b: 270ff). Former WTO head Renato Ruggiero (in Aga Khan, 1998: 27) has denied that the WTO wishes to police the world, declaring reassuringly that the world needs 'builders, not policemen'.

None of these depictions is accurate. Whilst the WTO is indeed a servicing secretariat, its rules and panel findings are deemed to be international law, often followed by many courts worldwide. Commitments are locked in by binding (above), and there is strong informal pressure to conform. Dispute panel decisions are mostly adhered to, enforced now by WTO-brokered sanctions of one member by another, and few negotiations, other than the famed Seattle Ministerial and earlier maritime transport talks, have broken down, although at the time of writing the Doha Round is stagnating and restive Third World members are demanding many changes or exemptions. At present the WTO is both a mild policeman and a persistent postman.

Ogre or umpire?

Anti-globalists variously accuse the WTO of being dominated by strong member states or by TNCs, of neglecting Third World members in practice, of being undemocratic, of using bullying tactics and of undermining national sovereignty, globalists denying these charges.[4] The truth is doubtless in-between. Officially the WTO represents member governments, each with one vote, while companies are merely recognised as NGOs, but companies appear to have much greater informal access to WTO bodies and member governments than do 'civil society' NGOs, with US TNCs having the greatest clout (Braithwaite and Drahos, 2000: 27). At the infamous Seattle Ministerial meeting, Bill Gates, on behalf of the WTO, sought some $10m in corporate sponsorships in return for access to delegates, a first for the WTO but a common practice for international conferences.[5]

The claim that the WTO's 'one-country-one-vote' system allows equal say and strengthens small countries (e.g. Legrain, 2002: 181) is simplistic. Much WTO work occurs in ad hoc meetings and proceeds mainly by consensus, which, rather than ensuring democracy, can push politics into back rooms. In the WTO there are at least two clear, undesirable symptoms of this. The first is domination by the 'Quad' (USA, EU, Japan and Canada), one US trade official declaring that 'the US basically sets the trade agenda, the EC constrains it' (Braithwaite and Drahos, 2000: 199). Compared with other countries, the USA chairs more committees on world bodies, levies more sanctions, starts and wins more WTO dispute cases and generally has more policymaking influence. The claim that WTO membership helps the weak is dubious, such states being much more likely to lose disputes than the strong (Braithwaite and Drahos, 2000: 183–4 and *passim*). Some forecast that US dominance will eventually bring the WTO down, US leaders often warning against too many defeats for their interests (see Rugman, 2000: ch. 2).

A second undesirable result of the consensus system is the alleged regular bullying of hesitant members. Ever since the Uruguay Round many Third World members have complained that they were rushed into acceptance of that agreement, and that at the ill-fated Seattle ministerial meeting bullying or small caucus tactics were used, especially by US delegates, to force a result (TWNF and TWN: various). Some commentators hold that it was Third World unrest with all this which derailed the Ministerial rather than the demonstrations or Clinton's advocacy of labour and environment standards, as grumpy Free Traders claimed (TWN 112–13, December 1999/January 2000).

Likewise regarding the Doha Ministerial, many critics and disillusioned delegates allege bullying, bribery (offers of aid or trade concessions) and 'Green Room' or 'Friends of the Chair' elite caucusing. One Third World delegate said: 'Wearing us down with fatigue is the typical tactic of the powerful at the WTO' (Reddy in TWN 112–13). Indeed, the final Ministerial Declaration pledged 'explicit consensus' for key Doha Round decisions, clearly implying that incomplete consensus has been used at other times.

The WTO maintains a UN-type accreditation list for trade-related international NGOs (TRINGOs), this status facilitating access to briefings, symposia, consultations and some trade negotiations, but 'civil society' NGOs complain that they get far less access than TNCs (Dunkley, 2000a). The WTO claims to be open and transparent, especially as most documents are placed on the Internet (up to 10,000 pages at a time!), but delays or withholding does occur and much decision-making is behind the scenes. Full participation in the WTO requires attendance at plenty of the two thousand or so formal, and innumerable informal, meetings held each year, but poor countries keep few or no permanent delegates at Geneva, while rich-country delegations even help with many WTO tasks. Thus the WTO is less open, democratic or helpful to the Third World than it claims, some supporters even urging less secrecy (e.g. Legrain, 2000: 200ff), while the former GATT head, Arthur Dunkel, has decried excessive business influence over the WTO and national governments (TWNF 1932/1999).

As regards the WTO's impact on national sovereignty, neither the anti-globalists' claims of crushing nor the globalists' picture of minimal, voluntary surrender is accurate. Technically, nations join the WTO voluntarily, but cabinets make the decisions, referenda on membership are never held, and polling shows public scepticism, along with some confusion, about Free Trade principles (see Chapter 4; Aaronson, 1996: 134ff and *passim*). In 1991, while their government was negotiating the Uruguay Round trade liberalisation proposals, a poll showed 71 per cent of Australians wanting to keep protection for local goods.[6] A Mori poll commissioned by *The Ecologist* (May 2000) found that 55 per cent of British respondents want protection for local companies and that more than 90 per cent favour protection over free trade where environmental, employment or health conditions are at stake. The USA, EU and IMF/World Bank often pressure countries to join the WTO. Withdrawal from the WTO by a later government is possible in principle, but difficult in practice once an economy has adjusted to MFN trade concessions. Hence, governments are consciously committing 'sovereignty suicide', but not entirely voluntarily.

Technically the WTO does not demand the surrender of policymaking sovereignty, claiming only to make 'member-driven' rules, but the WTO's brief is now so wide-ranging that much intrusion occurs by stealth: harmonisation under TBT/SBS can gradually evolve undesirable standards or policies, the TRIMs Agreement constrains controls over TNCs, GATS limits the promotion of local services, and so forth. Despite Legrain's (2002: 185) boast that Fidel Castro is a 'fan of the WTO', Castro has actually condemned the WTO system as unfair, unbalanced and hostile to development sovereignty (TWNF, no. 1753/1998).

Globalists often recommend that countries be pressured or 'shamed' into conformity with WTO or other global agreements, the WTO and pro-global governments seeking to do this through various channels, including blandishments by WTO leaders, support for pro-global interests, inter-country peer pressure, the invoking of WTO agreements as grounds for ignoring protests against free trade, and the WTO's trade-policy monitoring procedures. Supposedly just consultative, the WTO's trade-policy review teams often berate members for alleged 'sins' such as continuing protection, discriminatory tax policies or inadequate (*sic*) privatisation. Malaysia has been queried for its tariff-aided vehicle development, Mauritius for its multi-functionality principle (see above) in agricultural protection, Slovakia for its food self-reliance policy, South Africa and Kenya for slow privatisation, Japan for hidden protection and FDI controls, Australia for suspiciously interventionist industry policy, and Bangladesh for its extensive state-owned services and limited services liberalisation.[7] Some of these queries are outside the WTO's generally accepted brief, arguably constituting a degree of informal coercion, and certainly betraying a strong Free Market Economic Rationalist bias.

In sum, the WTO system seems antipathetic to democracy and national sovereignty because of the 'single undertaking' rule which makes most agreements compulsory (Box 8.1); the built-in agenda which forces continuing negotiations in some areas; the 'binding' system (see above); the GATS once-and-for-all listing system (see above); and the secrecy, supposedly for diplomatic and strategy reasons, of trade negotiations. These prevent adequate public scrutiny and may preclude future governments from changing policies, even should they have an electoral mandate to do so.

Particular criticism is directed at the WTO's dispute settlement system, which has ruled against several environmental measures, a Canadian law promoting local magazine content, India's cheap generic drugs policy and motor industry local content requirements, South Korean safety laws, Australian quarantine laws, Indian trade balancing duties and, most notoriously, an EU banana import quota system which favoured poor countries (see Box 8.3).

Box 8.3 The Banana War

This story is about one of the WTO's most crucial cases to date, which involved five different WTO agreements, embroiled almost a third of WTO member countries and for many people has brought the WTO into great disrepute. In 1997 a WTO panel heard arguments by the USA and some Central America (CA) countries against the EU's complex, multitiered banana import regime, which favoured, as a form of aid, the small, often impoverished, African, Caribbean and Pacific (ACP) banana-exporting countries.

The main protagonists, the EU and USA, produce virtually no bananas, the EU acting on behalf of poor nations, some of them ex-colonies, the US openly acting on behalf of the giant, mainly US, TNCs which grow most CA bananas. Carl Lindner, head of Chiquita, the largest of these TNCs, is known to have donated over $5 million to the two main US political parties during the Banana War (Hertz, 2002: 110–11).

NGOs have convincingly shown that CA bananas are mostly grown on huge plantations with massive inputs of insecticides; arduous, dangerous working conditions; and recently declining pay. CA plantation workers ingest insecticide at eight times the world average, with 20 per cent of males rendered sterile in some places. ACP bananas are mostly produced on small freehold farms, some being organic, often in reasonable living conditions. CA production costs are half to one-third of ACP levels, but some say about equal when health, exploitation or other 'external' costs are counted (Ransom, 2001: ch. 4; Smith, 2002).

Several mainstream econometric studies of a banana free-trade option for the EU found startling results. Under free trade, EU consumers and some CA producers would be better off, but after considering factors such as revenue losses to governments and massive losses to ACP producers, there would be a global *loss* of welfare unless CA banana export prices fell by an improbable 18–30 per cent (Preville, 1999). These studies confirm the core argument of this book, that gains from free trade are contingent, not guaranteed.

The WTO panel conceded that there were many 'economic and social effects' of the case, thus granting ACP and CA countries more rights of submission and attendance than is usual for third parties, but social and environmental issues were given no consideration whatsoever. The panel, like the WTO itself, assumed that more trade and freer trade is always best, ignoring the above-mentioned econometric studies, even though most of these studies were publicly available at the time (cited in Preville, 1999).

On 22 May 1997 the panel ruled on four major grounds, mostly under GATT and GATS, that the EU's banana policy was illegally discriminatory. In September the WTO's Appellate Body confirmed this, with minor legal adjustments.

In a largely unnoticed element of the case, the EU policy was overruled partly on the grounds that it breached the MFN and National Treatment provisions of GATS (Articles II and XVII) by restricting the supply of goods when the EU had already listed 'wholesale trade services' for liberalisation under GATS. The panel ruled (7.285 at p. 1038) that 'GATS encompasses any measure ... [even if] it regulates other matters but nevertheless affects trade in services'.

The potential implications of this are staggering. First, it appears to mean that any policy or law which indirectly affects a service listed under GATS could be challenged, so that GATS is a 'potent new weapon not limited to the concept of trade in services qua services', but including the service of providing *goods* (Dillon, 1999: 217). Second, it appears to introduce an element of 'entrapment' whereby a country which lists some service may find that this affects later laws – in this case the EU's listing of wholesale trade affected its right to influence banana imports.

The EU refused to alter its banana import regime substantially, though some officials wanted to, and the WTO authorised the USA to levy almost $200 million of punitive duties against a range of EU exports.

Many commentators and NGOs have criticised the inordinately narrow, technocratic nature of the panel decision, but this is clearly an outcome of the WTO's restrictive dispute-settlement system and narrow trade focus. Even leading Free Trader Jagdish Bhagwati (quoted in WTO, 2000b: 187) said of the case that free trade does not require 'that we ride at breakneck speed and with reckless regard (*sic*) over the economies of small and poor nations'.

Sources: Dillon, 1999; Hertz,2002: 103ff; Smith, 2002: 40–41; *New International-ist* 317, October 1999; Preville, 1999; WTO, 2000b (for Panel and Appellate Body decisions); Ransom, 2001.

Certainly dispute panels have also more 'progressively' over-turned an extended US trade boycott of Cuba and a US subsidy system for tax-haven-based TNC exporters, as well as backing a French ban on Canadian asbestos imports. But anecdotal evidence suggests that countries sometimes avoid progressive measures for fear of a WTO case. So the WTO disputes system is a two-edged sword, with the socially progressive edge much the blunter, and with trade issues always trumping other factors, irrespective of their philosophical basis (Dillon, 1999: 209; Box 8.3). Thus the WTO may be more umpire than ogre, but its umpiring has a strong pro-trade bias. This narrowing of the WTO's focus, in comparison with its broader official goals, may be due to its entering a more institutionalised, bureaucratic phase of its develop-ment, but also reflects its ideological, pro-market world view, which is now being widely questioned.

The Global Free Trade Project

The WTO's grand goal is a Hullian-style, liberal, relatively free-trading global order, or what I call the Global Free Trade Project. The WTO is not a de facto world government, as some assert, because its basis is too narrow and unpopular. Vanuatu, for in-stance, recently dropped its membership application because the WTO's farm and goods liberalisation demands were too onerous (Ransom, 2001: 26–7). But it sees itself as the agent of a Free Trade, Free Investment enlightenment which is to be achieved with the utmost urgency. This project is now a historic obsession, the WTO (quoted p. 189, above) and other globo-euphorists unabashedly proclaiming it a panacea (see also, World Bank, 2002). Free Trade Fundamentalists (e.g. Bergsten in WTO, 2000b: 167–8) declare the project inevitable because a 'competitive liberalisation race' is necessary to attract footloose capital, while one US WTO official (quoted above, p. 188) insists that the world must liberalise until it Americanises.

However, I argue in this book that the Global Free Trade Project and its associated mythology are misguided because they are based on several false assumptions, notably the alleged equivalence of goods and services and the claim that trade universally leads to growth and equity; because the populace has not been consulted about the project and probably disapproves; because its agenda is business- rather than democracy-led (Shiva, quoted p. 188, above); because it entails social changes about which there is no consensus; and because its goals, such as those implied by Bergsten and the US WTO official quoted above, are questionable ideals for the human race. Moreover, the WTO's blatant claim (above, p. 188) that wars and poverty are due to a lack of globalisation is dishonest and palpably ludicrous!

Alternatives: Global Free Trade versus Co-operative World

Most alternative visions centre around cooperation between societies which are more economically sovereign than is implied by the Global Free Trade Project. Elsewhere (Dunkley, 2000b: ch. 12) I have enumerated the alternatives to Free Trade as Managed Trade, Fair Trade and Self-Reliant Trade, with variations and combinations of these possible.

Managed Trade means that nations would still trade extensively, but in a controlled way through trade intervention, so as to tailor external forces to domestic requirements. The forms of trade intervention may include many types of protection, industry policy, import substitution (Chapter 6), planned development and sundry versions of 'strategic trade' policy (see Chapter 3). Managed Trade is usually advocated on Keynesian grounds such as a stable balance of payments and demand growth, as well as on more radical grounds such as planned industrial development, controlled sustainable development, avoidance of the social or structural costs brought by trade liberalisation and the right to national sovereignty in shaping the society people want.

Managed Trade has been practised far more frequently than Free Trade, including during the two highest growth eras in human history – the late nineteenth century and around 1950–75 (see Chapter 4 above). If the substantial trade intervention and domestic regulation of those eras did not directly *cause* the growth (though see Chapter 6 and Chang, 2002), then these practices clearly did not greatly *inhibit* it, and in any case the virtues of growth as a prime human goal are questionable (see Chapter 5).

There are three inconsistent meanings of *Fair Trade*: the WTO's sense of avoiding 'unfair' protectionism, schemes for buying Third World commodities at 'fair' or non-exploitative prices (I call this Fair Price Trading), and policies to prevent countries from abusing labour, the environment or human rights to gain a trading advantage (I call this Social Clause Fair Trade). Today there are many Fair Price Trading schemes run by NGOs, especially for coffee and cocoa, with the products sold through NGO co-ops, shops, mail order or the like, though as yet on a very small scale. The anecdotal NGO literature suggests that such schemes can markedly improve the incomes and living conditions of beneficiaries, and could feasibly be used more extensively in aid programmes. Advocates of Social Clause Fair Trade propose some form of 'social clause' in trade agreements which would enable WTO members to sanction other members for exploitative policies. In general, Fair Trade should consist, passively, of anti-exploitative structural clauses in the WTO and, more actively, of nationally based, but perhaps UN-directed, Fair Price Trading schemes (see Ransom, 2001).

Self-Reliant Trade entails the principle that nations trade only as a necessary supplement to a democratically self-determined development model. This suggests an intensive form of Managed Trade with protection, regulation and planning systems directed specifically at sectors and policies required to create the sort of society people want (see Chapter 7 above). This has been by far the most common form of trade policy throughout human history (see Chapter 4).

Rather than an elite-enforced opening up of global trade and capital flows, these alternative forms of trade can facilitate more cooperative relations between securely sovereign societies. Any alternative world order should be based on these rather than on dogmatic Free Trade.

A More Participatory, Cooperative World Order

Proposals for 'reform' of the present world order abound, indicating extensive dissatisfaction. Free Traders mostly want wider and deeper liberalisation, though some would accept an environmental body to supplement the WTO and mild curbs on speculative capital flows. Interventionists and Human Development theorists tend to favour cautious liberalisation, mildly Managed Trade, more development aid, curbs on speculative capital flows and a more open WTO.

The most radical proposals come from Community-Sovereignty activists, especially in NGOs, who agree with some of the above but also advocate a more flexible, transparent WTO, more mechanisms for Third World participation, more formal NGO involvement, social clauses (above), a separate but linked body for the environment, less trade-dominated decision-making and so forth (see Dunkley, 2000a for details).

I argue that proposals for 're-forming' the world trading order should begin with two factors seldom considered: first, that the present order is based on various mythologies and incorrect assumptions, as outlined in this book, and, second, that the trading system should be aimed more at achieving world consensus goals than it is at present. I thus propose the following three principles for re-formation: (1) that the benefits of Free Trade be seen as contingent, not universal or guaranteed, and that the costs of freer trade be acknowledged and measured (see Chapter 2); (2) that each country be able to pursue a range of requisite trade measures, of the sort outlined above, within the context of a loose multilateral agreement, so as to be able to shape their own development paths (see Chapter 5); (3) that the world trading system primarily seek to pursue cooperatively the key goals of social justice, environmental protection and cultural integrity.

I thus propose that the WTO or any successor body retain the principles or functions of multilateral rule-making, MFN, transparency, dispute settlement and trade negotiations (reduced in scope), but abandon or greatly modify those of National Treatment, 'single undertaking', continuing liberalisation and binding.

More specifically, I propose the following detailed changes. The present world elite will reject most of these, but some are practicable even in the short term, all are feasible in the longer term and NGOs will continue to demand these sorts of innovations (see Dunkley, 2000a).

1. *Article XX extensions*   The main exceptions clause of GATT should have addenda allowing the following: sanctions (import restrictions or withdrawal of concessions) for failure to observe core labour standards (see above); resource or environmental preservation measures in relation to both products and processes, with the environment emphasised more strongly than in the present XX(g); cultural protection; sanctions for enforcement of multilateral environmental agreements; and sanctions for extreme human rights abuse (based on UN resolutions). Article XX should also have a rider ensuring that these externalities are given priority over trade, because at present WTO panels often overrule an externality measure on technicalities such as allegedly being discriminatory or

unduly trade restrictive. Such a rider would acknowledge that dealing with the externality is more important than ensuring maintenance of trade levels.

2. *Alternative agriculture* The Agreement on Agriculture should clearly recognise the multi-functional role of farming, the right to protection for purposes of food security and the need to facilitate conversion to organic methods.

3. *Development packages* A clause should be added to GATT allowing members to devise development or self-reliance 'packages' of carefully planned measures, as alternatives to IMF/World Bank SAPs, and enabling the WTO to approve the requisite protection on 'infant industry' or other such grounds (see Dunkley, 2000b: 260).

4. *NGO accreditation* The WTO should accredit a reasonable range of credible NGOs for extended tasks such as observation at all trade negotiations, consultation with committees, input to research programmes, advice to dispute panels and membership of relevant panels.

5. *Extended voting* Formal votes, allowed for at present but seldom used, should be required for a wider range of issues, including final approval of trade agreements.

6. *Abolition of 'single undertaking'* For reasons discussed above, the 'single undertaking' clause, which makes most WTO agreements compulsory, should be discontinued, or at least the contentious TRIPs, GATS and TRIMs agreements should be made 'plurilateral' (non-compulsory).

7. *National WTO consultative bodies* Major WTO decisions begin with member governments but are usually made secretly at cabinet level. To counter this undemocratic practice the WTO should require members to form in-country, broadly based consultative bodies to debate national trade and WTO policy, scrutinise proposed trade agreements and advise parliaments on such matters. In case consensus is not reached, citizen-initiated referenda should be available for major trade agreements.

8. *Decennial rounds* Given periodic references to 'negotiation fatigue' and Third World impatience with seemingly perpetual trade talks, I propose that trade negotiation rounds be held at decennial intervals (every ten years) and that the present automatic 'built-in' agendas be abolished.

9. *Amnesty on bindings* For reasons discussed above, I argue that bindings are undemocratic and I propose a decennial amnesty on tariff bindings, GATS listings and other locked-in commitments so that new generations have the option of revising trade policies of previous governments.

10. *Quadripartite representation* For a broader WTO representation system, country delegations could consist of four persons – one each from government, employers, unions and 'civil society' (NGOs). This would entail large meetings, but no greater than for the ILO which has two delegates from government, with one each from employers and unions. Large quadripartite assemblies would only be required at two points: on the proposed national WTO consultative bodies (No. 7, above) and at annual or biennial WTO General Council meetings, which would thence appoint (more democratically) all other WTO units.

11. *Link to the UN* In time the WTO or any successor body should ideally be linked to the UN, as the original ILO, IMF and World Bank were meant to be (see Dunkley, 2000b: ch. 12; 2000a); should work consistently with UN resolutions; and should coordinate with other UN bodies such as the ILO for labour issues, the UN Environment Programme or other environmental research bodies and possibly the United Nations Educational Scientific and Cultural Organisation (UNESCO) for cultural issues. WTO research should include examining the wider social or other impacts of trade liberalisation, which it rarely does at present.

12. *Reformed IMF/World Bank* The WTO or any successor should continue to work with other world bodies, as at present, but the IMF should be re-formed into a more stabil-

ising, less dictatorial world central bank of the sort envisaged by Keynes. Ideally, the World Bank should be abolished in favour of UN development agencies, these being briefed to promote more participatory, grassroots development models (Chapter 5), including ISI and self-reliant options (Chapters 6 and 7), in cooperation with NGOs. The WTO's brief must be to allow trade policies consistent with any such models approved by the UN. Criteria for assistance should include conformity with human rights, labour standards and world environmental agreements, plus the production of a feasible appropriate development plan (see Proposal 3, above).

The Global Free Trade elite will resist such proposals as backward-looking, but I argue they are broadening, democratising measures, at least some of which are essential if disgruntled WTO member countries, NGOs and other critics are to be assuaged. More importantly, it is possible to create a fairer, more cooperative world of the kind advocated in this book, one based on what I have called the 'Community-Sovereignty' vision, but these sorts of changes will be required if we are to do so.

Conclusion

This chapter has argued that the WTO is both a mild policeman and a, for some exasperatingly, persistent postman. It is *not* an ogre but *is* a biased umpire, with a near-obsessive preoccupation with trade. The WTO's claim to focus equally on Third World development and 'sustainable development' is ludicrous, as it clearly holds these to be subsidiary to trade expansion.

Certainly the WTO is formally a mediating, servicing, member-driven body, but it also has now been vested with capacities to pressure members, force some agendas, facilitate the disciplining or sanctioning of members and is not above attempting to inveigle its own preferred trade negotiation results. Although members theoretically retain the autonomy to regulate matters such as industries, standards and the environment, WTO disciplines and disputes rulings do introduce constraints by stealth. Furthermore, implicitly recognising that globalisation is not inevitable or irreversible, the WTO seeks to lock in liberalisations in order to prevent future governments from reversing them, other world bodies doing likewise in their own jurisdictions. This is potentially creating an inflexible, non-consensual, undemocratic world order.

TNCs do not dominate the WTO, but they do heavily influence government in major countries, and these in turn, especially the USA, do dominate the WTO. The WTO's Global Free Trade Project is unduly business-dominated, is based on many Free Trade myths, as criticised in this book, and is inadequately set in the context of wider issues. For many, this project is symbolised by regular corporate pressure on the US government to seek economic 'regime change' in other countries, especially in Japan, or by the remarks of former US trade representative Carla Hills who once advocated prying markets (countries) open with a crowbar 'so that our private sector can take advantage of them' (see Dunkley, 2000b: 226). There will be no consensus about the WTO and its Free Trade adventure until such attitudes change, or until the WTO and other world institutions are broadened and democratised in ways proposed in this chapter.

Notes

1. Aaronson, 1996: 174 passim; Dunkley, 2000: ch. 2; Braithwaite and Drahos, 2000: ch. 7)
2. *The Age* (Melbourne), 13 February 2001: 1; 31 March 2001: 5. General: Monbiot, 2000: esp. chs 1, 2 and 9; Barlow, 2001.
3. Braithwaite and Drahos, 2000: 77; Linsu Kim in ICTSD, November/December 2002; Chang, 2002: 83ff.
4. Accusations: Mokhiber and Weissman, 1999a; Danaher and Burbach, 2000. Responses: Sampson in Aga Khan, 1998; WTO, 2001, 2002; Legrain, 2002.
5. Mokhiber and Weissman, 1999b; *Weekend Australian*, 7–8 August 1999: 39.
6. *The Age* (Melbourne), 15 May 1991: 16.
7. See recent WTO *Annual Reports*, Trade Policy Review section.

CHAPTER 9

CONCLUSION

The central theme of this book is that the two-century-long debate over Free Trade versus Protection has not been about truth versus falsity, as Free Market ideologues so often portray it, but about rival ideologies and world-views. To the extent that the debate follows the mainstream economists' unwritten rule that whichever policy can produce the higher income level at any one time or the faster economic growth over time, then truth or falsity can be judged to some degree. But I argue that free trade is less superior (if superior at all) in this regard than Free Traders claim, that improvements in growth or general living standards are often the result of domestic factors rather than freer trade or globalisation, that growth often causes increased trade or globalisation rather than the reverse, and that, in any case, income or growth criteria alone are far too narrow. If wider non-economic criteria are also used, then policy systems based on Protection, or wide-ranging trade intervention, are much more justifiable and are arguably superior to Free Trade.

The key conclusions of the book are that: (1) the now famous, world-dominating claim that free trade and globalisation can, relative to protection, provide superior income, growth, prosperity and equity performances is largely mythological; (2) the reality is that today's worldwide thrust for free trade and globalisation is a pro-business, ideological, politically motivated movement which ignores the extensive and 'non-consensual' economic, social, environmental and cultural costs of these policies; (3) many alternative ideas and policy options are available but are largely ignored by the world's Free Market Economic Rationalist elite. I have outlined three alternative streams of thought about trade and development issues: Market Interventionism, Human Development and Community-Sovereignty, as well as three alternative trade strategy systems: Managed Trade, Fair Trade and Self-Reliant Trade.

These alternatives are not mutually exclusive, but I primarily identify with the Community-Sovereignty stream and advocate the concept of Self-Reliant Trade, arguing particularly, in Chapters 6 and 7, that this is more feasible than is generally realised. I have also sketched out, mainly in Chapter 8, the elements of an alternative world trading order which would be more compatible with Self-Reliant Trade and with alternative models of development than the one currently being constructed by the WTO. In Box 9.1 I briefly summarise the main arguments against Free Trade and globalisation touched upon throughout the book, though the list is by no means complete.

I have used the 'myth versus reality' device partly as an entertaining approach and partly because I genuinely believe that, after two centuries or more, Free Trade doctrine has accumulated many shibboleths worthy of critical scrutiny. I will not recount all the myths I claim to have identified, but two stand out.

First, at the theoretical level most zealous globalists believe that free trade brings a direct stream of guaranteed income increases for virtually all people in all countries at all times. But this is more myth than reality. The 'gains from trade' process is actually an indirect, contingent, swings-and-roundabouts mechanism which relies on many questionable assumptions and corollaries, proceeds through some complex redistribution channels, notably 'consumer surplus' and elimination of 'inefficiency triangles', then finishes with several forms of indirect 'dynamic gains' from trade. As a result, I argue that gains from trade are uncertain and contingent on many circumstances, especially when non-economic criteria are invoked, with overall losses possible, and countries may differ in their capacities to gain from trade. Even many mainstream economists, including some of the great theorists, admit that certain people and countries can lose, unless compensated; that net losses for a nation are possible; and that Free Trade doctrine is stronger in practice than theory. US economist Rachel McCulloch (1999) thus quips that the doctrine is more about religion than science!

Second, at the level of practice the actual value of these gains from trade are less clear cut than is usually claimed, many economists admitting that the 'static gains' from inefficiency reduction (see Figure 2.1) are very small in practice and that the longer-term 'dynamic gains' are very uncertain. The myth of trade as an 'engine of growth' does not wholly accord with the evidence, which suggests that self-reliant 'import-substitution' can often bring more, or at least adequate, growth (see Chapter 6); that free trade or general globalisation can induce undesirable forms of development, with many social costs (Chapter 5); and that the resultant structural change is usually non-consensual, or undemocratic.

Overall, I do not claim that Free Trade doctrine is 'in ruins', as some assert, but I do argue that it is fundamentally flawed in so far as it is less certain in theory and the benefits of trade more contingent in practice than Free Traders allow. I agree with most of the arguments against Free Trade in Box 9.1, but consider its greatest failing to be its tendency to induce non-consensual change in society, often with very high non-economic costs (Box 9.1, Group IV).

As an alternative, I do not advocate a return to very high protective barriers such as the 500 per cent tariffs or the like which some countries have used, for these can have their own costs. Nor do I agree with export subsidies as a form of trade intervention because these are designed to break into other countries' markets rather than truly protect one's own. I suggest that nations should have the right to permanent use of some protection, not just temporary 'infant industry' forms, and to self-reliant trading and development models for purposes of achieving democratically selected goals. I also propose that the prime goals for policymaking and development should not be narrow conventional ones such as growth, trade liberalisation, trade expansion or the like but broad social ones, preferably the groupings of goals I have referred to as social justice, environmental sustainability and cultural integrity. I have proposed some changes in the world trading system to reflect such goals, to allow wider participation in trade decision-making and to increase the autonomy of nations within a new, more cooperative order.

Throughout the book I make a crucial distinction between what I call 'integrative globalism' and 'cooperative internationalism'. Globalists often imply, unfairly in my view, that anti-globalists oppose most links between countries, while globo-euphorists attribute an endless array of 'good things' to globalisation, which is equally nonsense. My concern is with the degree of 'deep integration' between nations being pushed by world bodies and global fatalists, a degree which is well-nigh unprecedented in human history and has brought people onto the streets around the planet. I believe that this trend will in time have massive social costs and ignores what I call the Gandhian Propensity in human nature, which is a natural desire to preserve autonomy and traditions, or the philosophy of what I call 'adaptive traditionalism'.

By contrast, cooperative internationalism, as I see it, wants harmonious links between societies, seeks some degree of international policy linkages on key issues such as human rights and the environment, and encourages sociocultural contacts between peoples, but all of these in a way which preserves the political, social and cultural sovereignty of each society. Such an ideal is quite feasible, but would require changes to the present world order of the sort I have outlined in Chapter 8. People will stay in the streets until the world's global elites begin to take such ideas more seriously.

Box 9.1   Summary of arguments against Free Trade

The following is a brief descriptive list of arguments frequently used against Free Trade doctrine, against free trade policy or in favour of at least some trade intervention. It is not exhaustive but covers the main issues, most of which have been touched on in this book or in Dunkley (2000b: ch. 6). Free Traders tend to accept only Group I and III arguments, the more Fundamentalist of them accepting just a few, only No. 1 or none at all. Certain mainstream economists accept some more radical economic arguments (Group II) but seldom many radical non-economic cases (Group IV). Protectionists tend to accept most of these arguments, though usually emphasising a select number, in accordance with their particular views.

Group I: Orthodox economic arguments

1. Terms of trade (large country case): where a country is large enough to influence price levels, its demand may raise world prices against its own interests, and an 'optimum tariff' may prevent this.

2. Infant industry: assistance to new activities; only some Free Traders accept this, and then just temporarily.

3. Externalities: these are side benefits or costs of economic activity, especially environmental problems; Free Traders accept trade intervention only where the externalities cannot be adequately controlled domestically.

4. Second best: where the best option, say domestic policy action, is not possible, trade intervention is next best and may be superior to free trade in terms of income.

5. Anti-dumping: duties on below-cost imports; most Free Traders agree but worry about duties being misused.

6. Revenue raising: 'revenue tariffs' are now barely acceptable to most Free Traders, who claim that plenty of other revenue sources are available.

Group II: Radical economic arguments

7. Trade balancing: protection may rectify a deficit, although Free Traders prefer exchange rate adjustment.

8. Employment: Keynes revived the Mercantilist case that protection may balance trade, boost demand and create employment; Free Traders reject this as a 'beggar-thy-neighbour' policy which hurts other countries; it is more likely to work when there is pre-existing unemployment which trade liberalisation would worsen, but which orthodoxy assumes away.

9. Catch-up: a radical Listian version of No. 2 (above) to help laggards keep up with leading countries; Free Traders say this means 'picking winners' and can be bungled; I have doubts about the goals involved (Chapter 5).

10. Dynamic comparative advantage: as comparative advantage can be 'cumulated', or consciously shaped over time (Chapters 2–4), protection may help create new competitive sectors, higher value-added activities and so forth, thus generating higher income or growth than free trade.

11. Increasing returns: protection may generate more income than free trade where potential new industries enjoy increasing returns (economies of scale).

12. Learning-by-doing: likewise when experience or learning effects improve productivity over time in new industries.

13. Wage stimulus: likewise again when protection raises wages and attracts labour into higher-returns manufacturing industries from agriculture (the 'Australian case' – see Chapter 3).

14. ISI-led development: likewise again when an 'import-substitution' model accelerates development (see Chapter 6).

15. Strategic trade: the possibility of higher income or accelerated growth when a Managed Trade Protectionist policy gives local firms a chance to reap benefits from innovations, seize 'first mover' advantages in new sectors, or obtain a share of monopoly profits in imperfectly competitive sectors – i.e. so-called 'rent-snatching' (Chapter 3).

16. Terms of trade (commodity dependency case): a country may suffer if its export prices grow more slowly than its import prices, and protection may help to limit imports or diversify into higher-price, higher-value-added sectors.

17. Adjustment costs: free trade may be economically worse than

protection if imports create or exacerbate unemployment or if displaced workers can only get lower-wage jobs.

18. Cheap or exploited labour – protection may help countries prevent their living standards from being undermined by imports based on 'cheap' (low-wage) or 'exploited' (wages below productivity) labour; I regard the 'cheap' labour case as invalid but the latter as partly valid (Chapter 5).

19. Infant government: tariffs or quotas may be a crucial source of revenue for governments of countries where income or property taxes are poorly developed; Free Traders want these developed as soon as possible.

20. Special circumstances: some economists have noted particular circumstances where protection apparently generates more income than free trade, such as where elasticities are unfavourable, insurance or other markets are poorly developed and so forth (see Dunkley, 2000b: 115ff).

Group III: Orthodox non-economic arguments

21. Defence: protection may be required to build defence industries and forestall military dependence on other countries; some Free Traders are sceptical because wars don't stop all trade and many industries try to sneak under the defence umbrella.

22. Food security: protection may be needed to ensure reasonable self-reliance in basic food staples; Free Traders say that imports can provide equal security and greater variety, but governments and NGOs doubt this.

23. Retaliation: sanctions and 'countervailing duties' (which the WTO allows against subsidies) may be economically justified if they succeed in having the 'offending' measures repealed.

Group IV: Radical non-economic arguments

24. General self-reliance: widespread protection may be needed for this; some Free Traders regard it as a legitimate, if misguided, goal.

25. Social costs of adjustment: trade-induced structural change may bring many adjustment costs such as relocation expenses, family

disruption, reskilling requirements, redundancies and associated psychological costs.

26. Community and regional maintenance: likewise, structural adjustment may have devastating impacts on communities and regions dependent upon affected industries, especially rural areas.

27. Cultural integrity: full free trade may cause a wide range of cultural displacements or at least undesirable encroachments, especially in the audio-visual and other service sectors.

28. National sovereignty: free trade and globalisation by definition compromise national sovereignty in many spheres; multilateral agreements like GATT reduce the flexibility of nations to select the compromises they wish to make, and thus are based on an unstated principle which I call 'sovereignty suicide'.

29. Environment: trade can have adverse direct and indirect impacts on the environment, which free trade may exacerbate (Chapter 5; Dunkley, 1999).

30. Uneven impacts: free trade may have more adverse impacts on particular groups than others, particularly minorities and women (Chapter 5); Free Traders say this requires targeted assistance policies rather than protection, but these might not help if entire regions and lifestyles have been affected, as is often the case in traditional rural areas.

31. Industry balance: protection may be required to maintain desired proportions of various industries: e.g. excessive erosion of the agricultural population may distort the social and value structures of society.

32. Subsidiarity: a European principle which holds that decisions should be made at levels as close as possible to the people or institutions affected; free trade and globalisation can jeopardise this goal in many ways.

33. Priority to Locals: my term for the Buddhist and Gandhian principle that local needs and people should be served before those more distant, a notion which globalisation compromises.

34. Special Status of Services: the Free Traders' claim that services are functionally equivalent to goods and hence are 'liberalisable'

is arguably false (Chapter 8); free-trade rules can thus jeopardise a country's service traditions and expose public services to
foreign, privatising influences.

35. Non-consensual change: in my view one of the key arguments against Free Trade is that, along with technological
innovation and many development processes, it induces changes
undemocratically or non-consensually, with many attendant
social costs and tensions.

References

Aaronson, S., 1996, *Trade and the American Dream*, University Press of Kentucky, Lexington.

Ackerman, F. et al. (eds), 2000, *The Political Economy of Inequality*, Island Press, Washington DC.

Adams, R., 1974, 'Anthropological Perspectives on Ancient Trade', *Current Anthropology* 15(3), September.

Adams, W. and J. Brock, 1986, *The Bigness Complex*, Pantheon, New York.

Adelman, I. and C. Morris, 1971, *Society, Politics and Economic Development*, Johns Hopkins University Press, Baltimore MD.

Aga Khan, S. (ed.), 1998, *Policing the Global Economy*, Cameron May, London.

Akyüz, Y. and C. Gore, 2001, 'African Economic Development in Comparative Perspective', *Cambridge Journal of Economics* 25.

Alcorta, L., 1994, 'The Impact of New Technologies on Scale in Manufacturing Industry', *World Development* 22(5).

Amann, E., 2000, *Economic Liberalization and Industrial Performance in Brazil*, Oxford University Press, Oxford.

Amin, S., 1990, *Delinking*, trans. M. Wolfers, Zed Books, London.

Amsden, A., 1989, *Asia's Next Giant*, Oxford University Press, New York.

Anand, S. and M. Ravallion, 1993, 'Human Development in Poor Countries: On the Role of Private Incomes and Public Services', *Journal of Economic Perspectives* 7(1), Winter.

Andrews, K., 1984, *Trade, Plunder and Settlement*, Cambridge University Press, Cambridge.

Angell, N., 1911, *The Great Illusion*, Heinemann, London.

Apffel Marglin, F., 1997, 'Counter-development in the Andes', *The Ecologist*, November–December.

—— and S. Marglin (eds), 1999, *Dominating Knowledge*, Clarendon Press, Oxford.

Aquino, C., 1998, *Changing the Rules of the Game*, Philippine Peasant Institute, Briefing Paper V1/4, December.

Armstrong, W., 1995, *Around the World with a King* (1904), Mutual Publishing, Honolulu.

Arndt, H., 1963, *The Economic Lessons of the Nineteen Thirties*, Cass, London.

Arthur, B., 1994, *Increasing Returns and Path Dependence*, University Of Michigan Press, Ann Arbor.

Arthur, B., 1998, 'Increasing Returns and the New World of Business', in D. Neef (ed.), *The Knowledge Economy*, Heinemann, Boston.

Athukorala, P. and S. Rajapatirana, 2000, *Liberalization and Industrial Transformation: Sri Lanka in International Perspective*, Oxford University Press, New Delhi.

Ayittey, G., 1991, *Indigenous African Institutions*, Transaction, New York.

Bagachwa, M.S.D. and F. Stewart, 'Rural Industries and Rural Linkages in Sub-Saharan Africa: A Survey', in F. Stewart et al. (eds), *Alternative Development Strategies in Sub-Saharan Africa*, Macmillan, London.

Bairoch, P., 1972, 'Free Trade and European Economic Development in the 19th Century', *European Economic Review* 3.

——— 1993, *Economics and World History*, Harvester Wheatsheaf, New York.

Balassa, B. and Associates, 1982, *Development Strategies in Semi-Industrial Economies*, Johns Hopkins University Press, Baltimore MD.

Barlow, M., 2001, in *Ecologist* 30(1).

Barratt Brown, M., 1995, *Africa's Choices*, Penguin, Harmondsworth.

Barrett, C., 1998, 'Immiserized Growth in Liberalized Agriculture', *World Development* 26(5).

Baumol, W. et al., 1989, *Productivity and American Leadership*, MIT Press, Cambridge MA.

Bello, W. and S. Rosenfeld, 1990, *Dragons in Distress*, Food First, San Francisco.

Ben-David, D., et al., 2000, *Trade, Income Disparity and Poverty*, WTO, Geneva.

Bennholdt-Thomsen, V., et al. (eds), 2001, *There is an Alternative*, Zed Books, London.

Berry, R. and W. Cline, 1979, *Agrarian Structure and Productivity in Developing Countries*, Johns Hopkins University Press, Baltimore.

Bhagwati, J., 1958, 'Immiserising Growth: A Geometrical Note', *Review of Economic Studies* 25.

——— 1978, *Foreign Trade Regimes and Economic Development: Anatomy and Consequences of Exchange Control Regimes*, Ballinger Press, Cambridge MA.

——— 1994, 'Free Trade: Old and New Challenges', *Economic Journal* (March).

——— 1998, *A Stream of Windows*, MIT Press, Cambridge MA.

——— (ed.), 1969, *International Trade*, Penguin, Harmondsworth.

Biersteker, T., 1980, 'Foreign Enterprise and Forced Divestment in LDCs', *International Organization*, 34(2), Spring.

Birdsall, N. and C. Rhee, 1993, *Does Research and Development Contribute to Economic Growth in Developing Countries?*, World Bank Policy Research Working Paper, no. 1221, November.

Blackburn, R., 1997, *The Making of New World Slavery*, Verso, London.

Blaug, M., 1985, *Economic Theory in Retrospect*, 4th edn, Cambridge University Press, Cambridge.

Bleaney, M. and D. Greenaway, 1993, 'Long-run Trends in the Relative Price of Primary Commodities and in the Terms of Trade of Developing Countries', *Oxford Economic Papers* 45.

Bowie, A. and D. Unger, 1997, *The Politics of Open Economies*, Cambridge University Press, Cambridge.

Braithwaite, J. and P. Drahos, 2000, *Global Business Regulation*, Cambridge University Press, Cambridge.

Braudel, F., 1982, *The Wheels of Commerce*, Fontana, London, 1985.

—— 1984, *The Perspective of the World*, Fontana, London.

Breslin, S., 1999, 'The Politics of Chinese Trade and the Asian Financial Crisis: Questioning the Wisdom of Export-Led Growth', *Third World Quarterly* 20(6).

Broadberry, S., 1986, *The British Economy Between the Wars*, Blackwell, Oxford.

Brogan, P., 1998, *World Conflicts*, 3rd edn, Bloomsbury, London.

Brokensha, D. et al. (eds), 1980, *Indigenous Knowledge Systems and Development*, University Press of America, Lanham MD.

Brown, L., 2003, *Eco-Economy*, Earthscan, London.

Bruton, H., 1989, 'Import Substitution', in H. Chenery and T. Srinivasan (eds), *Handbook of Development Economics*, Vol. II, North Holland, Amsterdam.

Buffie, E., 2001, *Trade Policy in Developing Countries*, Cambridge University Press, Cambridge.

Burger, J., 1990, *The Gaia Atlas of First Peoples*, Gaia Books, London.

Buzaglo, J., 1984, *Planning the Mexican Economy*, Croom Helm, London.

Cain, P., 1982, 'Communications', *Explorations in Economic History* 19.

Capie, F. (ed.), 1992, *Protectionism in the World Economy*, Edward Elgar, Cheltenham.

Carey, H. (1967 [1851–2]) *The Harmony of Interests*, Augustus M. Kelley, New York

—— (1963 [1858]), *Principles of Social Sciences*, 3 vols, Augustus M. Kelley, New York.

Carr, M. (ed.), 1988, *Sustainable Industrial Development*, IT Publications, New York.

Chandra, N., 1997, 'Trade, Technology and Development', in D. Nayyar (ed.), *Trade and Industrialisation*, Oxford University Press, New Delhi.

Chang, H.-J., 2002, *Kicking Away the Ladder*, Anthem, London.

Chickering, A.L. and M. Salahdine (eds), 1991, *The Silent Revolution*, International Centre for Economic Growth, San Francisco.

Ching, Lim Li, 2002, 'Sustainable Agriculture is Productive', *Third World Resurgence* 143–4, July/August.

Chun, H.-T. and J. Park, 1997, 'The North Korean Economy: A Historical Assessment', in D.-S. Cha et al. (eds), *The Korean Economy 1945–1995*, Korean Development Institute, Seoul.

Clark, D., 1987, 'Trade and Industry in Barbarian Europe till Roman Times', in M. Postan and E. Miller (eds), *The Cambridge Economic History of Europe*, Vol. 2, Cambridge University Press, Cambridge.

Clark, R., and C. Kirkpatrick, 1992, 'Trade Policy Reform and Economic

Performance in Developing Countries', in R. Adhikari et al. (eds), *Industrial and Trade Policy Reform in Developing Countries*, Manchester University Press, Manchester.

Clerides, S. et al., 1998, 'Is Learning by Exporting Important?', *Quarterly Journal of Economics*, August.

Cobb, C. and J. Cobb, 1994, *The Green National Product*, University Press of America, Lanham.

Cobden, R., 1995, *Speeches on Questions of Public Policy*, Vol. 1, Routledge, London.

Corden, M., 1994, *Economic Policy, Exchange Rates and the International System*, Oxford University Press, Oxford.

Cornia, G., 1994, 'Neglected Issues in the Decline of Africa's Agriculture', in G. Cornia and G. Helleiner (eds), *From Adjustment to Development in Africa*, St Martin's Press, New York.

Cowen, M. and R. Shenton, 1996, *Doctrines of Development*, Routledge, London.

Cracknell, B., 1992, 'New Wine in Old Bottles', in R. Adhikari et al. (eds), *Industrial and Trade Policy Reform in Developing Countries*, Manchester University Press, Manchester.

Crouzet, F., 1964, 'Wars, Blockade, and Economic Change in Europe, 1792–1815', *Journal of Economic History* 24.

——— 1980, in *Explorations in Economic History* 17.

Crystal, D., 2000, *Language Death*, Cambridge University Press, Cambridge.

Cunningham, W., 1914, *The Case Against Free Trade*, John Murray, London.

Curtis, M., 2001, *Trade for Life*, Christian Aid, London.

Currie, J. et al., 1971, 'The Concept of Economic Surplus and its Use in Economic Analysis', *Economic Journal*, December.

Daly, H., 1996, *Beyond Growth*, Beacon Press, Boston.

——— and J. Cobb, 1994, *For the Common Good*, Beacon Press, Boston.

Danaher, K. and R. Burbach (eds), 2000, *Globalize This!*, Common Courage Press, Monroe ME.

Daniels, P., 1999, in *Cambridge Journal of Economics* 23.

Davis, S. and W. Partridge, 1994, 'Promoting the Development of Indigenous People in Latin America', *Finance and Development*, March.

DeLancey, V., 1986, 'Cameroon Agricultural Policy: The Struggle to Remain Self-Sufficient', in M. Tetréault and C. Abel (eds), *Dependency Theory and the Return of High Politics*, Greenwood, New York.

Demaziere, C. and P. Wilson (eds), 1995, *Local Economic Development in Europe and the Americas*, Mansell, London.

Denny, C., 2000, in *Guardian Weekly*, 21–27 September.

Destler, I. and J. Odell, 1987, *Anti-Protection*, Institute for International Economics, Washington.

Diamond, S. (ed.), 1964, *Primitive Views of the World*, Columbia University Press, New York.

Dillon, S., 1999, 'Fuji–Kodak, the WTO and to the Death of Domestic Political Constituencies', *Minnesota Journal of Global Trade* 8(2), Summer.

Dixit, A. and V. Norman, 1980, *Theory of International Trade*, Cambridge University Press, Cambridge.

Dixon, R., 1997, *The Rise of Languages*, Cambridge University Press, Cambridge.

Dluhosch, B. et al., 1996, *International Competitiveness and the Balance of Payments*, Edward Elgar, Cheltenham.

Dodaro, S., 1991, 'Comparative Advantage, Trade and Growth: Export-Led Growth Revisited', *World Development* 19(9).

Doughney, J., 2002, *The Poker Machine State*, Common Ground, Melbourne.

Douthwaite, R., 1996, *Short Circuit*, Resurgence, Dartington.

Dove, M. (ed.), 1988, *The Real and Imagined Role of Culture in Development*, University of Hawaii Press, Honolulu.

Dowrick, S., 1994, 'Openness and Growth', in P. Lowe and J. Dwyer (eds), *International Integration of the Australian Economy*, Reserve Bank of Australia, Sydney.

———— 1997 'Trade and Growth: A Survey', in J. Fagerberg et al. (eds), *Technology and International Trade*, Edward Elgar, Cheltenham.

Drescher, S. and S. Engerman (eds), 1998, *A Historical Guide to World Slavery*, Oxford University Press, New York.

Drèze, J. and A. Sen, 1989, *Hunger and Public Action*, Clarendon, Oxford.

———— 1995, *India: Economic Development and Social Opportunity*, Oxford University Press, New Delhi.

Dumont, R., 1988 [1962], *False Start in Africa*, Earthscan, London.

Duncan, C. and D. Tandy (eds), 1994, *From Political Economy to Anthropology*, Black Rose Books, Montreal.

Dunkley, G., 1992, *The Greening of the Red*, Pluto, Sydney.

———— 1993, *People for Change*, VUT and CAA, Melbourne.

———— 1995, 'Is There a Case for Import Controls?', *Journal of Economic and Social Policy* 1(1), Summer.

———— 1996, *Belaboured Playing Fields*, 1st CITER Conference, APEC Studies Centre, Melbourne.

———— 1999, *Greening Trade or Trading the Green*, 4th CITER Conference, APEC Studies Centre, Melbourne.

———— 2000a, *INGOs, LINGOs, DINGOs and TRINGOs: Trade the WTO and the Interest of Civil Society*, 5th CITER Conference, APEC Studies Centre, Melbourne. www.apec.org.au.

———— 2000b, *The Free Trade Adventure*, Zed Books, London; 1st edn, Melbourne University Press, Melbourne, 1997.

Edelman, M. and R. Oviedo 1993, 'Costa Rica: The Non-Market Roots of Market Success', *Report on the Americas* 26(4), February.

Edwards, S., 1998, 'Openness, Productivity and Growth: What Do We Really Know?', *Economic Journal* 108, March.

Ellis, F., 1988, *Peasant Economics*, Cambridge University Press, Cambridge.

Elvin, M., 1973, *The Pattern of the Chinese Past*, Stanford University Press, Stanford.

Emmerij, L., 2000, 'Current Economic and Financial Policies and their Social

Consequences', in M. Metzger and B. Reichenstein (eds), *Challenges for International Organizations in the 21st Century*, Macmillan, London.

Evans, H.D., 1989, *Comparative Advantage and Trade*, St Martin's Press, New York.

Fabayo, J. et al., 1994, in *Scandinavian Journal of Development Economics*, March/June.

Fagerberg, J. 1988, 'International Competitiveness', *Economic Journal* 98, June.

Ffrench-Davis, R. et al., 1993, 'Trade Liberalization and Growth: The Chilean Experience, 1973–89', in M. Agosin and D. Tussie (eds), *Trade and Growth*, St Martin's Press, New York.

Fielden, 1992, in F. Capie (ed.), 1992, *Protectionism in the World Economy*, Edward Elgar, Cheltenham.

Fieldhouse, D., 1999, *The West and the Third World*, Blackwell, Oxford.

Figes, O., 1996, *A People's Tragedy*, Pimlico, London.

Finley, M.I., 1999, *The Ancient Economy* (1973), University of California Press, Berkeley.

Fontaine, J.-M. (ed.), 1992, *Foreign Trade Reforms and Development Strategy*, Routledge, London.

Foreman-Peck, J., 1979, 'Tariff Protection and Economies of Scale', *Oxford Economic Papers* 31(2), July.

Forster, P. and S. Maghimbi (eds), 1995, *The Tanzanian Peasantry*, Avebury, Aldershot.

Foster, G., 1973, *Traditional Societies and Technological Change*, Harper & Row, New York.

Francis, D., 1994, *Family Agriculture*, Earthscan, London.

Frank, A.G., 1998, *Re-Orient*, University of California Press, Berkeley.

Freeman, C., 1998, 'The Economics of Technical Change', in D. Archibugi and J. Michie (eds), *Technology, Globalisation and Economic Performance*, Cambridge University Press, Cambridge.

Frey, B. and A. Stutzer, 2000, 'Happiness, Economy and Institutions', *Economic Journal* 110, October.

Friedman, T., 1999, *The Lexus and the Olive Tree*, HarperCollins, London.

Funes, F. et al. (eds), 2002, *Sustainable Agriculture and Resistance*, Food First, Oakland.

Galbraith, J. and M. Berner, (eds), 2001, *Inequality and Industrial Change*, Cambridge University Press, Cambridge.

Galtung, J. et al. (eds), 1990, *Self-Reliance*, Bogle-L'Ouverture, London.

Ganuza, E., L. Taylor and R. Vos (eds), 2000, *External Liberalisation and Economic Performance in Latin America and the Caribbean*, UNDP, New York.

Gandhi, M.K., *The Collected Works of Mahatma Gandhi (CW)*, Ministry of Information and Broadcasting, New Delhi (100 Vols).

——— 1962, *Village Swaraj*, ed. H. Vyas, Navajvan, Ahmedabad.

Garnsey, P. et al. (eds), 1983, *Trade in the Ancient Economy*, Chatto & Windus, London.

Gates, B., 1996, *The Road Ahead*, Penguin, Harmondsworth.

Gelernter, D., 2001, 'Computers and the Pursuit of Happiness', *Commentary*,

January.

Gerefi, G. and M. Korzeniewicz (eds), 1994, *Commodity Chains and Global Capitalism*, Praeger, London.

Gimpel, J., 1994, *The End of the Future*, Adamantine, London.

Gittleman, M.B. and E.N. Wolff, 1995, 'R&D Activity and Cross-Country Growth Comparisons', *Cambridge Journal of Economics* 19.

Gomes, L., 1987, *Foreign Trade and the National Economy*, Macmillan, London.

Gomory, R. and W. Baumol, 2000, *Global Trade and Conflicting National Interests*, MIT Press, Cambridge MA.

Goodman, E. et al. (eds), 1989, *Small Firms and Industrial Districts in Italy*, Routledge, London.

Grampp, D., 1987, 'Peace and Trade: The Classical vs. the Marxian View', in H. Visser and E. Schoorl (eds), *Trade in Transit*, Kluwer, Dordrecht.

Granto, J., et al. 1996, 'The Effect of Cultural Values on Economic Development', *American Journal of Political Science* 40(3), August.

Green, D., 1995, 'Flexibility and Repression', in F. Rosen and D. McFadyen (eds), *Free Trade and Economic Restructuring in Latin America*, Monthly Review Press, New York.

Greenaway, D. and D. Sapsford, 1994, 'What Does Liberalisation Do for Exports and Growth', *Weltwirtschaftliches Archiv* 130(1).

Griffin, K., 1999, *Alternative Strategies for Economic Development*, 2nd edn, Macmillan, London.

Grossman, G. (ed.), 1992, *Imperfect Competition and International Trade*, MIT Press, Cambridge MA.

Group of Lisbon, 1995, *Limits to Competition*, MIT Press, Cambridge MA.

Hahn, F., 1982, 'Reflections on the Invisible Hand', *Lloyds Bank Review* 144, April.

——— 1998, 'Reconsidering Free Trade', in G. Cook (ed.), *The Economics and Politics of International Trade*, Routledge, London.

Hancock, G., 1989, *Lords of Poverty*, Atlantic Monthly Press, New York.

Hansson, G. (ed.), 1993, *Trade, Growth and Development*, Routledge, London.

Harrison, A. and G. Hanson, 1999, 'Who Gains from Trade Reform? Some Remaining Puzzles', *Journal of Development Economics* 59.

Hayami, Y. (ed.), 1998, *Toward the Rural-Based Development of Commerce and Industry*, World Bank, Washington.

Healy, J., 1990, *Endangered Minds*, Touchstone, New York.

Held, D. et al. (eds), 1999, *Global Transformations*, Polity, Cambridge.

Helleiner, G., 1972, *International Trade and Economic Development*, Penguin, Harmondsworth.

——— 1986, 'Outward Orientation, Import Instability and African Economic Growth: An Empirical Investigation', in S. Lall and F. Stewart (eds), *Theory and Reality in Development: Essays in Honour of Paul Streeten*, Macmillan, London.

——— (ed.), 1994, *Trade Policy and Industrialisation in Turbulent Times*, Routledge, London.

Herskovits, M., 1952, *Economic Anthropology*, Knopf, New York.

Hertz, N., *The Silent Takeover*, Arrow, London, 2002.

Hines, C., 2000, *Localisation*, Earthscan, London

Hirst, F. (ed.), 1903, *Free Trade and Other Fundamental Doctrines of the Manchester School*, Harper, London.

Hirschman, A., 1945, *National Power and the Structure of Foreign Trade*, University of California Press, Berkeley, 1969.

――― 1977, *The Passions and the Interests*, Princeton University Press, Princeton.

Hoff, K. and J. Stiglitz, 2001, 'Modern Economic Theory and Development', in G. Meier and J. Stiglitz (eds), *Frontiers of Development*, Oxford University Press, New York.

Holtfrerich, C.-L., 1989, *Interactions in the World Economy*, Harvester Wheatsheaf, New York.

Howe, C., 1996, *The Origins of Japanese Trade Supremacy*, Crawford House, Bathurst.

Hudson, M., 1992, *Trade, Development and Foreign Debt*, Pluto, London.

Hwang, E.-G., 1993, *The Korean Economies*, Clarendon Press, Oxford.

ILO/WEP, 1984, *Improved Village Technology for Women's Activities*, ILO and WEP, Geneva.

International Centre for Trade and Sustainable Development (ICTSD), *Bridges Between Trade and Sustainable Development (Bridges)*, Bi-monthly.

Inglehart, R., 2000, 'Globalization and Postmodern Values', *The Washington Quarterly*, Winter 2000.

IPCC, 1996, *Climate Change 1995*, Cambridge University Press, Cambridge.

Irwin, D., 1991a, 'Mercantilism as Strategic Trade Policy', *Journal of Political Economy* 99(6).

Irwin, D., 1991b, 'Was Britain Immiserised During the Industrial Revolution?', *Explorations in Economic History* 28.

――― 1996, *Against the Tide*, Princeton University Press, Princeton.

――― 1998, 'The Smoot–Hawley Tariff: A Quantitative Assessment', *Review of Economics and Statistics* 80.

James, J., 1986, 'Bureaucratic Engineering and Economic Men: Decision-making for Technology in Tanzania's State-owned Enterprises', in S. Lall and F. Stewart (eds), *Theory and Reality in Development: Essays in Honour of Paul Streeten*, Macmillan, London.

Jamison, A., 2000, 'Globalisation and the Revival of Traditional Knowledge', in J. Schmidt and J. Hersh (eds), *Globalization and Social Change*, Routledge, London.

Johnson, A. and T. Earle, 1987, *The Evolution of Human Societies*, Stanford University Press, Stanford.

Joy, B., 2000, 'Why the World Does Not Need Us', *Wired*, April.

Judd, D., 1996, *Empire*, Harper Collins, London.

Kaino, L. (ed.), 1995, *The Necessity of Craft*, University of Western Australia Press, Perth.

Kaldor, N., 1978, *Further Essays on Applied Economics*, Duckworth, London.

――― 1989, *The Essential Kaldor*, ed. F. Targetti and A. Thirlwall, Duckworth,

London.

Kaplinsky, R., 1991, 'Industrialization in Botswana', in C. Colclough and J. Manor (eds), *States or Markets*, Clarendon, Oxford.

──── 2001, 'Globalisation and Unequalisation', in O. Morrissey and I. Filatotchev (eds), *Globalisation and Trade*, Cass, London.

Kavoussi, R., 1985, 'International Trade and Economic Development', *Journal of Developing Areas* 19, April.

Keen, S., 2001, *Debunking Economics*, Zed Books, London.

Kenny, C., 1999, 'Does Growth Cause Happiness, or Does Happiness Cause Growth?', *Kyklos* 52(1).

──── and D. Williams, 2001, 'What Do We Know About Economic Growth?', *World Development* 29(1).

Kerr, C. et al., 1971, *Industrialism and Industrial Man*, Penguin, London.

Keynes, J.M., 1931 [1930], 'Economic Possibilities for our Grandchildren', in J.M. Keynes, *Essays in Persuasion*, Macmillan, London.

──── 1933, 'National Self-Sufficiency', *New Statesman*, 8 and 15 July.

──── 1936, *The General Theory of Employment Interest and Money*, Macmillan, London, 1967.

Khan, H. and E. Thorbecke, 1988, *Macroeconomic Effects and Diffusion of Alternative Technologies within a Social Accounting Matrix Framework*, Gower, Aldershot.

Kindleberger, 1992, 'The Rise of Free Trade in Western Europe, 1820–1875', in F. Capie (ed.), *Protectionism in the World Economy*, Edward Elgar, Cheltenham.

King, J., 1988, *Economic Exiles*, Macmillan, London.

──── 2002, *A History of Post Keynesian Economics Since 1936*, Edward Elgar, Cheltenham.

──── (ed.) 2003, *The Elgar Companion to Post Keynesian Economics*, Edward Elgar, Cheltenham,

Kitson, M. and J. Michie, 2000, *The Political Economy of Competitiveness*, Routledge, London.

──── and S. Solomou, 1990, *Protectionism and Economic Revival*, Cambridge University Press, Cambridge.

Klein, H., 1999, *The Atlantic Slave Trade*, Cambridge University Press, Cambridge.

Kofman, J., 1997, *Economic Nationalism and Development*, Westview, Boulder.

Koot, G., 1987, *English Historical Economics 1870–1926*, Cambridge University Press, New York.

Kravis, I., 1970, 'Trade as a Handmaiden of Growth', *Economic Journal*, December.

Krueger, A.O., 1974, 'The Political Economy of the Rent-Seeking Society', *American Economic Review* 64(3), June.

Krueger, A., 1978 *Foreign Trade Regimes and Economic Development: Liberalization Attempts and Consequences*, Ballinger Press, Cambridge MA.

──── 1997, 'Trade Policy and Economic Development: How We Learn', *American Economic Review* 87(1), March.

Krugman, P., 1987, 'Is Free Trade Passé?', *Economic Perspectives* 1(2), Fall.

——— 1991, *Geography and Trade*, MIT, Cambridge MA.

——— 1994, *Rethinking International Trade*, MIT Press, Cambridge, MA.

——— 1995, 'Growing World Trade: Causes and Consequences', *Brookings Papers on Economic Activity* 1.

——— 1998, *Pop Internationalism*, MIT Press, Cambridge MA.

——— 1999, 'The Narrow and Broad Arguments for Free Trade', in T. Brewer (ed.), *Trade and Investment Policy*, Vol. 1, Edward Elgar, Cheltenham.

——— and Obstfeld, 1994, *International Economics*, 3rd edn, Harper Collins, New York.

Kumar, N. and N. Siddharthan, 1997, *Technology, Market Structure and Internationalisation*, Routledge, London.

Lall, S., 1996, *Learning from the Asian Tigers*, Macmillan, London.

Lane, R., 2000, *The Loss of Happiness in Market Democracies*, Yale University Press, New Haven.

Lea, D.A.M. and D.P. Chaudhri, 1983, *Rural Development and the State, Contradictions and Dilemmas in Developing Countries*, Methuen, London and New York.

Legrain, P., 2002, *Open World*, Abacus, London.

Lerner, D., 1958, *The Passing of Traditional Society*, Free Press, New York.

Levine, R. and D. Renelt, 'A Sensitivity Analysis of Cross-Country Growth Regressions', *American Economic Review* 82(4), September.

List, F., 1841, *The National System of Political Economy*, Augustus M. Kelley, New York, 1966.

Little, I. et al., 1970, *Industry and Trade in Some Developing Countries*, Oxford University Press, London.

Liu, Jin-Tan, 1999, 'Export Activity and Productivity: Evidence from the Taiwan Electronics Industry', *Weltwirtschaftliches Archiv* 135(4).

Lockwood, M. and P. Madden, 1997, *Closer Together: Further Apart*, Christian Aid, London.

Lovins, A. et al., 2003, *Small is Profitable*, Earthscan, London.

Lutz, M., 1999, *Economics for the Common Good*, Routledge, London.

MacAndrews, C. and L.S. Chia (eds), 1982, *Too Rapid Rural Development*, Ohio University Press, Athens OH.

McAfee, K. (ed.), 1991, *Storm Signals*, South End Press, Boston.

McCloskey, D., 1992, 'Magnanimous Albion: Free Trade and British National Income, 1841–1881', in F. Capie (ed.), *Protectionism in the World Economy*, Edward Elgar, Cheltenham.

McCulloch, R., 1999, 'The Optimality of Free Trade: Science or Religion', in T. Brewer (ed.), *Trade and Investment Policy*, Vol. 1, Edward Elgar, Cheltenham.

Maddison, A., 1994, 'Explaining the Economic Performance of Nations, 1820–1989', in W. Baumol et al. (eds), *Convergence of Productivity*, Oxford University Press, Oxford.

——— 1995, *Monitoring the World Economy 1820–1992*, OECD, Paris.

Madeley, J., 2002, *Food for All*, Zed Books, London.

Malinowski, B., 1921, 'The Primitive Economies of the Trobriand Islanders', *Economic Journal* 31.

Maneschi, A., 1998, *Comparative Advantage in International Trade*, Edward Elgar, Cheltenham.

Mansfield, E., 1994, *Power, Trade and War*, Princeton University Press, Princeton.

Marin, D., 1989, in D. Audretsch et al. (eds), *The Convergence of International and Domestic Markets*, North-Holland, Amsterdam.

Mariti, P., 1993, in M. Humbert (ed.), *The Impact of Globalisation on Europe's Firms and Industries*, Pinter, London.

Marshall, A., 1920, *Principles of Economics*, 8th edn, Macmillan, London.

——— 1923, *Industry and Trade*, Macmillan, London.

Marshedi, M. and E. Setty, 1988, *Small-Scale Cottage Industries in Bangladesh*, Asian Institute of Technology, Bangkok.

Marx, K., 1967 [1867], *Capital*, International Publishers, New York.

——— and F. Engels, 1967, *The Communist Manifesto*, Penguin, London.

Mehmet, O., 1995, *Westernizing the Third World*, Routledge, London.

Mehrotra, S. and R. Jolly (eds), 1997, *Development with a Human Face: Experiences in Social Achievement and Economic Growth*, Clarendon Press, Oxford.

de Mello, L., et al., 1999, 'Computable General Equilibrium Models, Adjustment and the Poor in Africa', *World Development* 27(3).

Mellor, J., 1986, 'Agriculture on the Road to Industrialisation', in J. Lewis and V. Kallab (eds), *Development Strategies Reconsidered*, Transaction Books, New Brunswick.

Michaely, M., 1977, 'Exports and Growth: An Empirical Investigation', *Journal of Development Economics* 4(1), March.

——— 1984, *Trade, Income Levels and Dependence*, North Holland, Amsterdam.

Mies, M. and V. Bennholdt-Thomsen, 1999, *The Subsistence Perspective*, Zed Books, London.

Milanovic, B., 2002, 'True World Income Distribution, 1988 and 1993', *Economic Journal*, January.

Mill, J.S., 1848, *Principles of Political Economy*, ed. D. Winch, Penguin, Harmondsworth, 1970.

Mokhiber, R. and R. Weissman, 1999a, '10 Reasons to Dismantle the WTO', 23 November, http://lists.essential.org/corp-focus.

——— 1999b, 26 October, http://lists.essential.org/corp-focus.

Monbiot, G., 2000, *The Captive State*, Pan, London.

Mosley, P., 2000, 'Globalisation, Economic Policy and Convergence', *The World Economy* 23(5) May.

Muller, J., 1993, *Adam Smith in His Time and Ours*, Princeton University Press, Princeton.

Murphy, S., 1990, *Why Gandhi is Relevant in Modern India*, Gandhi Peace Foundation, New Delhi.

Musson, A.E., 1992, 'The Manchester School and Exportation of Machinery', F. Capie (ed.), *Protectionism in the World Economy*, Edward Elgar, Cheltenham.

Mytelka, L., 1983, 'The Limits of Export-Led Development', in J. Ruggie (ed.), *The Antinomies of Interdependence*, Columbia University Press, New

York.

Ndlovu, L., 1994, *The System of Protection and Industrial Development in Zimbabwe*, Avebury, Aldershot.

Nell, E., 1998, *The General Theory of Transformational* Growth, Cambridge University Press, Cambridge.

Nettle, D. and S. Romaine, 2000, *Vanishing Voices*, Oxford University Press, Oxford.

Nisbet, R., 1969, *Social Change and History*, Oxford University Press, New York.

Norberg-Hodge, H., 1991, *Ancient Futures*, Rider, London.

Ocampo, J. and L. Taylor, 1998, 'Trade Liberalisation in Developing Economies', *Economic Journal* 108, September.

Olaniyan, R., 1996, *Foreign Aid, Self-Reliance and Economic Development in West Africa*, Praeger, Westport.

Olson, M. and C. Harris, 1959, 'Free Trade in "Corn"', *Quarterly Journal of Economics* 73.

O'Rourke, K., 2000, 'Tariffs and Growth in the Late 19th Century', *Economic Journal* 110, April.

—— and J. Williamson, 1999, *Globalization and History*, MIT Press, Cambridge MA.

Oxfam, 2002, *Rigged Rules and Double Standards*, Oxfam, Oxford.

Papageorgiou, D., M. Michaely and A. Choksi (eds), 1991, *Liberalizing Foreign Trade*, 7 vols, Blackwell, Oxford.

Park, Jim-Do, 1992, 'Export-led Industrialisation and the Crisis of Korean Agriculture', in T. Iwasaki et al. (eds), *Development Strategies for the 21st Century*, Institute of Development Economics, Tokyo.

Peake, G. (ed.), 1995, *The Penguin Dictionary of Ancient History*, Penguin, Harmondsworth.

Pearce, J., 2001, *Small is Still Beautiful*, Harper Collins, London.

Pedersen, P. et al. (eds), 1994, *Flexible Specialisation*, IT Publications, London.

Peters, E., 1996, 'From Export-Oriented to Import-Oriented Industrialization', in G. Otero (ed.), *Neoliberalism Revisited*, Westview, Boulder CO.

Pietilä, H., 1997, 'The Triangle of the Human Economy', *Ecological Economics* 20.

Piore, M.J., and C.F. Sabel, 1984, *The Second Industrial Divide*, Basic Books, New York.

Polanyi, K., 1957 [1944], *The Great Transformation*, Beacon Press, Boston.

—— 1977, *The Livelihood of Man*, ed. H. Pearson, Academic Press, New York.

—— et al. (eds), 1957, *Trade and Market in the Early Empires*, Free Press, Glencoe IL.

Poirine, B., 1993, *Three Essays from French Polynesia*, Centre for South Pacific Studies, University of New South Wales, Sydney.

Pool, R., 1997, *Beyond Engineering*, Oxford University Press, New York.

Prasch, R., 1996, 'Reassessing the Theory of Comparative Advantage', *Review of Political Economy* 8(1).

Pratten, C., 1991, *The Competitiveness of Small Firms*, Cambridge University Press, Cambridge.

Pretty, J., 1995, *Regenerating Agriculture*, Earthscan, London.

Preville, C., 1999, *How Will Free Trade Impact on Net Global Economic Welfare?*, Institute of Social Studies, The Hague, June.

Pritchett, L., 1992, 'Measuring Outward Orientation in the LDCs: Can it be Done?', *Journal of Development Economics* 49, 1996.

——— 1997, 'Divergence, Big Time', *Journal of Economic Perspectives*, Summer.

Progler, Y., 2001, in *Third World Resurgence* 112–113, January.

Pryor, F., 2000, 'Internationalization and Globalization of the American Economy', in T. Brewer et al. (eds), *Globalizing America*, Edward Elgar, Cheltenham.

Puttnam, D., 1997, *The Undeclared War*, HarperCollins, London.

Pyke, F. and W. Sengenberger (eds), *Industrial Districts and Local Economic Regeneration*, International Institute for Labour Studies, Geneva, 1998.

Raghavan, C., 2002, *Developing Countries and Services Trade*, Third World Network, Penang.

Rahnema, M. and V. Bawtree (eds), 1997, *The Post-Development Reader*, Zed Books, London.

Rajan, V. (ed.), 1993, *Rebuilding Communities: Experiences and Experiments in Europe*, Resurgence, Totnes.

Rambo, A.T., 1982, 'Malaysia', in C. MacAndrews and L.S. Chia (eds), *Too Rapid Rural Development*, Ohio University Press, Athens OH.

Ramirez, F. (ed.), 1988, *Rethinking the Ninteenth Century*, Greenwood Press, New York.

Ransom, D., 2001, 'Fair Trade', *New Internationalist* 334, May.

Rattso, J. and R. Torvik, 1998, 'Zimbabwean Trade Liberalisation: Ex Post Evaluation', *Cambridge Journal of Economics* 22.

Reese, D., 1998, *The Prospects for North Korea's Survival*, Oxford University Press, Oxford.

Ricardo, D., 1971 [1817], *Principles of Political Economy and Taxation*, ed. R.M. Hartwell, Penguin, Harmondsworth.

Richards, P., 1985, *Indigenous Agricultural Revolution*, Hutchinson, London.

Riddell, R. (ed.), 1990, *Manufacturing Africa*, James Currey, London.

Riedel, J., 1984, 'Trade as the Engine of Growth in Developing Countries, Revisited', *Economic Journal* 94, March.

Rist, G., 1997, *The History of Development*, Zed Books, London.

Robinson, J., 1962, *Economic Philosophy*, Penguin.

Robinson, R. and J. Gallagher, 1967, *Africa and the Victorians*, Macmillan, London.

Rock, M., 1995, 'Thai Industry Policy: How Irrelevant Was it to Export Success?', *Journal of International Development* 7(5)

——— 1999, 'Reassessing the Effectiveness of Industrial Policy in Indonesia: Can the Neoliberals be Wrong?', *World Development* 27(4).

Rodriguez, F. and D. Rodrik, 1999, *Trade Policy and Economic Growth: A Sceptic Guide to the Cross-National Evidence*, National Bureau of Economic

Research, Cambridge MA.

Rodrik, D., 1995, 'Getting Interventions Right: How South Korea and Taiwan Grew Rich', *Economic Policy* 20, April.

——— 1999a, *The New Global Economy and Developing Countries*, Policy Essay No. 24, Overseas Development Council, Washington DC.

——— 1999b, 'Where Did All the Growth Go?', *Journal of Economic Growth* 4.

——— 2001, 'Trading in Illusions', *Foreign Policy*, March/April.

Rosecrance, R., 1986, *The Rise of the Trading State*, Basic Books, New York.

Rosset, P., 1999, in *The Ecologist*, December.

——— and M. Benjamin, 1994, *The Greening of the Revolution*, Ocean Press, Melbourne.

Rowthorn, R. and J. Wells, 1987, *De-Industrialisation and Foreign Trade*, Cambridge University Press, Cambridge.

Rubner, A., 1987, *The Export Cult*, Gower, Aldershot.

Rugman, A., 2000, *The End of Globalization*, Random House, London.

Sabel, C. and J. Zeitlin (eds), 1997, *World of Possibilities*, Cambridge University Press, Cambridge.

Sahlins, M., 1974, *Stone Age Economics*, Tavistock, London.

Sahu, S., 1998, *Technology Transfer, Dependence and Self-Reliance in the Third World*, Praeger, Westport.

Samatar, A., 1999, *An African Miracle*, Heinemann, Portsmouth.

Samuelson, P., 1974, *Foundations of Economic Analysis*, Atheneum, New York.

——— 1996, 'Trade Theory and the Problem of Unemployment', in R. Hinshaw (ed.), *The World Economy in Transition*, Edward Elgar, Cheltenham.

——— 1999, 'A Coming Erosion of Advanced Nations' Well-Being from World Trade?', in R. Sato et al. (eds), *Global Competition and Integration*, Kluwer, Boston.

Sayigh, Y., 1991, *Elusive Development*, Routledge, London.

Schmitz, H., 1999, 'Collective Efficiency and Increasing Returns', *Cambridge Journal of Economics* 23.

Schneider, C. 1993, 'Chile: The Underside of the Miracle', *Report on the Americas* 26(4), February.

Schumacher, E.F., 1973, *Small is Beautiful*, Abacus, London, 1974.

Seavoy, R., 2000, *Subsistence and Economic Development*, Praeger, Westport.

Sediri, S., 1970, *Trade and Power*, Rotterdam University Press, Rotterdam.

Sen, A., 1983, 'Development: Which Way Now?', *Economic Journal*, December.

——— 1999, *Development as Freedom*, Oxford University Press, Oxford.

Senghaas, D., 1985, *The European Experience*, Berg, Leamington Spa.

Shapiro, H., and L. Taylor, 1990, 'The State and Industrial Strategy', *World Development* 18(6).

Shiva, V. 2000, in *The Ecologist*, September.

Shuman, M., 1998, *Going Local*, Free Press, New York.

Silberberg, E., 1972, 'Duality and the Many Consumer's Surpluses', *American Economic Review* 62.

Simkin, C.G.F., 1968, *The Traditional Trade of Asia*, Oxford University Press, London.

Singer, H. and P. Alizadeh, 1988, 'Import Substitution Revisited in a Darkening External Environment', in S. Dell (ed.), *Policies for Development*, Macmillan, London.

Skinner, E., 1996, 'Traditional Institutions and Economic Development: The Mossi Naam', in A.Yansane (ed.), *Development Strategies in Africa*, Greenwood Press, Westport CT.

Smith, A., 1776, *The Wealth of Nations*, ed. E. Cannan, 2 vols, Methuen, London.

Smith, J., 2002, in *The Ecologist*, April.

de Soto, H., 1989, *The Other Path*, Harper and Row, New York.

Sridharan, E., 1996, *The Political Economy of Industrial Promotion*, Praeger, Westport.

Srinivasan, T. and J. Bhagwati, 2001, 'Outward-Orientation and Development: Are Revisionists Right?', in D. Lal and R. Snape (eds), *Trade, Development and Political Economy*, Palgrave, London.

Steedman, I. (ed.), 1979, *Fundamental Issues in Trade Theory*, St Martin's Press, New York.

Stein, H., 1994, 'The World Bank and the Application of Asian Industrial Policy to Africa: Theoretical Considerations', *Journal of International Development* 6(3).

Steven, M., 1983, *Trade, Tactics and Territory*, Melbourne University Press, Melbourne.

Stewart, F., 1978, *Technology and Underdevelopment*, Macmillan, London.

────── et al. (eds), 1992, *Alternative Development Strategies in Sub-Saharan Africa*, Macmillan, London.

────── 1995, *Adjustment and Poverty*, Routledge, London.

Streeten, P., 1982, 'A Cool Look at "Outward-Looking" Strategies for Development', *The World Economy* 5(1).

──────, 2001, *Globalisation: Threat or Opportunity?*, Copenhagen Business School Press, Copenhagen.

────── 1990, 'Comparative Advantage and Free Trade', in A. Khan and R. Sobhan (eds), *Trade, Planning and Rural Development*, Macmillan, London.

────── 1996, 'Free and Managed Trade', in S. Berger and R. Dore (eds), *National Diversity and Global Capitalism*, Cornell University Press, Ithaca.

────── 1998, 'Globalization: Threat or Salvation?', in A. Bhalla (ed.), *Globalization, Growth and Marginalization*, Macmillan, London.

Stoeckel, A., et al., 2000, *Productivity, Risk and the Gains from Trade Liberalisation*, Pelham Papers 9, Melbourne Business School, Melbourne.

Stretton, H., 1999, *Economics: A New Introduction*, UNSW Press, Sydney.

Sutcliffe, B., 2003, *A More or Less Unequal World?*, Working Paper 54, Political Economy Research Institute, University of Massachusetts, Amherst.

Sylos-Labini, P., 2001, *Underdevelopment*, Cambridge University Press, Cambridge.

Talalay, M., 2000, 'Technology and Globalization: Assessing Patterns of Interaction', in R. Germain (ed.), *Globalisation and its Critics*, Macmillan, London.

Taylor, L., (ed.), 1993, *The Rocky Road to Reform*, MIT Press, Cambridge MA.

—— 2001, *External Liberalization, Economic Performance and Social Policy*, Oxford University Press, Oxford.

—— (ed.), 1988, *Varieties of Stabilisation Experience*, Clarendon Press, Oxford.

Teitel, S., 1993, *Industrial and Technological Development*, Inter-American Development Bank, Washington DC.

—— and F. Thoumi, 1986, 'From Import Substitution to Exports', *Economic Development and Cultural Change* 34(3).

Thacker, S., 2000, *Big Business, the State and Free Trade: Constructing Coalitions in Mexico*, Cambridge University Press, Cambridge.

Thaman, R., 1982, 'Deterioration of Traditional Food Systems', *Journal of Food and Nutrition* 39(3).

Third World Network (TWN), *Third World Resurgence*, Penang, bi-monthly.

Third World Network Features (TWNF), Third World Network, Penang, News Service.

Thirlwall, A.P., 2002, *The Nature of Economic Growth*, Edward Elgar, Cheltenham.

Thomas, H., 1997, *The Slave Trade*, Macmillan, London.

Thomas, H. et al. (eds), 1991, *Small-Scale Production*, IT Publications, London.

Thomas, J.J., 1992, *Informal Economic Activity*, Harvester, New York.

Thurnwald, R., 1932, *Economies in Primitive Communities*, Oxford University Press, Oxford.

Thurow, L., 1992, *Head to Head*, Allen & Unwin, Sydney.

Todaro, M., 2000, *Economic Development*, 6th edn, Longman, London.

Toner, P., 1999, *Main Currents in Cumulative Causation*, Macmillan, London.

Trainer, T., 1995, *The Conserver Society*, Zed Books, London.

—— (ed.), Annual, *State of the World*, Worldwatch Institute, Washington.

Trocki, C., 1997, *Opium, Empire and the Global Political Economy*, Routledge, London.

Tyson, L., 1992, *Who's Bashing Whom*, Institute for International Economics, Washington DC.

United Nations Conference on Trade and Development (UNCTAD), *Trade and Development Report,* (annual), UN, New York..

—— *World Investment Report 2000*, UN, New York.

United Nations Development Programme (UNDP), *Human Development Report* (annual), UN, New York..

United Nations Environment Programme (UNEP), 1999, *Trade Liberalisation and the Environment*, UN, New York.

Van Vugt, W., 1988, 'Running from Ruin', *Economic History Review 2nd Series* 41(3).

Verhelst, T., 1990, *No Life Without Roots*, Zed Books, London.

Viljoen, S., 1936, *The Economics of Primitive Peoples*, Staples, London.

Vreeland, J., 2003, *The IMF and Economic Development*, Cambridge University Press, Cambridge.

Wade, R., 1990, *Governing the Market*, Princeton University Press, Princeton.

Warren, D. et al. (eds), 1995, *The Cultural Dimension of Development*, IT Publications, London.

Weber, T., 'Gandhi, Deep Ecology, Peace Research and Buddhist Economics', *Journal of Peace Research* 36(3), 1999.

Whatmore, S. et al. (eds), 1991, *Rural Enterprise*, Fulton, London.

White, G., 1982, 'North Korean Juiche: The Political Economy of Self-Reliance', in M. Bienefeld and M. Godfrey (eds), *The Struggle for Development*, Wiley, Chichester.

Wiarda, H. (ed.), 1999, *Non-Western Theories of Development*, Harcourt Brace, Fort Worth.

Williamson, J., 1997, 'Globalization and Inequality, Past and Present', *World Bank Research Observer*, August.

World Bank, *World Development Report* (WDR), Washington DC (annual).

—— 2002, *Globalization, Growth and Poverty*, Washington DC.

Whalen, C. (ed.), 1996, *Political Economy for the 21st Century*, M.E. Sharpe, Armonk.

Wichterich, C., 2000, *The Globalized Woman*, Zed Books, London.

Wignaraja, G., 1998, *Trade Liberalisation in Sri Lanka*, Macmillan, London.

Williams, J., 1929, 'The Theory of International Trade Reconsidered', *Economic Journal*, June.

Womersley, M., 1998, 'Sustainable Development in Scotland', in A. McQuillan and A. Preston (eds), *Globally and Locally*, University Press of America, Lanham.

Wood, A. and K. Jordan, 2001, in O. Morrissey and I. Filatotchev (eds), *Globalisation and Trade*, Frank Cass, London.

World Bank, 1993, *The East Asian Miracle*, World Bank, Washington.

—— *World Development Indicators 1999*, World Bank, Washington.

World Trade Organisation (WTO), *Annual Reports* (*AR*).

—— 2000a, *Trade, Development and the Environment*, WTO, Geneva.

—— 2000b, *Dispute Settlement Reports 1997*, Cambridge University Press, Cambridge.

—— 2001, *Trading into the Future*, 2nd edn, WTO, Geneva.

—— 2002, *10 Common Misunderstandings About the WTO*, WTO, Geneva.

Young, A., 1928, 'Increasing Returns and Economic Progress', *Economic Journal*, December.

Zagler, M., 1999, *Endogenous Growth, Market Failures and Economic Policy*, Macmillan, London.

INDEX

Numbers in italics refer to figures and tables

absolute advantage, 19, 36
adaptive traditionalism, 224
adjustment costs 226
Africa, 68
    alternative technologies, 181
    Banana War, 210–12
    co-operative communalism, 129
    self-reliance, 169
    slave trade, 71
agglomeration, of units, 175
agriculture, 78–9
    alternative, 217
    cash crops in Malaysia, 130–31
    farm protection, First World, 195
    food tariffs and, 195
    industry and, 140
    manifest destiny and, 87
    neglect of, 121–3
    North Korea, 169
    organic, 124–5
    self-reliance, 181–2
    small farms, 123–4
    traditionalism, 128
agriculture-first interventionists, 121
AIDS, TRIPs and, 200
alternative agriculture, 217
alternative development, 167, 183–5
alternative technology (AT), 180–81
amnesty on bindings, WTO and, 218
Anti-Corn Law League, 75
    see also Corn Laws

anti-dumping, 225
arbitrage, 21
asymmetric information, 104
audio-visual liberalisation, 204
Australia
    case for Protection, 53
    WTO and, 208
autarkic lifestyles, as satisfactory, 127
autocentric, European countries as,
    164
autonomous savings behaviour, 101

Bairoch, Paul, 77–8
Banana War
    GATS and, 198–9
    WTO and, 210–12
beggar-thy-neighbour exports, 154
    protectionism and, 84
benefits of free trade
    unilateral, 41–2
    universal, 41
bindings, WTO and, 194, 218
biopiracy, TRIPs and, 200
Botswana, self-reliance, 169–70
Brazil, ISI and, 152
Bretton Woods, 189
Buddhist economics, 16
    self-reliance and, 166

Cameroon, self-reliance, 170
Carey, Henry, 51

Caribbean, Banana War and, 210–12
Castro, Fidel, 208
Central America (CA), Banana War and, 210
cheap labour, competitiveness and, 177
Chile, exports, 153
China, 68
  opium trade, 72
  self-reliance, 171
Clark, David, 63
classical economists, 12
clustering, of units, 175
co-operative world order
  proposals for, 215–19
  versus global free trade, 213–15
Cobden, Richard, 76, 79, 81
communal villages, Tanzania, 169
community integrity, self-reliance and, 167
community
  as lost cause, 125–34
  theories of, 102
Community-Sovereignty theory, 15–16, 19, 58, 102
  competitiveness and, 177
  traditions and, 131
comparative advantage, 18, 22–6
  arguments against free trade, *226*
  competitiveness and, 179
  as natural, 70
  origins of, 70
  phases of, 57
  self-reliance and, 168
  shaping of, 74
  slave trade and, 71
  as volatile, 45
compensation, lump-sum, 37
competitive advantage, 24
competitiveness, global, chimera of, 176–7
computable general equilibrium (CGE) models, 85, 143–4, 145–6
computers, self-reliance and, 179–80
consumer surplus, 30, *32–3*, 97–8
co-operative communalism, in Africa, 129
co-operative internationalism, 224

Corn Laws, repeal of, 74–5, 79
corruption, liberalisation and, 143
creative destruction, development as, 100
cross-country regressions, 149–50
Cuba
  human development indicators, 115
  organic agriculture, 125, 182
cultural barriers, 9
cultural integrity, 228
cultural separation, 68
culture
  as lost cause, 125–34
  WTO and, 204
cumulative causation, 57

Daly, Herman, 58
dead-weight losses, 29, 35–6
  DUP and, 143
  from protection, 142
decentralising technologies, alternative technologies and, 181
deep integration, 4, 224
Dependency Marxists, self-reliance and, 165
Depression, Great (1930s), 83–6, 189
development
  alternative packages, 217
  costs of, 132–3
  economics of, 103
  growth and, 99
  as inevitable evolutionary progress, 99–100
  invention of, 98–100
  modest expectations and, 127
directly unproductive profit-seeking activity (DUP), 142–3
  dead-weight loss and, 143
diseconomies of scale, self-reliance and, 175
division of labour, 19, 63
Doha Round, GATT
  allegations of bullying at, 207
  issues for consideration, 203–5
  trade in goods, 195
  TRIPs, 200
  WTO and, 192, 195, 205–6

drug production, generic, in Third World, 200
dynamic comparative advantage, 56, 60
dynamic gains, 30, 31, 100
    problems with, 33

East Asia, ISI models, 157
East Asian Tigers, 151–2
Eastern Europe, ISI and, 151
econometric models, 143–4
economic arguments against free trade, 225
economic growth, trade and, *148*
economies of scale, self-reliance and, 174–5
employment
    arguments against free trade, 226
    full, 37
    liberalisation and, 195
    low-cost imports and, 113
engine of growth, 76, 103
environmental issues, 117–18
    arguments against free trade, 228
    GATS and, 197
    Kuznets curve, 117
    sustainability, 131
    WTO and, 202–3
equilibrium, linguistic, 133
EU, Banana War and, 210–12
exploitation, labour standards and, 202
exploited labour, 112, 114
export pessimism, 138
    lock-in problem and, 106
export-orientation (EO), 136–59
export-orientation industrialisation (EOI), 137
exports, as cult, 136–59
external resource usage, self-reliance and, 167
externalities, 37–8

fair trade, definitions of, 214
farming, *see* agriculture
female traditional roles, 119–20
first mover advantage, 57
fishing, 124
flexible specialisation, 176

alternative technologies and, 181
food security, 227
food tariff cuts, 195
foreign direct investment (FDI)
    development and, 111
    exports and, 139
France, trade liberalisation agreements and, 75
Free Market Economic Rationalism, 1, 12
Free Marketeers, 1–2
    IS–EO debate and, 155–8
free trade
    arguments against, 225–9
    beneficence myth and, 76–80
    benefits of, 41–2
    definition of, 9
    dissent from, 48–62
    as doctrine, 22–4
    five myths of, 8–11
    imperialism of, 73
    as natural activity, 66–70
Friedman, Thomas, 1
full employment, 37

gains from trade, 19, 26–34, 60
    development and, 100
    to locals, 39
Gandhi, Mahatma, 15, 81, 97
Gandhi–Schumacher approach, traditions and, 131
Gandhian Propensity, 65, 67, 69, 95, 102, 224
    definition of, 10
    self-reliance and, 166, 168
Gatesian nightmare, self-reliance and, 179–80
General Agreement on Tariffs and Trade (GATT)
    core assumptions of, 190
    Uruguay Round (1986–93), 3, 190
    WTO and, 192
    see also Doha Round; Uruguay Round
General Agreement on Trade and Services (GATS)
    Banana War and, 210–12
    details of, *197–8*

single undertaking clause and, 217
General Trade Analysis Project
  (GTAP), 145
Geneva Consensus, 138
global free trade, versus co-operative
  world, 213–15
Global Free Trade Project, 26, 29,
  189–91
  WTO and, 212–13
global instability, speculation and, 104
global supply chains, 110
globalisation
  competitiveness and, 176–7
  critique of, 97–134
  as deep integration, 4
  exports and, 136
  as 'in-your-face', 4–5
  myths about, 5–8
  poverty and, 108–12
  reversing destructive impacts of,
    129
  self-reliance and, 161
globo-euphoria, 3–4
goods trade, WTO and, 194–6
government failure, 44
grain, price collapse of, 78–9
green development, 182–3
green Gandhianism, 182–3
green revolution, organic farming and,
  124–5
green trade, 117–18
gross domestic product (GDP)
  human development and, 114–15
  manifest destiny and, 93–5
growth
  as confused with development, 99
  engine for, 42
  Free Marketeers and, 105
  trade and, 148

Hamilton, Alexander, 50
happiness, r-curve pattern and, 115
Harberger triangles, 27–9, 28, 76, 85,
  142
Havana Conference (1946), 189
health TNCs, 199
Hechscher and Ohlin (HO)
  hypothesis, 21–2

historical economists, 52
Hull, Cordell, 189
Human Development (HD) theorists,
  13–14, 102, 108
  GDP and, 114–15

IMF reforms, WTO and, 218–19
immiserising growth, 77
imperfect competition, 56, 145, 146
imperial expansion, opium trade and,
  72
import-substitution (IS), 106, 136–59
import-substitution industrialisation
  (ISI), 137
  arguments against free trade, 226
  Tiger growth and, 151–2
import substitution, then export
  (ISTE), 157
increasing returns sectors, 56
Index of Sustainable Economic
  Welfare (ISEW), 117
India
  human development indicators,
    115
  industrial districts, 176
  IS–EO debate, 157
  ISI and, 152
  modest expectations, 127
  opium trade, 72
  removal of traditional society, 126
  self-reliance, 171
indigenous institutions, self-reliance
  and, 170
indigenous peoples, reversing
  destructive impacts, 130
Indonesia
  alternative technologies, 181
  IS–EO debate, 156–7, 157
industrial districts, 175
  self-reliance and, 175–6
Industrial Revolution, 67, 70
industrial stagnation, 77
industrialisation, 97
  agriculture and, 121
  linked with export-orientation,
    137
industry policy, 155–8
inefficiency, triangles of, 29

inequality, globalisation and, 108–12
infant industry protection, 50, 101, 138, 140
   exports and, 139
   trade liberalisation and, 195
informal sector, self-reliance and, 173
information technology (IT), self-reliance and, 179–80
integrative globalism, 224
intellectual property rights, WTO and, 199–200
Intermediate Technology Group, 16
International Trade Organisation (ITO), 189
internet disillusion, self-reliance and, 180
interventionists, 101
   agriculture-first, 121
   growth analysis and, 105
intra-firm trade (IFT), 89
intra-industry trade (IIT), 60, 89
   self-reliance and, 162–3
investment
   growth and, 141
   IT and, 180
invisible hand theory, 12, 19
Iraq War, 2
Ireland, 79
Islamic fundamentalism, rise of, 7
isolationist experiments, self-reliance and, 168
Italy, industrial districts and, 176
Ivory Coast
   exports and, 153
   self-reliance and, 170

Kaldor, Nicholas, 13, 55
Keynes, John Maynard, 13, 48, 54–6, 163, 189

labour
   arguments against free trade, 227
   costs, 23
   competitiveness and, 177
   as exploited, 112–13
   low wages as fair, 114
   markets, globalisation and, 111
   standards, WTO and, 202

languages, 132–3
Latin America, self-reliance and, 171
law of one price, 21
learning-by-doing, 36, 60, 226
Legend of the Thirties, 83–6, 189
linguistic Darwinists, 132–3
List, Friedrich, 50
local development, self-reliance and, 173
local film quotas, 204
local needs, self-reliance and, 166
local participation, agriculture and, 123–4
lock-in, 105–6
low-cost imports, 113
lump-sum compensation, 37

Malaysia, agricultural cash crops, 130–31
male–female economic roles, 119–20
Malthus, Thomas, 50
managed trade, 213–14
market intervenionist approach, 13
   mercantilists and, 49
marketing boards, agriculture and, 122
Marx/Marxism, 14, 48, 51–2, 161
   Indian traditional society and, 126
   self-reliance and, 165
   war and, 81
Mercantilists, 3, 19, 49
Mexico, exports and, 153
migration, trade as substitute for, 21
mobility of factors, internal, 36–7
modernisation, women and, 119
Most Favoured Nation (MFN), 191
Multilateral Agreement on Investment (MAI), 204

national sovereignty, self-reliance and, 164, 167
national system theory, 51
national treatment, WTO and, 191
natural barriers, 9
neo-classical models, 12, 145
New Growth Theory, 61
new international economic theory (NIET), 59–61
NGO accreditation, alternative, 217

Nigeria, self-reliance and, 170
Nike syndrome, 113
no learning effects, 35–6
non-economic arguments, against free
    trade, 227
North Korea, self-reliance, 168–9
not-quite-free trade, rise of, 43–6

one-country-one-vote, WTO, 206
opium trade, 72
opportunity costs, 23
organic agriculture, 124–5
    self-reliance and, 181–2
oversupply, 107

Pacific countries, Banana War and,
    210–12
Pacific Paradox, 128
path dependence, 57
    self-reliance and, 172, 179
peace, global, 81–3
pecuniary economies, self-reliance
    and, 175
perfect competition, 35
Peru, self-reliance, 173
Polanyi, Karl, 66–70
pollution, 117–18
    agriculture and, 121
    havens, 118
population control, 50
Portugal, trade with Britain, 73–4
poverty
    globalisation and, 108–12
    vicious circles of, 103
'priority to locals' principle
    arguments against free trade, 228
    self-reliance and, 166
producer surplus, 27
    definition of, 32
productivity gains, 31
propensities, clash of, 64–6
protection/protectionism, 8, 49
    benefits from, 77–8
    campaigns for, 52–3
    dead-weight loss from, 142
    definition of, 9
    Harberger triangle and, 28
    in 1930s, 84–6

IS–EO debate and, 155–8
Keynes and, 54–6
as natural activity, 3
not-quite-free trade and, 43–4
psychic income, 30, 32, 97, 100
public choice, vested interests and,
    42
purchasing power parity (PPP), 93–4
    effects of, 94
    human development and, 114–15

quadripartite representation, WTO
    and, 218
quota protection, 142

r-curve, 116
    human development and, 114–17
relative opportunity costs, 20
rent seeking, 44, 142
rent snatching, 56, 60
research and development (R&D)
    competitiveness and, 178
    dynamic growth and, 140
Ricardo, David, 20
    model of, 23
risk premium gains, 31, 34
Robinson, Joan, 55
rural-based development, self-reliance
    and, 173

Sanitary and Phytosanitary (SPS)
    measures, product standards and,
    201
Say's Law, 146
scale economies, 105–6
    self-reliance and, 174–5
Schumacher, E.F., 16, 161, 166, 182
Schumpeter, Joseph, 99–100
scientific measures, product standards
    and, 201
Seattle Ministerial meeting, 206,
    207
'second best' theorem, 44, 225
self-reliance, 227
    case for, 165–7
    definition of, 163–5
    feasibility of, 167–72
    lineage of, 162–3

as option, 161–86
rationality of, 172–83
self-reliant trade, 80, 215
service exports, *88*
services, trade in, 196–9
slave trade, 71–2
Corn Laws and, 79
Smith, Adam, 3, 18, 63
on comparative advantage, 18,
19–22
Smith/Ricardo approach, 12
Smithian Propensity, 64–5, 66, 69, 95,
103
definition of, 10
self-reliance and, 168
social accounting matrix (SAM), 145,
146
soil depletion, 52
South Korea, ISI and, 152
special and differential (S&D)
treatment, WTO and, 191, 193
specialisation, flexible, 176
specific factors model, 46
Sri Lanka, exports, 153
static gains, 31, 34, 100
Stolper–Samuelson theorem, 22, 114
structural adjustment programmes
(SAPs), inequality and, 110
structural models, 145, 146
subsidiary principle, self-reliance and,
166
subsidisation, export, 137
sustainable development
environment and, 202–3
WTO, 117–18
sustainably organised systems, 131
sweatshops, 112–13

Tanzania, self-reliance and, 169
tariff protection, 142
technical barriers to trade (TBT),
WTO and, 201
techno-global theory, myths and, 161
technology, 86
global competitiveness and, 176–7
imported, 169
innovation and, 99
terms of trade, 29, 106–7, 225, 226

Thailand, IS–EO debate and, 156–7
Third Italy, industrial districts and, 176
Third World
alternative technologies and, 181
generic drug production, 200
global supply chains and, 110
liberalisation and, 195–6
Tigers, East Asian, 151–2
TINA (there is no alternative),
challenges to, 11–16
total factor productivity (TFP),
competitiveness and, 177
trade
changing nature of, 89–90
economic growth and, *148*
loss of innocence of, 70–75
and markets embedded, 66–70
as natural activity, 66–70
as obsession, 3–4
as substitute for migration, 21
terms-of-trade problem, 106
as universally beneficial, 70–5
trade balance
arguments against free trade, 225
competitiveness and, 177–8
trade determinism, 3–4, 103
1930s and, 84–5
trade in goods, WTO and, 194–6
trade in services, WTO and, 196–9
trade liberalisation agreements
after 1860, 75
corruption and, 143
employment and, 195
exports and, 136
France, 75
infant industry protection and, 195
rush of enlightenment, 139–40
Third World and, 195–6
trade ratios, *92*
Trade-Related Aspects of Intellectual
Property Rights (TRIPs)
single undertaking clause, 217
WTO and, 192, 199–200
trade-related international NGOs
(TRINGOs), WTO and, 207
Trade-Related Investment Measures
(TRIMs) agreement, 204
single undertaking clause, 217

tradition, as lost cause, 125–34
traditional indigenous peoples,
    reversing destructive impacts, 130
traditional roles, female, 119–20
traditional societies, 102
transnational corporations (TNCs)
    GATS and, 197
    Health and, 199
    water utilities and, 197
'Trojan Horse' fears, 196–7, 198
Truman, Harry, 97

unilateral benefits, 41–2
unit cost gaps, labour and, 112–13,
    202
urban bias, agriculture and, 121
urbanisation, women and, 119
Uruguay Round, GATT
    allegations of bullying at, 207
    WTO and, 190–91
USA
    as autarkic, 164
    Banana War and, 210–12
    health TNCs and, 199
    TRIPs and, 199
    WTO and, 188

values, as lost cause, 125–34
virtue, necessity of, 76–80
voluntary arm's-length trade, 38
voting, WTO and, 217

wage stimulus, arguments against free
    trade, 226
war, 81–3

Washington Consensus, 104, 138, 140
wasteful trade, 89–90
water, GATS and, 197, 198
women, globalisation and, 119–20
World Bank, WTO and, 218–19
World Bank SAPs, exports and, 154
world industrial/manufacturing
    production, growth in, 91
World Institute for Development
    Economics Research (WIDER),
    141, 150
world parity pricing, 122
world trade, 88
    growth in, 91
    predicted decline in, 86
World Trade Organisation (WTO),
    188–220
    Banana War and, 210–12
    details of, 192
    environment and, 202–3
    foundation assumptions, 189–91
    Global Free Trade Project and,
        212–13
    labour standards and, 202
    as policeman of trade, 205–6
    product standards and, 201–2
    sustainable development and,
        117–18
    trade in goods and, 194–6
    trade in services and, 196–9
    TRIPs and, 199–200

Zimbabwe
    ISI and, 152
    self-reliance and, 170

ABOUT THE AUTHOR

Dr GRAHAM DUNKLEY is an economist at the Victoria University of Technology, Melbourne, Australia. He has been a Visiting Fellow at the University of Warwick in the UK. His wide-ranging interests and activities include policy development work with various environmental organisations and also, over many years, with the Australian Labor Party as well as trade unions and labour research bodies. He has travelled extensively in Europe and Asia, has had experience in project work with Community Aid Abroad (Oxfam Australia), and is a commentator in the Australian media. He is the author of *The Free Trade Adventure: The WTO, the Uruguay Round and Globalism – A Critique* (Zed Books, 2000; Melbourne University Press, 1997); and *The Greening of the Red: Sustainability, Socialism and the Environmental Crisis* (Pluto Press, Australia, 1992).

About this Series

'Communities in the South are facing great difficulties in coping with global trends. I hope this brave new series will throw much needed light on the issues ahead and help us choose the right options.'

MARTIN KHOR, *Director,*
Third World Network, Penang

'There is no more important campaign than our struggle to bring the global economy under democratic control. But the issues are fearsomely complex. This Global Issues series is a valuable resource for the committed campaigner and the educated citizen.'

BARRY COATES, *Director,*
World Development Movement (WDM)

'Zed Books has long provided an inspiring list about the issues that touch and change people's lives. The Global Issues series is another dimension of Zed's fine record, allowing access to a range of subjects and authors that, to my knowledge, very few publishers have tried. I strongly recommend these new, powerful titles and this exciting series.'

JOHN PILGER, *author*

'We are all part of a generation that actually has the means to eliminate extreme poverty world-wide. Our task is to harness the forces of globalization for the benefit of working people, their families and their communities – that is our collective duty. The Global Issues series makes a powerful contribution to the global campaign for justice, sustainable and equitable development, and peaceful progress.'

GLENYS KINNOCK, *MEP*

THE GLOBAL ISSUES SERIES

Already available

Walden Bello, *Deglobalization: Ideas for a New World Economy*

Robert Ali Brac de la Perrière and Franck Seuret, *Brave New Seeds: The Threat of GM Crops to Farmers*

Oswaldo de Rivero, *The Myth of Development: The Non-viable Economies of the 21st Century*

Graham Dunkley, *Free Trade: Myth, Reality and Alternatives*

Joyeeta Gupta, *Our Simmering Planet: What to Do about Global Warming?*

Nicholas Guyatt, *Another American Century? The United States and the World since 9/11*

Martin Khor, *Rethinking Globalization: Critical Issues and Policy Choices*

John Madeley, *Food for All: The Need for a New Agriculture*

John Madeley, *Hungry for Trade: How the Poor Pay for Free Trade*

A.G. Noorani, *Islam and Jihad: Prejudice versus Reality*

Riccardo Petrella, *The Water Manifesto: Arguments for a World Water Contract*

Peter Robbins, *Stolen Fruit: The Tropical Commodities Disaster*

Vandana Shiva, *Protect or Plunder? Understanding Intellectual Property Rights*

Harry Shutt, *A New Democracy: Alternatives to a Bankrupt World Order*

David Sogge, *Give and Take: What's the Matter with Foreign Aid?*

Paul Todd and Jonathan Bloch, *Global Intelligence: The World's Secret Services Today*

In preparation

Peggy Antrobus, *The International Women's Movement: Issues and Strategies*

Greg Buckman, *Globalization: Tame it or Scrap It? Mapping the Alternatives of the Anti-Globalization Movement*

Julian Burger, *First Peoples: What Future?*

Ha-Joon Chang and Ilene Grabel, *Reclaiming Development: An Alternative Economic Policy Handbook*

Koen de Feyter, *A Thousand and One Rights: How Globalization Challenges Human Rights*

Susan Hawley and Morris Szeftel, *Corruption: Privatization, Transnational Corporations and the Export of Bribery*

Roger Moody, *Digging the Dirt: The Modern World of Global Mining*

Edgar Pieterse, *City Futures: Confronting the Crisis of Urban Development*

Toby Shelley, *Oil and Gas: What Future? What Consequences?*

Kavaljit Singh, *The Myth of Globalization: Ten Questions Everyone Asks*

Vivien Stern, *Crime and Punishment: Globalization and the New Agenda*

Nedd Willard, *The Drugs War: Is This the Solution?*

For full details of this list and Zed's other subject and general catalogues, please write to: The Marketing Department, Zed Books, 7 Cynthia Street, London NI 9JF, UK or email Sales@zedbooks.demon.co.uk

Visit our website at: www.zedbooks.co.uk

Participating Organizations

Both ENDS A service and advocacy organization which collaborates with environment and indigenous organizations, both in the South and in the North, with the aim of helping to create and sustain a vigilant and effective environmental movement.

> Nieuwe Keizersgracht 45, 1018 VC Amsterdam, The Netherlands
> Phone: +31 20 623 0823   Fax: +31 20 620 8049
> Email: info@bothends.org   Website: www.bothends.org

Catholic Institute for International Relations (CIIR) CIIR aims to contribute to the eradication of poverty through a programme that combines advocacy at national and international level with community-based development.

> Unit 3, Canonbury Yard, 190a New North Road, London N1 7BJ, UK
> Phone +44 (0)20 7354 0883   Fax +44 (0)20 7359 0017
> Email: ciir@ciir.org   Website: www.ciir.org

Corner House The Corner House is a UK-based research and solidarity group working on social and environmental justice issues in North and South.

> PO Box 3137, Station Road, Sturminster Newton, Dorset DT10 1YJ, UK
> Tel.: +44 (0)1258 473795   Fax: +44 (0)1258 473748
> Email: cornerhouse@gn.apc.org   Website: www.cornerhouse.icaap.org

Council on International and Public Affairs (CIPA) CIPA is a human rights research, education and advocacy group, with a particular focus on economic and social rights in the USA and elsewhere around the world. Emphasis in recent years has been given to resistance to corporate domination.

> 777 United Nations Plaza, Suite 3C, New York, NY 10017, USA
> Tel. +1 212 972 9877   Fax +1 212 972 9878
> Email: cipany@igc.org   Website: www.cipa-apex.org

Dag Hammarskjöld Foundation The Dag Hammarskjöld Foundation, established 1962, organises seminars and workshops on social, economic and cultural issues facing developing countries with a particular focus on alternative and innovative solutions. Results are published in its journal *Develpment Dialogue*.

> Övre Slottsgatan 2, 753 10 Uppsala, Sweden.
> Tel.: +46 18 102772   Fax: +46 18 122072
> Email: secretariat@dhf.uu.se   Website: www.dhf.uu.se

Development GAP The Development Group for Alternative Policies is a Non-Profit Development Resource Organization working with popular organizations in the South and their Northern partners in support of a development that is truly sustainable and that advances social justice.

927 15th Street NW, 4th Floor, Washington, DC, 20005, USA
Tel.: +1 202 898 1566   Fax: +1 202 898 1612
E-mail: dgap@igc.org   Website: www.developmentgap.org

Focus on the Global South Focus is dedicated to regional and global policy analysis and advocacy work. It works to strengthen the capacity of organizations of the poor and marginalized people of the South and to better analyse and understand the impacts of the globalization process on their daily lives.

C/o CUSRI, Chulalongkorn University, Bangkok 10330, Thailand
Tel.: +66 2 218 7363 Fax: +66 2 255 9976
Email: Admin@focusweb.org   Website: www.focusweb.org

IBON IBON Foundation is a research, education and information institution that provides publications and services on socio-economic issues as support to advocacy in the Philippines and abroad. Through its research and databank, formal and non-formal education programmes, media work and international networking, IBON aims to build the capacity of both Philippine and international organizations.

Room 303 SCC Bldg, 4427 Int. Old Sta. Mesa, Manila 1008, Philippines
Phone +632 7132729   Fax +632 7160108
Email: editors@ibon.org   Website: www.ibon.org

Inter Pares Inter Pares, a Canadian social justice organization, has been active since 1975 in building relationships with Third World development groups and providing support for community-based development programs. Inter Pares is also involved in education and advocacy in Canada, promoting understanding about the causes, effects and solutions to poverty.

221 Laurier Avenue East, Ottawa, Ontario, KIN 6PI Canada
Phone +1 613 563 4801   Fax +1 613 594 4704
Email: info@interpares.ca   Website: www.interpares.ca

Public Interest Research Centre PIRC is a research and campaigning group based in Delhi which seeks to serve the information needs of activists and organizations working on macro-economic issues concerning finance, trade and development.

142 Maitri Apartments, Plot No. 28, Patparganj, Delhi 110092, India
Phone: +91 11 2221081/2432054   Fax: +91 11 2224233
Email: kaval@nde.vsnl.net.in

Third World Network TWN is an international network of groups and individuals involved in efforts to bring about a greater articulation of the needs and rights of peoples in the Third World; a fair distribution of the world's resources; and forms of development which are ecologically sustainable and fulfil human needs. Its international secretariat is based in Penang, Malaysia.

121-S Jalan Utama, 10450 Penang, Malaysia
Tel.: +60 4 226 6159   Fax: +60 4 226 4505
Email: twnet@po.jaring.my   Website: www.twnside.org.sg

Third World Network–Africa TWN–Africa is engaged in research and advocacy on economic, environmental and gender issues. In relation to its current particular interest in globalization and Africa, its work focuses on trade and investment, the extractive sectors and gender and economic reform.

2 Ollenu Street, East Legon, PO Box AN19452, Accra-North, Ghana.
Tel.: +233 21 511189/503669/500419   Fax: +233 21 511188
Email: twnafrica@ghana.com

World Development Movement (WDM) The World Development Movement campaigns to tackle the causes of poverty and injustice. It is a democratic membership movement that works with partners in the South to cancel unpayable debt and break the ties of IMF conditionality, for fairer trade and investment rules, and for strong international rules on multinationals.

25 Beehive Place, London SW9 7QR, UK
Tel.: +44 (0)20 7737 6215   Fax: +44 (0)20 7274 8232
Email: wdm@wdm.org.uk   Website: www.wdm.org.uk

THIS BOOK IS ALSO AVAILABLE
IN THE FOLLOWING COUNTRIES

CARIBBEAN

Ian Randle Publishers
11 Cunningham Avenue
Box 686, Kingston 6,
Jamaica, W.I.
Tel: 876 978 0745/0739
Fax: 876 978 1158
email: ianr@colis.com

EGYPT

MERIC
(Middle East Readers'
Information Center)
2 Bahgat Ali Street,
Tower D/Apt. 24
Zamalek
Cairo
Tel: 20 2 735 3818/3824
Fax: 20 2 736 9355

FIJI

University Book Centre,
University of South
Pacific,
Suva
Tel: 679 313 900
Fax: 679 303 265

GHANA

EPP Book Services,
PO Box TF 490,
Trade Fair,
Accra
Tel: 233 21 778347
Fax: 233 21 779099

MAURITIUS

Editions Le Printemps
4 Club Road
Vacoas

MOZAMBIQUE

Sul Sensações
PO Box 2242,
Maputo
Tel: 258 1 421974
Fax: 258 1 423414

NAMIBIA

Book Den
PO Box 3469
Shop 4
Frans Indongo Gardens
Windhoek
Tel: 264 61 239976
Fax: 264 61 234248

NEPAL

Everest Media Services,
GPO Box 5443
Dillibazar
Putalisadak Chowk
Kathmandu
Tel: 977 1 416026
Fax: 977 1 250176

NIGERIA

Mosuro Publishers
52 Magazine Road
Jericho
Ibadan
Tel: 234 2 241 3375
Fax: 234 2 241 3374

PAKISTAN

Vanguard Books
45 The Mall
Lahore
Tel: 92 42 735 5079
Fax: 92 42 735 5197

PAPUA NEW GUINEA

Unisearch PNG Pty Ltd
Box 320, University
National Capital District
Tel: 675 326 0130
Fax: 675 326 0127

RWANDA

Librairie Ikirezi
PO Box 443
Kigali
Tel/Fax: 250 71314

SUDAN

The Nile Bookshop
New Extension Street 41
PO Box 8036
Khartoum
Tel: 249 11 463 749

TANZANIA

TEMA Publishing Co. Ltd
PO Box 63115
Dar Es Salaam
Tel: 255 22 2113608
Fax: 255 22 2110472

UGANDA

Aristoc Booklex Ltd
PO Box 5130,
Kampala Road
Diamond Trust Building
Kampala
Tel/Fax: 256 41 254867

ZAMBIA

UNZA Press
PO Box 32379
Lusaka
Tel: 260 1 290409
Fax: 260 1 253952

ZIMBABWE

Weaver Press
PO Box A1922
Avondale
Harare
Tel: 263 4 308330
Fax: 263 4 339645